I0760110

HITLER'S CROATIAN ALLY

HITLER'S CROATIAN ALLY

THE CROATIAN ARMY AND THE BATTLE FOR YUGOSLAVIA, 1941-1945

Figure 1. The Croatian 369th Infantry Division cloth shield. A red-and-white chequerboard shield with the name 'Hrvatska' (Croatia) above in white thread on a black cloth background.

DR ANTONIO J. MUÑOZ

FRONTLINE
BOOKS

HITLER'S CROATIAN ALLY
The Croatian Army and the Battle for Yugoslavia, 1941-1945

First published in Great Britain in 2025
by Frontline Books
An imprint of
Pen & Sword Books Ltd
Yorkshire - Philadelphia

ISBN 978 1 03612 805 0

A CIP catalogue record for this book is available from the British Library

Typeset by Lapiz Digital
Printed and bound in the UK by CPI Group (UK) Ltd,
Croydon, CR0 4YY.

The Publisher's authorised representative in the EU for product safety is Authorised Rep Compliance Ltd., Ground Floor, 71 Lower Baggot Street, Dublin D02 P593, Ireland.
www.arccompliance.com

For a complete list of Pen & Sword titles please contact
PEN & SWORD BOOKS LTD
47 Church Street, Barnsley, South Yorkshire, S70 2AS, England
E-mail: enquiries@pen-and-sword.co.uk
Website: www.pen-and-sword.co.uk
or
PEN & SWORD BOOKS
1950 Lawrence Rd, Havertown, PA 19083, USA
E-mail: uspen-and-sword@casematepublishers.com

This book is dedicated to the Ukrainian victims of Russian aggression.

CONTENTS

LIST OF PLATES

LIST OF FIGURES, MAPS AND TABLES

Figures and Maps

Tables

AUTHOR'S NOTE

As an academician, I have been trained to write works that are fully noted, so as to provide the reader with only fact-based references that justify any conclusions drawn from those facts. I decided in this case to do away with the hundreds (and sometimes thousands) of reference annotations that would normally appear in any academic study. I did this for the sake of writing a free-flowing study, unencumbered with the minutia of reference detail that often distracts a reader's eyes from the story. In order to avoid this 'page clutter', I decided to keep the notes to a bare minimum. Those readers out there who are more scholastically inclined, and who wish to study the topic further, can refer to the select bibliography of primary and secondary sources that I have prepared at the end of this work. There they will find the references that were used to write this book. History, without its academic requirements, tends to be more compelling and entertaining, as opposed to clogging the storyline with hundreds of footnotes. The key to writing history successfully, is to keep the reader's attention focused on the narrative. Further still, if an author has the ability to place the reader in the middle of that story, as if he/she is witnessing the events as they happened, the writer will have succeeded in achieving something that is very rare and often does not occur in history books: capturing the reader's imagination and interest.

The story of the Armed Forces of the Independent State of Croatia (*Nezavisna Država Hrvatska* – NDH) during the Second World War is important because the events that occurred in Croatia and the rest of what used to be Yugoslavia then, had a direct effect on the manner in which that Balkan nation disintegrated in the early 1990s, and continues to affect its history today. The long memories, intolerance and vendettas that are so prevalent in the people of this region of Europe are still affecting their history. Currently, the issue that is plaguing the former Yugoslavia lies in the establishment of the nation-state of Bosnia-Herzegovina; a loose confederation which is a hodgepodge of two basic ethnic groups: Muslims and Serbs. The Serbs, who are part of this artificially-created nation, based on the Dayton Accords, live in what they call the *República Srpska* (Serb Republic).[1] To a certain extent, it is a politically autonomous region that recently has passed a law that says that in certain cases, *República Srpska* will ignore laws and decisions made by the High Representative for Bosnia & Herzegovina, Christian Schmidt.[2] Obviously, allowing the governing members of *República Srpska* to ignore the decisions and laws of the state of Bosnia-Herzegovina would be effectively ending that nation state. This, of course, is the intent of the Serbian legislative body's decree. The ultimate goal is an eventual separation from Bosnia-Herzegovina and absorption of *República Srpska* into the nation of Serbia. The nationalist element in Serbia is far stronger than the Serbian minority who wish to live in peace in a democracy. Serbians can't seem to get rid of their expansionist and chauvinistic tendencies. It seems that these proclivities are very much imbedded in their psyche. Adding to the problem are outside political interests that have seeped into the equation. An example of this is Victor Orbán, the authoritarian leader of Hungary. Orbán has taken on the cause of the Serbian legislators by claiming that the politicians running *República Srpska* merely wish to create a more 'democratic' state. He claims that the High Representative for Bosnia & Herzegovina is nothing less than a dictatorial ruler. Those who know how Orbán has turned Hungary from a democratic nation into a dictatorship, find his complaint quite cynical.

It is obvious to all (including Orbán), that the ultimate goal of the Serbian politicians in Bosnia-Herzegovina is to create a 'Greater Serbia' by physically joining with the existing Serbian nation. Once again, we see the single-minded dream of wanting to create a 'Greater Serbia.' A dream that helped to spark the First World War. As that war was starting, an English reporter wrote an opinion piece in the London *Times* during the summer of 1914. At a time when virtually all of the people of the United Kingdom were fully behind supporting France, Russia and Serbia, this one reporter wrote an editorial that ran contrary to everything that was being written in every other article, about who was at fault for the war. The reporter commented that had it not been for Serbia's desire to expand its territorial borders – a desire that threatened the national borders of the Austro-Hungarian Empire, then Austria would not have felt that it needed to take action against the Serbian nation. He ended the piece by commenting that if the Serbian nation were to be ripped out of Europe, and dragged into the middle of the Atlantic Ocean, then sunk to the bottom of the sea, Europe would breathe cleaner air.

Although this opinion-piece was quite harsh, one wonders if Serbia's belligerent history was the cause of such extreme thought. Given the expansionist aspirations of many a Serbian government in the nineteenth, twentieth and twenty-first centuries, perhaps one can understand how this British reporter reached such a drastic opinion of the Serbian nation. Given the current events unfolding in the Balkans today, it appears that the dream of a 'Greater Serbia' is still very much alive. Today the Hungarian dictator, Victor Orbán, is openly supporting Serbia. Why is Orbán so keen on aiding the Serbian cause? Because, as the saying goes, 'birds of a feather, flock together.' It is simply one authoritarian regime (Hungary) helping to support another dictatorship (Russia), by aiding its friend and ally (Serbia). Hungary is the only NATO country that has not come to the aid of beleaguered Ukraine, and continues to have very close ties with the Russian despot, Vladimir Putin of the Russian Federation. In fact, Victor Orbán has done his very best to impede NATO's attempt to help supply Ukraine with weapons to defend against Russian aggression. The Serbians, who have always supported Russia in any and all ways, are therefore being politically assisted by Hungary – Russia's only friend in NATO.

The United States, which supports Ukraine, and which sees Orbán's meddling for what it is, has put pressure on his dictatorship to keep its nose out of the politics of Bosnia-Herzegovina. As a result of his actions, Victor Orbán has become a pariah within NATO and the European nations. His isolation has become so well known, and his support for Russia and Serbia so pronounced, that the dictator of Belarus, Alexander Lukashenko, another one of Putin's lackies, has recently invited the Hungarian autocrat to visit his country as a way to help counter that isolation. In another region of the former Yugoslavia, in Kosovo, Serbian nationalism is also causing trouble by stirring up anti-Muslim and anti-Albanian hatred. Unfortunately, it would seem that the Balkan ghosts of the past are once again resurfacing. Perhaps they never fully went away. Whether another war is on the horizon or not is not yet certain. What is certain, is that the 'Balkan troubles' that have plagued that region of Europe for hundreds of years, are still very much with us today; and the unfortunate history of the Balkans is very much tied to its future. What will happen next will depend very much on the decisions taken by the leaders of the nations who call the Balkans home. Sadly, recurring history has shown us that in the end, most of the Balkan people have chosen war over compromise.

Antonio J. Muñoz,
25 October 2023

FOREWORD

In November 1918 the Habsburg Empire was on the brink of collapse. This supranational empire, where different nations, races and religions had lived together in harmony, had fought for its survival fiercely and courageously for four years to the utter surprise of its enemies in London, Paris and St. Petersburg. When everything seemed lost a Croat officer, Field Marshal Svetozar Boroevic de Bojna, wanted to help his Austrian Emperor-King, Karl, in his desperate situation and to regain Karl's freedom of action by occupying Vienna with the well-disciplined Army of the Isonzo. But this last act of fidelity and heroism never occurred. Boroevic's plan was the last attempt of resistance of a supranational idea against secessionism and nationalism, which began to rule the fate of the countries emerging from the ruins of the Danube monarchy. The *'pax austriaca'* which, when recalled nostalgically, looked like a paradise of multi-national diversity in European unity, was not replaced by a balanced and just post-war order, but by the Treaty of Versailles and its version of peace.

The Kingdom of Yugoslavia – until 1929 it was named the Kingdom of the Serbs, Croats and Slovenes – was the heir of the ruined Austro-Hungarian double monarchy in the Balkans. It gained the territories of southern Styria, Krajina, Croatia, Slavonia, Bosnia-Herzegovina, and the bulk of Dalmatia. This 'product of Versailles' was an ethnic hodgepodge which contained Serbians (45 per cent of the population), Croatians, Slovenians, Germans, Hungarians, Romanians, Bulgarians, Greeks, Albanians, and Turks. Nearly until the end of the state, the kingdom's leadership never considered giving the minorities a chance to participate meaningfully in the government. Serbian centralism dominated over Croatian and Slovenian wishes for autonomy and federalism. Their unfulfilled hopes created an explosive mixture. In 1929, internal tensions in Yugoslavia caused the dismissal of the parliament and the establishment of a dictatorship by the Serbian King.

Five years later the first nationalist reaction to this dictatorship exploded. Croatian extremists murdered the Serbian king, Alexander I, in Marseille, France. Only in August 1939 did Belgrade concede to address the 'Croat question', and gave the Croatians some independence, although this move was too little and too late to really achieve a reconciliation between the Serbs and Croats, or to assure the Kingdom of Yugoslavia's survival in the field of international policy. Mussolini's attack on Greece on 29 October 1940 changed the map and balance of power in the Balkans. Hitler decided to act, when the Greek counter-attacks drove the Italians back and entered Italian-controlled Albania. Hitler needed stability on his southeastern flank for his upcoming invasion of the Soviet Union. In 1940 National Socialist Germany had no territorial claims in Yugoslavia, but wanted to trade with her for its economic resources, and was therefore interested in a stable southern Slavic state. Germany therefore planned to integrate Yugoslavia into its Axis system.

The Belgrade government and Prince Paul hesitated, basically because they feared internal unrest if Yugoslavia would side with Berlin and Rome. Finally, German pressure and the promise to support Yugoslav claims for the Greek port of Saloniki turned the scale. On 25 March 1941 the Yugoslavian prime minister, Cvetkovic, signed the treaty initiating Yugoslavia into the Axis fold. The ink on this treaty had just dried, when two days after its signing, a pro-Western *coup* toppled the Cvetkovic Administration and King Peter II ascended to the Serbian throne. The *coup* was clearly anti-German, a fact which was confirmed by isolated excesses against German individuals and institutions. The National Socialist leadership in Berlin reacted swiftly, uncompromisingly, and brutally. Already on 27 March Hitler had given orders to smash the Yugoslav state and to destroy Belgrade using the *Luftwaffe* (German Air Force). German units massed in Hungary, Romania, and Bulgaria. The attacking forces – composed of the 12th and 2nd German Armies – had air support of about 900 planes. The offensive against Yugoslavia and Greece began on 6 April 1941. Italian troops and from 11 April on also, Hungarian troops assisted the German forces. The Yugoslav Army with its forces made up of different nationalities broke down, not only from enemy pressure, but also because of internal frictions.

The Croatian ultra-nationalists Pavelić and Kvaternik (who was a former Colonel in the Croatian army) proclaimed an independent state in Zagreb beginning on 10 April. The Kingdom of Yugoslavia surrendered on 17 April. The victors now divided the country. Germany gained northern Slovenia and occupied old Serbia and the

Banat, while Italy annexed southern Slovenia and parts of Dalmatia. It occupied Montenegro and western Macedonia and enlarged Albania, which had been an Italian-occupied territory since 1939. Hungary gained the Backs and Baranya triangle, while Bulgarian troops entered eastern Macedonia. This swift victory led the victors to arrogance and overconfidence, especially when dealing with the Serbians. Hitler thought that in the German-held territories a three-division occupation force would be sufficient. New states and para-states emerged from the bankrupt estate of Yugoslavia. Being under Italian protection the Independent State of Croatia, welcomed in the beginning by most of its inhabitants, had 6,300,000 people (1943), only 3,300,000 of them Catholic Croats whereas two million were Serbs and the rest 'other' nationalities. The German occupation government in Serbia, which had 4,450,000 inhabitants in 1941, tolerated an indigenous government with a very limited authority, headed by General Milan Nedic beginning in August 1941.

Small Montenegro, which had been independent from 1878 to 1918, had only 435,000 inhabitants and no government at all. Originally the Italians had planned to place the son of the last King of Montenegro on the throne, but installed an Italian 'High Commissioner' in the town of Cetinje instead, when the King's son refused their offer. The stage for the future drama was now set. Occupation troops of the four Axis forces, German National Socialists and Italian Fascists, Croatian nationalists and Croatian communists, Serbian monarchists and Serbian Stalinists, Montenegrin separatists and Bosnian autonomists, exiled Russian followers of the Tsar and Allied secret agents, Slovenian patriots and Macedonian revolutionaries, Catholics, Orthodox pan-Slavs, Muslims and Jews all acted on this tragic stage, set in the former territory that was known as the Kingdom of Yugoslavia. Ethnic, social, religious and national conflicts overlapped and combined in a tangle that was really impossible to unravel. An elaborate policy of peaceful resettlement would have been necessary to smooth out all of these diverging tendencies and interests, or to subordinate them to a common, universal idea. But National Socialist Germany, the leading power of the Axis, was totally unfit for the role of mediator. The daring exploits of the German tank divisions through Europe had not been followed by an inspiring or universal theory or doctrine.

The idea of anti-Semitism and anti-Communism, combined with propaganda of the superiority of Germans might have attracted a minority in Europe, but were extremely useless for an ideology of integration into a European federation of states because they denied the equality of nations and designed a racist hierarchy as the New

Order of Europe. There was no place for Jews and Slavs in this vague 'New Order'. Not all Slavs were destined for extermination, but they could not expect a special place in 'new' Europe. The former lawyer Dr Ante Pavelić, leader of the radical *Ustaše* movement, which had been founded in 1929, wanted to extinguish the stain of south-Slavic origin of his people and encouraged scientists and publicists to 'prove' the non-Slavic origin of the Croatian people. But no one in Berlin was interested in this, because the Balkans was a political and military side-show and Pavelić, the leader of this new Croatia, was not an equal partner. As far as a politically convincing solution was concerned the *Reich* fell short, but there remained Fascist Italy, which was less totalitarian than National Socialist Germany and which had not made racial hatred the doctrine of its state. Italy made attempts to wage war, not only militarily but also to intensify its political manoeuvring in order to introduce a new solution on a European level. This was especially true between the years 1942 to 1943.

A 'European Carta' should have guaranteed the prosperity, sovereignty and freedom of all nations under Axis control, but the National Socialists committed to the ways of terror and unforgiveness turned down this project. It is also doubtful if Rome would have been able to play the role of the honest mediator and find a just supranational settlement, because it considered the Balkans and especially the southern Slavic area as its own sphere of interest. Without a uniting string, without an obligatory idea and without a strong central power, the southern Slavic area relapsed into the old, partly atavistic pattern of behaviour. A kind of bloody and tribal warfare erupted with cruel excesses against other national or ethnic groups and wide spread banditry (you were not able to distinguish some partisan units from gangs of bandits). In some part of the country a '*bellum omnium contra omnes*' raged and considerable areas were a deadly 'no man's land'. An important reason for this was that the various provinces had been influenced by different rules and occupiers and as a result, the southern Slavic area had never developed into a united land. Romans, Byzantines, Venetians, and Turks had ruled at different times, but had never been able to extinguish the various national aspirations for independence or fantasies of superpower status.

Even in Macedonia, which was partitioned between Bulgaria, Greece and Serbia, the dream of a Global Empire of Alexander the Great was still very much alive. Irredentism, chauvinism, religious and ideological hatred, all formed the breeding ground of the tragedy in Yugoslavia. The German intervention was only the beginning of a much bigger war, which in reality was composed of civil wars, national wars of liberation, wars of conquest, religious wars and wars of extermination. The radical Croat *Ustaše* movement's unwillingness to forgive the Serbs was a decisive reason for the brutality of the conflict. The *Ustaše* used deportation, forced baptism, and terror against the Serbs. Whole villages were razed. The massacres assumed such proportions that even the German occupation government protested. The concentration camps in Croatia became real killing fields, Jasenovac being the most notorious. After the war the Communist propaganda took hold of this subject and maintained that between 700,000 and 1,500,000 people, most of them Serbs, had been killed in Jasenovac alone. The Serbian Titoists tried to prove the 'Genocidal nature' of the Croatian people with this false information. Impartial research has now revealed that the number of victims in Jasenovac amounted to around 80,000 people.

The Serbs' response to the *Ustaše* brutality was counter terror. Their actions far exceeded the legitimate defensive actions and were also directed against those non-involved Muslims, who were slaughtered in the thousands. The old hatred against the century-long Turkish occupation resurfaced once again. The communist partisans, who became the strongest force in Yugoslavia at the end of the war, finally murdered because of ideological reasons. Their targets were the political opponents, the class enemy, and the occupation troops. Yugoslavia became a slaughterhouse. The eyewitness, Fitzroy MacLean, a British officer, described the tortured country as a place 'of burning villages, desecrated churches, massacred hostages, and mutilated bodies'. The tactic of the occupation forces to react with mass executions to the Communist and Monarchist guerrilla movements further escalated the situation. The Axis troops were numerically too weak to 'pacify' the southern Slavic area and therefore soon fell back to relying on indigenous forces.

Montenegrin and Serbian volunteer corps, ethnic German units, a Tsarist corps, Croatian divisions of the *Wehrmacht* (German Armed Forces), and Bosnian divisions of the *Waffen SS* came into existence. No other theatre of operations in the Second World War saw a similar great number of foreign units fighting side by side with the Germans. The motives of the Serbian, Bosnian, Montenegrin, and Macedonian volunteers were manifold as were their different uniforms which they wore. The least of them were National Socialists. Most of them fought for the autonomy or national liberty of their region and against Communism, but often with sympathy for the Western Allies. After extensive source study Dr Antonio J. Muñoz has described these events, this kaleidoscope of heroism and treason, rivalry and intrigue in detail with knowledge, fairly and – if this is possible at all – outlined it with great objectivity. It is good that an American author has written about this subject. Not only because of the physical distance separating him from the region in question, but also because Americans have been entangled in the Balkan troubles of this century far less than Europeans, and this is a decisive requirement for an unprejudiced description and appraisal of the southern Slavic tragedy.

After September 1943 matters became more dramatic and complicated when Italy changed sides. Now Italians fought each other in the Balkans – followers of Mussolini, allied with the Germans, against the remains of the Italian occupation forces, which had sided with the Partisans (the same Partisans who had territorial claims against Venetia, Giulia, and Triest). Remnants of the *Regia Aeronautica,* Badoglio's cobelligerent air force, made supply drops to Tito, who reached out for Italian territory and Carinthia. But it also started fomenting trouble within the Axis forces. The relationship between Benito Mussolini's new *Republica Sociale Italiane* and the Independent State of Croatia reached an absolute low, because of Croatian territorial claims in Istria and Dalmatia.

The *Duce* didn't even send an ambassador to Zagreb. To add to the confusion, new combatants entered the Yugoslav theatre in the beginning of 1943. These were General Helmuth von Pannwitz's Cossacks – allied to the Germans and fanatical anti-Communists. The likewise anti-Communist Slovenian Home Guard (*Slovensko Domobranstvo*), which comprised the core of the Slovenian Catholic youth, came into existence in the recently established '*Operationszone Adriatisches Küstenland*' (Zone of Operations Adriatic Coast), under Nazi Party District Leader Friedrich Rainer.

This formation also had strong sympathies for the Western Allies – but these didn't land in Yugoslavia, neither in Montenegro nor in Dalmatia or Istria. Winston Churchill's attitude towards Yugoslavia was especially ambiguous. On the one hand he left the country to Stalin, because he had conceded to limit British influence in post-war Yugoslavia to 10 per cent. On the other hand, he tried to persuade US President Roosevelt into a landing in the Balkans. When he didn't succeed in this, he tried everything to snatch the Dodecanese Islands, especially Rhodes, during the Italian collapse in 1943, to win over Turkey. Turkey should have conquered the Balkans before the Soviets entered that area, and in this way could have secured it for the West. But the German Armed Forces foiled an Allied takeover of the Dodecanese, although it had to fight against six-fold superior forces. Until 1945 Churchill did nothing to oppose communism in Yugoslavia's domestic policy. He was only interested in who had killed more Germans – the

Chetniks or the Communists under Tito. Churchill cut off support for the pro-Western Chetnik leader Draza Mihailovich, when the communists proved to be more effective in this respect.

British support for Tito and Stalin reached its climax in April/May 1945, when the British turned over to their mortal enemies by trickery and force the tens of thousands of Cossacks, Croats, Slovenians, Serbs and Montenegrins who bad fought on the German side. Communist Yugoslavia, which was initially based on terror, didn't last half a century. Today after the international community's diplomatic recognition of Slovenia and Croatia, which was enforced by Vienna and Bonn/Berlin, the Balkans is once again aflame. The chauvinistic theory of a 'Greater Serbia', being one of the initiating factors that caused the First World War, now covers Bosnia-Herzegovina with violence and terror. The Serbian aggression is a war against central Europe. The starting point is nearly the same as it was in 1914: Vienna and Bonn/Berlin sympathizing with the unfortunate Bosnia-Herzegovina, whereas London, Paris and Russia side with Serbia – even though not always openly. Yugoslavia, being an artificial product of Allied diplomacy, has brought its inhabitants no lasting luck. Hatred rules again and the idea of a federation of nations, religions and races with equal rights is also only a chimera again. A supranational and acceptable idea, a written consensus, which guarantees cultural and ethnic diversity, is lacking. The words Leo Valiane wrote for the Italian daily *Corriere delia Sera* on 24 May 1980 are still valid: 'Austria-Hungary is irrevocably gone and nobody strives for its restoration, but until today the vacuum it has left behind has not been filled out.'[1]

Dr Hans Werner Neulen,
Neckargemund

Chapter 1

BACKGROUND TO THE BALKANS

Why do we need to know the Balkan past?

In order to understand the actions taken by Croats, Serbs, and Bosnian Muslims during the Second World War, as well as how outside powers such as Hungary, Austria, Italy, Germany and Russia interacted with these people, one must first understand how the people of this region of Europe came together and how religion, politics and war shaped their psyche. For this, we must look to the past and learn how it all came together, and why it did so as it did. The story of the Second World War in the Balkans, and in particular, in the former Yugoslavia, is the story of old vendettas never forgotten, of a war within a war, within a war, and of conflicting rivalries and goals. The secret to understanding this is hidden in the Balkan past.

The Balkan Peninsula from the Bronze Age to the Iron Age

Ever since the Bronze Age, the region of the Balkan Peninsula has had its own brand of troubles that have been particular to this part of Europe. The crux of the matter is the manner in which the Balkan Peninsula and its people came together. Even before the rise of the Roman Empire, the Balkans was a hotbed of troubles for the people that populated the region and those who migrated there. The Illyrians were the first to settle in the Balkan Peninsula, settling in the northern region of the Balkans around 3000 BC. The Greeks, whose first wave of settlers came into the peninsula around 2000 BC, moved south, eventually establishing the Mycenaean period in Greek history (1600–1100 BC). These Greeks were called the Dorians. The Minoans, who had settled principally on the island of Crete around 5000 BC, eventually spread to the surrounding islands. It is believed that they had come from the western part of Anatolia (present-day western Turkey). Interaction between the Minoans and Dorian Greeks initially occurred during the Mycenaean period. It is then that the first conflict takes place between the Minoans and the Mycenaean Greek city states, like Sparta and Athens.

It is during the Mycenaean period that Homer's classic stories take place, the most famous being the 10-year war and siege of Troy, which was not actually on the Balkan Peninsula, but was located on the northwestern coastline of Anatolia. Meanwhile, contact between the Illyrians and Mycenaean Greeks was limited, mainly due to distance. This changed after the end of the Dark Age in Greek history (1200–900 BC). This saw the emptying of many Greek city states on the Peloponnesian and Euboean regions of Greece. The period that followed, known as the Archaic Period (800–500 BC) saw the arrival of two more waves of Indo-European (Greek) settlers: the Aeolians, and the Ionians. For the most part, Aeolians settled on the islands of the Aegean Sea, while the Ionians settled along the western coastline of Anatolia. The Dorians also settled the island of Crete and surrounding islands – the former home of the Minoans, who disappeared from history during the Dark Age period in Greek history. It is believed that a cataclysmic environmental event occurred on the island of Thera. Today the island of Thera is called Santorini. It's believed that a volcanic eruption on Thera/Santorini destroyed the Minoan civilization and brought about the Dark Age in Greek history. This environmental phenomenon was most likely what scientists refer to as a 'super-volcano' that erupted around 1,200 BC.

The Classical Period of Greek history (500–336 BC) followed the Dark Age. Thracians arrived in the southeastern region of the Balkans through Anatolia around the fifth century BC. Similarly, Dacians (initially called Getae), who are considered proto-Thracians, arrived in the northwestern region of the Balkans around the same time. The Dacians and Thracians were a mixture of Indo-European farmers, some of whom were described as having blue eyes and red hair. It is during the classical period in Greek history that art, architecture, drama, mathematics, science and philosophy reached its zenith in Greek culture. All the while, constant fighting occurred between the Greek city states, as well as with Macedonia, which also had to contend with the wild Illyrian tribes to the north, and the Thracians to the east. Add to this chaos, Persia, which invaded the Balkan peninsula twice: in 490 and 480 BC

The rise of Alexander the Great

Then in 336 BC, the Macedonian king, Philip II, was assassinated by one of his own personal guards, Pausanias of Orestes. Immediately his son, Alexander, assumed control. Thereupon, several Greek city states who had been vassals of Macedonia rebelled. Alexander moved quickly to crush the rebellion, and reestablish Macedonian hegemony over the Greek city states. Knowing that rebellion would erupt again, Alexander resolved to eliminate the threat, by accusing Darius III, the Persian king, of being complicit in the assassination of his father, Philip II. This accusation did two things. First, it gave the young Macedonian king the pretext for invading the Persian Empire. Secondly, it forced the Greek city states who were vassals of the Macedonians to provide troops for the campaign. Troops that otherwise, might have been used against Macedonia in another uprising.

We will never truly know who, if anyone, was behind the assassination of Philip II. Certainly, there were many possible culprits. Philip II had taken a second, much younger wife, who had given him a child. Those who accuse Olympias, the mother of Alexander the Great, say that she was fearful that King Philip would appoint that other child as his heir over Alexander. Others will claim that what inspired Pausanias to kill his king was the taunting and ridicule that Philip's uncle-in-law, Attalus, threw at Pausanias one evening, during a typical Macedonian drinking party. Bisexuality was common during the Greek classical period, and, according to the story, King Philip II had sexual relations with Pausanias. The insult was not that they had a homosexual encounter at the party. The mocking that Attalus heaped on Pausanias was that Philip had 'roughly handled' Pausanias. In effect, all but raping him during the banquet.

Some recent scholars discussing this possibility have claimed that assassinating Philip II was way out of proportion to the humiliation that Pausanias may have felt, and therefore the theory has been made suspect. There is also the possibility that the conspiracy might have involved several Greek city states who loathed to be under the thumb of Macedonia and its ambitious king. In particular, historians have pointed an accusing finger at Athens and Thebes. While this is a possibility, it also has not been completely proven. A few scholars say it could have been Alexander himself who plotted his father's own demise, so he could assume control. Finally, although Alexander was looking for an excuse to invade Persia, by accusing Darius III of being behind his father's murder, that possibility could have actually been true. It was no secret that long before Alexander thought of invading and conquering the Persian Empire, Philip II had already conceived of it. Philip II had finally defeated the wild Illyrian tribes in 357 BC. For centuries, Macedonia had been the kingdom that had kept the Illyrians from invading the Greek city states further south, though those Greek city states never appeared to show any gratitude to the Macedonians. On the contrary, Athenian politicians would often claim that the Macedonians were not Greek at all – an obvious insult to the Macedonians.

The was no love lost between Macedonia and the Greek city-states. After the northern Macedonian border was considered safe, Philip II then involved himself in the Third Sacred War, gaining greater power as a result. Later, he conquered most of the Greek city states in 338 BC The only powerful state that was not compelled to join the League of Corinth created by Philip (which the Greek city states were forced to join), was Sparta. Philip II sent a threatening letter to the Spartans in which he wrote that he would send his army into the Peloponnese and if the Spartans lost, he would turn Sparta into a subjugated state. The Spartans answered Philip's demand by sending him a letter of their own. In it, their one-word reply was: 'If.' Philip took the hint and left the Spartans alone. Nevertheless, by 336 BC Philip II was in almost complete control of the southern part of the Balkan Peninsula, so he was in a position to threaten the Persian Empire. It is possible therefore, that Darius III may have been involved in Philip's assassination, in order to prevent the Macedonian king from carrying through on his plan. Whichever is the case, his death brought about a drastic change in the history of the Balkan Peninsula, when his son, Alexander of Macedon, assumed power. After the death of Alexander in 323 BC, several Greek city states once again rebelled against Macedonian rule, but were quickly put down. The empire that Alexander had created however, fractured into various kingdoms, all of them ruled by his former generals, and all of whom often fought one another.

Pax Romana

The next significant event to alter the history of the Balkans, was the invasion of the region by the Romans in the second century BC. The Romans took some time to conquer the numerous Greek city states as well as the various empires established after the death of Alexander the Great, but in the end they did, expanding Roman power into the eastern Mediterranean Sea. For the next five centuries, Rome would rule the entire Mediterranean basin region virtually unopposed. In the second century AD the people that eventually became the Bulgarians, made their appearance. They were of Turkic origin from the Hunnic-Onogur tribe, and had moved to the southeastern region of the Balkans from Central Asia. Their arrival presaged the arrival of a larger mass migration of people from Central Asia. This began with the arrival of the Huns in the third century AD. For 200 years, these nomadic and warlike people from the central Asian steppes invaded eastern and central Europe, displacing numerous Germanic tribes who could not oppose them and affecting the Roman Empire, initially indirectly, but later directly. The Hunnic invasion of Europe was a principal cause for the so-called Crisis of the Third Century within the Roman Empire and the beginning of that Empire's fall.

The Germanic tribes, who had been a bothersome issue for the Romans, had always been held back by the might of the Roman legions. However, once dozens of these tribes were displaced from their former German lands, they had only one place to move to: Roman territory. Where before, the Roman Army could handle the incursion of one, two or even three Germanic tribes into Roman territory, now dozens of tribes were invading Roman lands at once, and this proved to be simply overwhelming. In 476 AD the western half of the Roman Empire fell, when the Germanic Sciri tribal king and former Roman auxiliary commander, Odoacer, conquered Rome and overthrew the 12-year-old emperor Romulus Augustulus. Odoacer ruled on the Italian peninsula until 493 AD, but from the very beginning, he did not control the entire western half of the Roman Empire. Instead, numerous Germanic tribes carved up whole sections of territory. These tribes included the Vandals, Visigoths, Franks, Burgundians, Alemanni, Cimbri, Teutons, Charudes, Jutes, and others. In the eastern half of the Roman Empire however, the Romans persisted. From this eastern half of the Roman Empire rose what we today call the Byzantine Empire.

The rise of the Byzantine Empire

The rise of the Byzantine Empire is directly related to Emperor Constantine I, who was the victor in a Roman civil war that ended in 311 AD when he defeated the second co-ruling emperor, Maxentius, at the Battle of the Milvian Bridge, just north of Rome, along the Tiber River. Although Emperor Constantine was not a Christian, he attributed his victory to the Christian God, so as a reward, in 313 AD, Constantine issue the famous Edit of Milan, granting all religions within the Roman Empire the right to worship freely without persecution. It should be noted that by 311 AD, Constantine's mother had already converted to Christianity, but he converted only on his deathbed in 337 AD. This implies that he was not a true believer, but that he merely used the up-and-coming Christian faith as a way to unite the people in his empire.

Constantine had a choice to make in 311 AD – whether to remain in Rome given that it was the classical capital of the Roman Empire, or move elsewhere. The eastern half of the Roman Empire had always been the richest, and the most populous. It was therefore with this in mind that Emperor Constantine I chose to live in the eastern half of the empire, in order to better control it. He built a new capital which he named after himself: Constantinople. Work on the city began in 322 AD, at the site of an existing fishing town that was called Byzantium. It is from the name of this small fishing town, upon which the city of Constantinople was built, that would eventually give the latter history of the Roman Empire its name: the Byzantine Empire. The city would continue to grow over the centuries, but by 326 AD the initial confines of the city had been established.

A year earlier, in 325 AD Emperor Constantine officiated, but did not take an active role in the Council of Nicaea. It was at the Council of Nicaea that many issues of the early Christian Church were adjudicated. For example, the Nicaean Creed was established. This is the prayer that all Catholics make when they partake of church services. It was also during the Council of Nicaea that the ideas of presbyter Arias, an Egyptian Christian priest, were branded a heresy. Arias believed that Christ was, at one point, a human being. But if one was to believe in the Trinity – that God, Jesus and the Holy Spirit were one and the same – then you could not accept the belief that Christ was human at any time. Arias was excommunicated from the Christian Church and banished into Goth lands. He took his revenge on the Christian leaders of the Church who had expelled him, by converting the Goths to his brand of Christianity: Aryan Christianity. Eventually, most of the Germanic tribes adopted Arianism instead of Catholicism. It was also at the Council of Nicaea that the New Testament to the Jewish bible was put together from the writings of the original apostles and early church patriarchs. Jews believe in the Old Testament (that is their bible), but Christians believe in both the Old and New Testament (which together forms the Christian bible).

The schism between Catholicism and Eastern Orthodox Christianity

The break between the Catholic Church in Western Europe and the Eastern Orthodox Church in Eastern Europe began with Bishop Leo, the Christian Bishop of Rome in 450 AD, who in that year wrote a letter to Bishop Flavius of Constantinople. At the time, the position of Pope in the Christian Church did not exist. In 450 AD there were five principal bishops in Christendom: the position of Bishop of Jerusalem, Bishop of Alexandria, Bishop of Antioch, Bishop of Constantinople and Bishop of

Rome. Leo wrote a *Tome*, a letter explaining the position of the Papacy in matters of Christology. In the letter, Leo argued among other things, that the interpretation of Matthew 16:18 in the New Testament was that Peter, one of the twelve original apostles of Jesus Christ, was the rock upon which Christ said would build his Church. Peter was martyred in Rome in 64 AD under the orders of Emperor Nero. Because Peter was the foundation of the Christian Church (according to his interpretation of Mathew 16:18), then Peter was the first head of the Christian faith, and by virtue, every other Bishop of Rome that followed him, was the head of the Christian Church on earth.

Obviously, this meant that Bishop Leo of Rome was claiming that he was above all the other Christian bishops, and therefore the head of the Christian Church. Leo began to call himself Pope Leo I, and a year later in 451 AD, at the Council of Chalcedon, he pushed forward that idea. The main purpose for the council had actually been to reassert the wisdom of the ecumenical Council of Ephesus, against the heresies of Eutyches and Nestorius, and their idea of a monotheistic God (single entity), which of course, ran contrary to the idea of the Holy Trinity (the Father, the Son, and the Holy Ghost). However, Leo I used the council and his *Tome* to push forward the idea that whoever was the Bishop of Rome, was also the head of the Christian faith (Pope). For the most part the bishops at the council, including most of the major Christian bishops, from Alexandria, Jerusalem, and Antioch, all acquiesced to Leo's argument. The only holdout was the Bishop of Constantinople, Flavius.

The argument became quite heated, with the effect that at one point Flavius retorted, 'If you want to call yourself Pope, and claim that you are the head of the Christian Church, then I'll call myself Patriarch of Constantinople, and the head of the Christian followers in the East.' The break between the western and eastern Christians did not occur immediately, but took hundreds of years to simmer and fester. During that time, the Christian Church in the West was developing customs separate from the Christian Church in the East. Even such mundane things like how a monk would cut his hair, or the issue of whether to use leavened or unleavened bread at mass, began to differentiate the Eastern Christian Church from the Western Christian Church. The final break occurred in 1054 AD and is forever immortalized in religious history as 'The Great Schism'. The distrust that existed between Catholicism and Eastern Orthodox Christianity lingered for hundreds of years. Eventually, the Croatians adopted Catholicism, while the Serbians embraced the Eastern Orthodox Church. Religion from this point on, was also a contributing factor to the issues that would divide these two people from each other. That mistrust that existed between the Catholic faith and Eastern Orthodox Christianity was passed onto the Serbs and Croats, adding to the existing animosity between these two peoples. Even today, some of this enmity can still be felt between both churches, although on the surface, and officially, they appear to show tolerance.

The rise of Islam, and the arrival of the Seljuk Turks

The rise of Islam from the Arabian Peninsula in the seventh century AD forever altered the history of the world. Islam spread quickly, and the first empire to fall to the green flag of Islam was the Sassanid Persian Empire. The Sassanid Empire fell in 651 AD. For hundreds of years, the Byzantine Empire had been fighting the Sassanid Empire, with no clear winner. When the empire fell, the news of its demise at the hands of Islamic forces was greeted with cheers and celebrations in Constantinople. That sense of euphoria was quickly shattered when Muslim forces began launching raids against the heartland of the Byzantine Empire in eastern and central Anatolia. A major struggle now developed between Islam and Christianity. While the Byzantines were able to hold off initial attacks by Muslim forces, Islam nevertheless spread east and west. Under the Rashidun Caliphate (632–661 AD), Islam spread to present-day Egypt, Libya, Syria, Iraq, the Holy Land, Persia and beyond. Under the Umayyad Caliphate (661–750 AD) Islam reached the western half of North Africa, into the Iberian Peninsula, as well as present-day Afghanistan and Pakistan, and parts of central Asia.

The arrival of another nomadic tribe to the Middle East from central Asia, the Seljuk Turks, in the ninth century AD, forever altered the equation in favour of Islam versus Christianity. Like most nomadic peoples who entered regions that were already occupied by agrarian societies, the Seljuk Turks gave up their nomadic ways and became farmers themselves. They would also take on the existing faith. When they entered the Middle East, they converted to Sunni Islam. The Seljuk Turks were a nomadic society that had developed an excellent cavalry. They retained that heritage when they settled down. Over time, the Seljuk Turks began to make inroads into Byzantine territories. Byzantium was always at a crossroads from where it was located. In the West, Catholic Christian knights fought the Byzantines in Italy and other Byzantine holdings. In the Balkans, the rise of the Serbian kingdom occurred at the expense of Byzantine territory. The same was true of the rise of the Bulgarian kingdom. In the East, it had first been the Parthians, then the Sassanid Persians who were the enemy, followed by Arab Muslims and then the Seljuk Turks. The history of the Byzantine Empire, in effect, was the history of enemies on all sides and constant warfare that, over time, wore down the Byzantine Empire.

The Byzantine Empire did not collapse immediately and did not fall simply on religious grounds. There were extenuating factors that helped hasten the demise of the Byzantine Empire and it all began in the eleventh century AD. The first was a weakness that was the creation of the Byzantines themselves. The *Dynatoi,* the powerful nobles, were the Byzantine aristocracy who often wielded political power through their offices in civil, religious, and military circles. In the beginning of the eleventh century, the *Dynatoi* engineered to get a Byzantine emperor elected, whom they could control. Through the emperor, laws were passed that were favourable to the nobility but economically damaging to the empire. For example, a law was passed that allowed the *Dynatoi* to obtain government lands for free, in exchange for a promise to give a portion of the proceeds from those cultivated lands to the Byzantine government treasury. The only problem with this was that the nobles took the land, and never gave any of the profits gained from the cultivation of those lands to the Byzantine treasury.

Towards the end of the reign of the Byzantine Emperor, Basil II, a decision was made by the emperor that would have far reaching and long-term economic consequences for the Byzantine Empire. The rule of Basil II, known also as 'the Bulgar slayer', is considered the height of Byzantine power and influence. During his almost 50-year reign (January 976–December 1025), he managed to defeat the Bulgarians after a 20-year struggle, and held off repeated incursions by the Fatimid Caliphate based in Syria. At the same time, he managed to control the southern tip of the Italian peninsula. There, he firmly held on to the important cities of *Brindisium* (Brindisi), *Tarento* (Taranto), *Bari,* and *Reghium* (Reggio). All of these military successes did not come cheap. The cost of fighting enemies on all sides is never cheap. By the end of his reign, the Byzantine treasury was nearly empty. Something had to be done. The decision was made in the summer of 1025 to begin to add non-precious metals to the Byzantine gold sovereign, which would feature the face of the emperor at minting.

Byzantine coins were valued above all other gold coins. This move allowed the Byzantine Empire to continue to pay for its numerous armies and navies, but the end-result of this act was to devalue the Byzantine coin, which in turn created inflation. Because of these various decisions, the economic base of the Byzantine Empire began to shrink. That in turn, made it harder for the later Byzantine Emperors to defend the empire. The final nail in the coffin, as it were, to the eventual demise of the Byzantine Empire was, like the other factors discussed above, an issue that was solely the making of the Byzantines themselves. This last aspect had to do with the nature of Byzantine rule. Throughout the history of the Byzantine Empire, court intrigues, military coups, and treachery ruled the day. The number of Byzantine Emperors who were overthrown, then were either killed or were blinded and sent to a monastery for the rest of his life, is Legion.

That is to say, that political intrigue was endemic in the nature of Byzantine rule, and this constant infighting among the various noble families, religious and economic rivals, all vying for power, helped to sap the strength of the empire and quicken its eventual demise. As President Abraham Lincoln once said, 'a house divided against itself, cannot stand'.[1] In fact, this division was so prevalent and constant in the history of Byzantine rule, that one can use the word 'Byzantine', as it has come to mean in the English language, someone or some group characterized by operating or behaving in a devious and usually surreptitious manner. The stage was set, therefore, for the confrontation between the Byzantine Empire, at the height of its power, and the Seljuk Turks at the end of the eleventh century. After Basil II died, Constantine VIII, who was the second son of Romanus II, was elected emperor. His reign lasted three years (December 1025–November 1028). His 'contribution' to the beginning of the decline of Byzantine power was to be distrustful of his leading generals, most of whom were extremely competent. Those who weren't executed were blinded and exiled. During his reign Romanus II had thus eliminated the best military talent that had been defending the empire.

Uninterested in the well-being of the empire, Romanus II was told by his advisors whom to pick as his successor. Apparently, the one qualifying factor that made Romanus III the perfect candidate to be the next emperor, was that he could be manipulated by the *Dynatoi*. During his reign Romanus III lowered the taxes on the aristocracy, which of course, was the point why he had been chosen as emperor. His reign however, was also brief, given that when he became emperor, he was already 60 years old. He reigned from November 1028 to April 1034. The next emperor was Michael IV, who had been the lover of the wife of Romanus III, Zoe. His reign was insignificant as well, given that his attempt to recover Sicily from the Catholic Frankish knights failed. He also suffered from bouts of epilepsy, which didn't help matters. Apparently, he had no formal education, and had to rely heavily on his court advisors. Again, his reign suited the *Dynatoi,* since he was pliable. He ruled from April 1034 to December 1041. The nephew and adopted son of Michael IV, Michael V, became the new emperor upon the death of Michael IV. His reign lasted only from December 1041 to April 1042. His mistake was to try and sideline the power and influence of his uncle's wife, Zoe. The courtiers sided with the 64-year-old Zoe. Before being banished, he was castrated and sent to a monastery, where he died that same year from an infection of the groin.

The next two individuals to rule the Byzantine Empire were women. Zoe ruled from 1042–50, although she supposedly ruled with her younger sister, Theodora. Zoe married Constantine IX in 1042. Although not officially emperor, Constantine IX was the actual decision-maker and therefore, ruler. When Zoe died, it was Theodora, who was officially given the title of empress. Her rule lasted from 1050–6. Thereafter Constantine IX assumed official control of the empire. According to the chroniclers, Constantine IX was only concerned with living a luxurious lifestyle, and thus ignored growing threats to the empire. As a result, he also alienated the military aristocracy, and favoured the merchant class. During his reign, the Pechenegs, who were a semi-nomadic Turkic group from Central Asia, invaded the Balkans from the northeast and threatened Byzantine territory. Simultaneously from the east, the Seljuk Turks began to make greater inroads into eastern Anatolia. Given his neglect of affairs of state, he had to contend with two military revolts against him, one from 1042–3 and the other in 1047, when the cousin of Constantine IX, who was a general, rebelled, but failed. The reign of Constantine IX is also marked by the first serious clashes with the Seljuk Turks.

After the death of Constantine IX, there followed three more emperors who reigned through the years 1056 to 1067. In January 1068 Romanus IV Diogenes became the Byzantine Emperor. His claim to fame would be that he presided over the defeat of Byzantine forces against the Seljuk Turks at the Battle of Manzikert in 1071. A capable general, he was betrayed twice. The first betrayal was during the battle itself. Knowing fully the threat that the Seljuk Turks posed, not only to the Byzantine Empire, but to Catholic Europe, Romanus IV had hired hundreds of Catholic knights and men-at-arms to fight alongside his men. He paid these Christian mercenaries handsomely, hoping that his magnanimity would guarantee their allegiance to Byzantium, if only for one battle. But that did not stop these Christian knights from walking away from the battlefield at a critical point in the battle, and thus handing a victory to the Seljuk Turks. The second betrayal was when Andronikos Doukas, who controlled the Byzantine Army reserve troops, saw that his emperor was in trouble, but nevertheless abandoned the battlefield, and quickly marched back to Constantinople, to declare Romanus IV dead, so he could become emperor. Romanus

IV was captured by Sultan Alp Arslan, who eventually ransomed him to the Byzantines. However, he was rebuffed by Andronikos Doukas. Once freed, Romanus IV gathered what forces he could and fought to regain his throne. He lost and was ordered blinded and exiled to a monastery by Doukas. The defeat of the Byzantines at the Battle of Manzikert in 1071 allowed the Seljuk Turks to obtain eastern and central Anatolia, which was the economic as well as the population base of the Byzantine Empire. With the 'heart' of the empire carved out, the fall of Byzantium was guaranteed. It took a long time for the empire to fall, but the end of the eleventh century was the beginning of the end for the Byzantine Empire. The rest was a slow, agonizing death that ended in 1453. A slow death by a thousand little cuts is the best way to describe the downfall of the Byzantine Empire.

The rise of the Ottoman Empire

In 1453, Constantinople finally fell to the Muslim forces of the 21-year-old Ottoman Sultan, Mehmet II. Thereafter followed several hundred years when Ottoman rule expanded throughout the Balkans, where many peoples, the Greeks, Bulgarians, Serbs, Wallachians, Croats and others lived. The Serbs in particular, were devastated when they had been defeated by the Ottomans in 1389, at the Battle of Kosovo. This was because after the battle, the Ottomans made it a point to wipe out every existing family member of the Serbian nobility. This had the effect of turning the Serbian nation into a leaderless class of peasant farmers. It took a long, long time for Serbian leaders to rise from the crowd. The Serbs never forgot, and never forgave the Ottoman Muslims for this. This is why for centuries, the Serbs have hated the Turks, and why for them, a Serbian Muslim is an abomination which they always seek to destroy. Croatia, which was also a target of Ottoman expansion, had been a vassal state of the Hungarian kingdom since the twelfth century. From the fourteenth century up to the end of the seventeenth century, the kingdom of Croatia struggled to defend itself from Ottoman invasion. The so-called Hundred Years' Croatian-Ottoman War lasted from 1493 to 1593, when the Ottomans were conclusively halted at the Battle of Sisak. There a combined army from the Habsburg lands, mainly from the Kingdom of Croatia and the Kingdom of Inner Austria, defeated an Ottoman Bosnian force. Nevertheless, the Ottomans continued to control large swaths of Croatian territory into the sixteenth and seventeenth century. The beginning of Ottoman decline occurred at the end of the seventeenth century, when a large Ottoman army was defeated at the Siege of Vienna in 1683.

The Austrians were saved by the arrival of French, German and Polish troops. Thereafter, the Ottomans began to slowly lose territories that they had previously conquered. Ironically, their decline mimicked the fall of the Byzantine Empire: a slow and agonizing death that lasted for hundreds of years.

Figure 2. General reference map of the Balkans in 1941. The major mountain ranges are listed. (Author's line drawing)

Chapter 2

THE BALKAN TROUBLES

The modern region of the Balkans and its people

The word 'Balkan' is derived from a Turkish word meaning mountain. As used by the English-speaking nations, however, the word refers to that peninsula of southeastern Europe lying between the Black and Adriatic Seas and extending south to the Mediterranean. To the north, the geographic boundary is less definite, but is generally accepted as the area south of the line of the Danube and Sava, west along the Kupa River, whence an imaginary line is drawn to the Adriatic port of Fiume. From north to south, the broad expanse of the Danube Basin gives way to the mountain ranges of Yugoslavia and Bulgaria. The remainder of the peninsula consists mainly of rugged mountains, broken occasionally by such features as the coastal lowlands of Albania, the area surrounding the Gulf of Salonika in Greece, and the lowlands of Turkish Thrace. The Balkan peoples have been in contact with the inhabitants of Asia Minor, the Hungarian Plain, Central Europe, and the highly developed Mediterranean civilizations for thousands of years. Nevertheless, it is still possible to distinguish such ethnic groupings as the Albanians, Serbs, Bulgars, Turks, Greeks and Vlachs, the last a semi-nomadic race of herdsmen being absorbed gradually into the various national states into which the Balkan area is divided. Occupied for centuries by Romans, Turks, Austrians, and Hungarians, the Balkan peoples were forced to adopt the methods of irregular warfare in the struggle against their oppressors. When not resisting foreign invaders, they battled one another or kept alive their fighting traditions in bitter blood feuds. The mountainous terrain of their peninsula, with few good roads or rail lines, hampered the countermeasures of regular forces and made possible sustained guerrilla operations.

The Demise of the Ottoman Empire

The history of the Balkans, beginning with the fall of the Byzantine capital, Constantinople, in 1453 and continuing into the seventeenth century, is one of continued Ottoman expansion. After the second siege of Vienna however, military fortunes began to turn for the Ottomans and a slow but steady decay in their power began. During the eighteenth century the Ottomans attempted to maintain what lands they had, but more and more rebellions began to appear. The first half of the nineteenth century saw these rebellions increase in tempo and number. The second half of the nineteenth century and beginning of the twentieth century saw further upheaval and much conflict in the Balkan Peninsula. Most of it was centred on the numerous independence movements of the many people there under Ottoman rule. The Ottoman Empire came to be known as the 'sick man of Europe'. The Ottomans ended up on the losing side of these struggles. Determined to prevent further erosion of their empire, a revolt occurred in 1908 that was supported both by university students and the Turkish military which finally overthrew the incompetent, lazy and corrupt Sultan, Abdul Hamid II from power, installing a constitutional government. However, the Sultan attempted a coup in April 1909 that eventually failed. This failed coup led to the establishment of a three-man military junta running what remained of the empire. This junta (nicknamed the 'three Pashas') governed Turkish lands until the end of the First World War. They were responsible for deciding to join the Central Powers (Germany and the Austro-Hungarian Empire) in October 1914. This proved to be a fatal blunder. After the Turkish defeat, all three were blamed for the loss in the First World War and the dismemberment of what remained of the Ottoman Empire. One by one, all three were assassinated. A constitutional government was organized but it was a former Ottoman Army officer, Mustafa Kemal, known as *Atatürk* (father of the Turks) who eventually led the Turkish nation during its conflict with Greece (1919–23) and beyond.

The Balkan land-grab

Meanwhile those Balkan nations who had cooperated with one another in seizing Ottoman lands eventually turned against each other. In 1908 the Austro-Hungarian Empire annexed the provinces of Bosnia and Hercegovina. These two regions had been formally under Ottoman rule, but had become semi-independent in 1878. Seeing the weakness of the 'sick man of Europe', the Austro-Hungarian emperor, Franz

Josef, seized the two provinces and made them a part of his empire. The agreement to annex the two provinces had actually been a part of the treaty signed by the Russian *Tsar*, the German *Kaiser*, and the Austro-Hungarian emperor, and referred to as the *Drei Kaiser Bund* (the League of the Three Emperors) in 1881. The problem arose when a new Tsar objected to the annexation in 1897. In 1908 the Russian Tsar relented, only if the Austro-Hungarian emperor would support the Tsar's request to open the Bosporus Strait and the Dardanelles to Russian warships. The Austro-Hungarian occupation of Bosnia and Hercegovina enraged the Serbians, who had designs on the sizable Serbian population that lived in those two regions. Serbian nationalists have always had the dream of establishing a 'Greater Serbia' by unifying all Serbian people into one large Serb state.

Of course, the substantial Bosnian Muslim and Croatian Catholic populations living in these two regions were not taken into consideration. Given that there was a sizable Serbian population under Austro-Hungarian rule was enough to drive these Serbian nationalists to anger. Conflict between both states seemed inevitable given the animosity and hatred that both the Serbs and Austro-Hungarians had for one another. While the annexation of Bosnia and Hercegovina had been a blow to the Serbian nationalist dream of a 'Greater Serbia', other conflicts were brewing in the Balkans. Conflict between the Ottoman Empire on one hand, and the nations of Greece, Serbia, Montenegro and Bulgaria on the other erupted into the First Balkan War (8 October 1912 to 30 May 1913). Additional allies against the Ottomans included volunteers from Albania and Russia's official declaration of war against the Ottoman Empire. The end result was the loss of additional Balkan territory by the Ottomans. Almost immediately a second conflict broke out. This turned out to be the Second Balkan War (June–August 1913); begun when Bulgaria, unhappy with the lands it had gained from the Ottomans after the First Balkan War, declared war on Serbia and Greece. Serbia and Greece had gotten the lion's share of the territories lost by the Ottomans after the First Balkan War. Bulgaria, seeing that it had received the 'scraps', sought a redress. However, things quickly worked against the Bulgarians. In this conflict, Romania quickly joined against Bulgaria, hoping to get in on the spoils by siding with the side with the superior numbers. The Ottoman Empire even joined in as well. Facing overwhelming numbers, Bulgaria was forced to sue for peace and lost all the lands gained in the First Balkan War. The city of Adrianople even had to be handed over to the Ottomans.

The Middle East in the aftermath of the Great War

The First World War destroyed four empires and reshaped all of Europe and the Middle East. In the Middle East, the British and the French were the winners. In 1916, even before the First World War had been won, France and England signed a secret pact, called the Sykes-Picot Agreement, whereby the Middle East would be divided amongst the two Entente powers after hostilities ended. Indeed, the French and British created new mandate states from the various peoples of the Middle East. The Arabs, who had only supported the Entente Powers because of vague promises made to them by Sir Henry McMahon, the British high commissioner for Egypt, were rightly angered after they realized that France and the United Kingdom were not going to leave the Middle East to its own affairs. After the war ended Prince Faisal temporarily occupied Damascus, thinking the British would permit an Arab state to be established in that region. The French unceremoniously expelled Prince Faisal and several hundred of his Arab guerrilla fighters from the Syrian capital.

Both Faisal's father, Hussein bin Ali al-Hashimi, the Sharif of Mecca, and his brother, Prince Abdallah, were livid. It was then that the Arabs realized they had been hoodwinked and betrayed by the British. Prince Abdallah decided to come to the aid of his brother, Prince Faisal, who had been humiliated by the French by being forced to leave the Syrian city. Abdallah began to move several thousand Arab fighters towards Damascus from the Arabian Peninsula. The Arab army was not a serious threat to the French in Syria, but it posed a very sensitive problem. The British and other Western nations were now becoming more and more dependent on oil. Instability in the region would have destabilized that supply of oil coming out of the Middle East. Seeing the danger, Winston Churchill, who in 1920 was Secretary of State for the Colonies in the Foreign Office, came up with a plan to defuse the French-Arab situation. It was Churchill who suggested appeasing the Faisal and Abdallah brothers by offering Faisal the kingship of Iraq, a newly created state. Iraq had been drawn on a map, somewhere in a London bureaucrat's table, over afternoon tea and biscuits. The frontiers of this new state had been drawn irrespective of the diverse peoples that they inadvertently forced together. The borders completely ignoring tribal boundaries and ethnic regions.

Of course, this was beneficial to the British. By including various groups into one kingdom, the British were assured that infighting between those groups would allow them the opportunity to be the real rulers behind the scene. It was the old tactic of divide and rule which had been so successfully employed by the British in creating their empire. Although Faisal was made king, London really ruled. His brother, Abdallah, was given a strip of worthless desert east of the Jordan River, that was similarly created by London bureaucrats. The nation of Jordan, as it is called today, was and is still dependent on foreign economic assistance to maintain its viability. Today, it is the United States and Saudi Arabia who prop up the Jordanian economy. In the past, it was the United Kingdom. Jordan had made attempts in the past to cultivate a domestic economy, and there was a move to grow fig trees as a cash crop. However, in 1964 the Israeli government began to divert water from the Jordan River that ultimately reduced the amount of water available for Jordanian consumption. Today water is at a premium for Jordanian farmers who are still willing to cultivate fig trees. To this day, the high cost of water is a major challenge facing small-scale farmers in Jordan. Water shortages and high costs are the most significant challenges for small-scale farmers, according to a study issued by the United Nations Food and Agriculture Organisation (FAO). But I digress. This mandate kingdom originally called Transjordan was and always remained an artificially-created state. But by creating Iraq and Transjordan/Jordan both Abdallah and Faisal were thrown a bone, and the Arab threat to the required peace that the British and French needed to extract the region's resources quickly fizzled out. The British and French were now free to dig up the region's oil without fear of interruption or chaos. The Suez Canal was also secure and British and French dominance of the region would hold until 1948.

Long memories and short tempers

As for the various peoples that comprised the Balkans, their future in the first half of the twentieth century would not be made any easier by the demise of the German, Russian, Austro-Hungarian and Ottoman Empire. Memories in the region of the Balkan Peninsula never forgot insults and slights that had occurred to their ancestors long ago. The people of the region carried these grudges and biases with them as the twentieth century passed. Past political upheavals and religious conflicts lay there, temporarily dormant, just below the surface. To their great detriment, old grudges and biases were a great part of the psyche of the Balkan people. Unfortunately, this is still true today, and most likely will be for the foreseeable future. Vendettas and murders involving honour still abound in this region of the world. In the case of Yugoslavia, in addition to 'normal' family or personal vendettas, the political, ethnic and religious hatred is centred on four groups who absolutely hate each other with a passion.

During the Second World War, these main groups were (1) the Serbian royalists of the Zbor movement;[1] (2) the royalist Chetniks led by Draža Mihailović, who was Josip Broz Tito's chief rival for power in the Second World War, and (3) the Croatians, including many former members of the *Ustaše* movement. Finally, Bosnian Muslims were the fourth group. The Serbians are Eastern Orthodox Christians, while the Croatians are ardently Catholic. The overwhelming majority of Slovenians are Catholic as well. In fact, most Slovenian homes to this day have a Christian cross that they place in the corner of one of the rooms in the house. The Slovenians refer to this as 'Christ's corner'. Although the Croatian Catholics tolerate the Muslims to a certain degree, it is an uneasy alliance which Croatians and Bosnian Muslims have forged against their common enemy, the Serbians. The Second World War in Yugoslavia was, for all intents and purposes, a war within a civil war, within a long-standing conflict between peoples who really did not want to live together. For the most part, this is still the case today.

Stacking the Deck

Which brings us to the Yugoslav state, known up until 1928 as the Kingdom of the Serbs, Croats and Slovenes. To say that Yugoslavia was an artificially-created state like Iraq and Transjordan (known simply as Jordan beginning in 1948), is an understatement. Given that during the First World War Serbia had been a member of the Entente powers and the Croatians and Bosnian Muslims had served in the Austro-Hungarian Army, the British and French made sure that Serbia would be the dominant power in this multi-ethnic, multi-religious, multi-cultural artificially-created state. The Slovenians, Croatians and Bosnian Muslims felt (rightly) that they had been handed a lousy deal. In fact, they had. The chauvinistic theory of a 'Greater Serbia', which had been partly responsible for the First World War, finally bore fruit in a state (Yugoslavia) that was dominated by the Serbs. The Serbian government was a parliamentary monarchy, with a Serbian king, even though a federalist system was also created. However, unlike in the United Kingdom, where the monarch is pretty much a figurehead, in Yugoslavia King Alexander I was an autocratic ruler. For example, he could appoint or fire the Prime Minister. Unlike the House of Lords and the House of Commons in the United Kingdom, the Serbian parliament was more a rubber stamp for the Serbian king than a check on his power.

As all autocratic rulers tend to do, any sign of political opposition or regional autonomy was ruthlessly crushed by the central royalist government. Political parties were banned and numerous newspapers were shut down for publishing articles deemed in opposition to the king and his authority. Naturally, whenever a nation experiences this kind of political repression, it is only normal that secret political and military organizations will be established, given that no one could speak truth to power without fearing arrest or worst. This is why Anarchism and Socialism grew in Tsarist-era Russia to such large numbers. This was because the Russian Tsar, being an autocrat, was absolutely opposed to any form of criticism of himself and his government. The same thing happened in Spain, where the king, the nobility and the landed gentry had their boots on the neck of the landless poor, which constituted the majority of the population in the country. One must also take into account human nature, which shows us that those in a society who are in a privileged position, will seek to hold onto those privileges at whatever cost. The Serbs where in a privileged position after the end of the First World War. They intended to keep that privilege, even if it meant treating the other peoples that made up Yugoslavia as second-class citizens.

To this unbalanced social equation, the people of Yugoslavia also had to contend with hundreds of years of religious intolerance and private vendettas. Life in Yugoslavia during the 1920s and 1930s became more and more politically toxic. In 1926, Stjepan Radić, the leader of the Croatian Peasant Party and the most popular Croatian politician of his time, was shot dead on the floor of the *skupština* (the House of the National Assembly). He had been killed by a fellow politician, Puniša Račić, a Serbian member of parliament from the region of Montenegro. The assassination of Radić was seen by many in Croatia as a declaration of war by the Serbs. This was especially true to most Croatians after Puniša Račić, who was tried and sentenced to 60 years in prison, quickly had his sentence reduced to 20 years and to 'house arrest'. The unfairness and injustice of this ruling merely rubbed salt into the open wound carried by the Croatian people.

The Serbian king, Alexander I, made matters worse when on 6 January 1929 he abolished the Yugoslav constitution. Henceforth his regime no longer had the trappings of legitimacy and popular sovereignty, but was simply a dictatorship. Solidifying Serbian dominance in the country, Alexander I quickly moved to create nine more *banonvinas* (regions), while also redrawing the existing thirty-three regions. The effect of this remapping of the country was that out of the forty-two regions that now made up Yugoslavia, the Serbs had majorities in all but three of them. Two regions were dominated by the Slovenians and the Croatians were dominant in only one region where they had a majority. Today in the United States we would call that partisan redistricting 'gerrymandering': the political manipulation of electoral district boundaries with the intent to create undue advantage for a party, group or socioeconomic class within the constituency. Clearly, the Serbian king had stacked the deck in favour of Serbia and Serbians at the expense of the Croatians, Slovenians, and Bosnian Muslims. The rise of the radical *Ustaše Stranka* (Ustashe Party) therefore, was due mostly to the repressive political atmosphere inside the Yugoslav state, especially beginning in 1929 when the king declared his dictatorship. It is not a coincidence that the *Ustaše* Party was established in that same year. By 1931 the terror of bombing and counter bombing, and further assassinations was causing chaos in Yugoslavia.

That same year King Alexander I wrote a new constitution that gave the king complete executive power, thus further alienating those who saw this move as yet another Serbian tactic of repression. In November 1932 the new head of the Croatian Peasant Party, Vladko Maček, demanded that the king dissolve the constitution of 1931 and make a new constitution that would be fair to all the peoples of Yugoslavia. This was not an unreasonable request. Nevertheless, he was immediately arrested and jailed. His declaration however, inspired Muslims, Slovenes and even the minority Hungarians to issue similar demands. Meanwhile, the number of assassinations and reprisals primarily between Croatians and Serbians now numbered in the hundreds. For every bomb that *Ustaše* fanatics planted, the Serbian-dominated police responded with equal speed and fury, fuelling even further resistance to the Yugoslav state. One can even argue that beginning in 1932 Yugoslavia was in a 'slow-burn' civil war.

The assassination of King Alexander I

In the month of October 1934, King Alexander I was in the French city of Marseilles, to sign a Franco-Yugoslav agreement that would pave the way for negotiations with the Italian Fascist dictator, Benito Mussolini, who was supporting the *Ustaše* attacks in Yugoslavia and was harbouring wanted members of that organization, the most important being Ante Pavelić, the *Ustaše* leader. On Tuesday, 9 October 1934 King Alexander I was assassinated by a member of the Inner Macedonian Revolutionary Organization (IMRO). IMRO was another radical political group that had sprung up in the Macedonian region of Yugoslavia and was supported by ethnic Bulgarians who were citizens of Yugoslavia. They sought to make Serbian Macedonia an independent state, but aligned with Bulgaria. French investigators discovered that the Hungarian government had assisted the assassin and that members of IMRO had been in contact with the Croatian Fascist leader, Ante Pavelić. Upon the death of King Alexander I, his cousin Prince Paul became regent for the young heir, Peter II, until he came of age. Prince Paul would rule until Alexander's son, reached the age of 18 and assumed the Serbian throne.

One cannot condone assassinations as a way to change regimes, but given the repression of the Yugoslav state and the fact that peaceful means were unavailable to alter the political reality of living in a tyrannical kingdom, it is no surprise that radical political groups would arise, seeking the ousting of the oppressor. The Roman term *Sic semper tyrannis* ('thus always to tyrants') were the bywords used to explain the radical step taken to try and alter the political equation of the Yugoslav state. This also occurred in Imperial Russia. Wherever you have political repression, where the people are not free to express themselves openly, what invariably occurs is the radicalization of a segment of that society who, because of state tyranny, join extreme and radical political parties and turn to violence as a means to political change. This is why in Tsarist Russia, communism and anarchism became so popular. This is why in Yugoslavia, fascism and communism became popular.

Hitler intervenes in the Balkans

It was Prince Paul who would have to deal with Germany's new leader, Adolf Hitler. By the spring of 1941, the Nazi leader had bullied and/or cajoled many states in central and southeastern Europe into either joining in his planned invasion of the USSR or remaining neutral in the war. In November 1940, the German *Führer* had compelled the leaders of Hungary, Romania, and Slovakia to join the Tripartite Pact. The Hungarians and Romanians would eventually provide entire armies for Hitler's Russian adventure. Even the puppet state of Slovakia, which had been created when the Czech regions became just two more German provinces (Bohemia and Moravia),[2] provided a few divisions for the Russian campaign. On 1 March 1941 Bulgaria signed the Tripartite Treaty. When Adolf Hitler, in the spring of 1941, demanded that Yugoslavia sign an accord with Germany, the prince regent of Yugoslavia balked. In the case of Yugoslavia, the Nazi leader saw its Prince Paul as the key to limiting British influence there. As stated earlier, Prince Paul was to rule until his nephew, Prince Peter II, could reach adulthood and assume the throne. Yugoslavia was therefore the 'missing piece' in Hitler's Balkan plan. However, that piece seemed to have been found by the Nazis leader when the Yugoslav regent reluctantly signed the Tripartite Treaty in the same month as the Bulgarians. On 25 March 1941 in Vienna, the prime minister of Yugoslavia, Dragiša Cvetković, signed the Tripartite Pact on behalf of Prince Paul. There were many reasons why Hitler wanted Yugoslavia as an ally. He needed to secure the right flank of the upcoming German invasion of the Soviet Union. He also needed to come to the aid of Benito Mussolini, whose army was floundering after the invasion of Greece in October 1940.

By December 1940 it was clear to anyone but a complete fool that Mussolini had blundered in attacking Greece. The smaller Greek army had actually pushed the Italian forces back into Albania. Hitler had been incensed that the Italians had opened the entire Mediterranean basin region to war in June 1940. The Italian decision had thus created a threat to Europe's underbelly, the Mediterranean basin. Hitler realized that he had to save his dubious Fascist friend. the Nazi leader approached the prince-regent of Yugoslavia with the offer of gaining territory for his country if Yugoslavia joined Germany in the invasion of Greece. Hitler offered the region of Salonika as a territorial temptation. Prince Paul courteously declined the offer, and once more cautioned the Nazi leader of the overwhelming pro-British sentiment felt by a majority of Serbians. The Serbs dominated the armed forces of Yugoslavia. That meant that the leadership of the Yugoslav Armed Forces were pro-British.

In the face of Prince Paul's warning, Hitler hesitated, then once again attempted to compel the Yugoslav regent with a combination of threats and ultimatums. The prince-regent was cautious and reluctant to signing a treaty with Nazi Germany. He was rightly concerned because his armed forces were overwhelmingly pro-Allied. The experiences of the First World War had seared a hatred of Germany, but especially Austria, on the Serbian people. Although Austria had been annexed by Germany in 1938, and made into just another German province, the Serbs hated Austria and Austrians, no matter what political alignment. That sentiment also applied for Germany. This Serbian hatred for these Germanic nations had been born during the First World War. The Serbian regent even prophesied that if he were to sign a treaty with the Third Reich, his own military would oust him from power within six months. Hitler listened to the prince regent's warnings and understood that he wasn't being lied to. The *Führer* therefore relented, and pledged to respect Yugoslavia's territorial borders. The Nazi regime let the European newspapers know that Nazi Germany would not violate

Yugoslavia's border or use its railway system to transport troops. However, after Hitler welched on the Munich Agreement, very few Europeans believed in the *Führer*'s promises, or German declarations of peaceful intentions. Reluctantly, Prince Paul signed the document on 25 March 1941.

Hitler's decision to invade Greece and Yugoslavia

Two days after Prince Paul signed the treaty with Germany, Yugoslav Air Force officers overthrew the prince-regent and installed the 17-year-old Peter II as the king of Yugoslavia. The prince-regent had been prophetic in his prediction that his government would be overthrown. He just didn't realize how quickly that would happen. The second thing which the military junta in Belgrade did after ousting Prince Paul and installing the young Peter II, was to annul the German-Yugoslav treaty. Those who were in attendance at the conference room in Berlin related how Hitler quickly became enraged and was soon seething with anger when he was told what had happened. His plan to keep Yugoslavia on his side or at the very least, neutral and out of the Allied camp had been thwarted. He believed that it was just a matter of time before Yugoslavia would invite British and Commonwealth forces into the country. Grudgingly, Hitler directed that the planned invasion of Greece should also include the conquest of Yugoslavia. The start date for the attack now had to be pushed back to 6 April 1941 in order to accommodate the conquest of that country. The German plan for the invasion of Greece was codenamed *Marita.* It had been ordered by Hitler in November 1940 – a month after Benito Mussolini's ill-fated invasion.

Once the *coup d'état* in Belgrade occurred, the plan was expanded to include Yugoslavia in Germany's invasion plan. Hitler's decision was not made simply because the Italian Army was losing and Mussolini needed to save face. Once the Italian dictator involved himself in the war, the 'soft underbelly' of Europe (the Mediterranean basin region) became an active war zone. The Italian war effort in North Africa was also being waged ineptly. In a meeting held on 18 November 1940 between Count Galeazzo Ciano, Mussolini's foreign minister (who was also Mussolini's son-in-law) and Hitler, the *Führer* expressed how unhappy he was at the way Mussolini was waging war.[3] The Italian invasion of Greece in October 1940 further destabilized the Axis military situation. British and Commonwealth forces soon entered Greek territory. This military move completely undermined Hitler's plans to safeguard his oil supply in Romania and Hungary.[4] It also threatened the right flank of the planned invasion of the Soviet Union. The *Führer* therefore, felt he had no other choice than to invade both of these Balkan nations in order to stabilize the Axis military situation. It was the German decision to invade Yugoslavia, that would give the Croatians the opportunity to establish their own state.

Chapter 3

THE INDEPENDENT STATE OF CROATIA

What kind of a Croatian state?

The establishment of an independent state had been a dream that most Croatians had been seeking for a long time. Many people had varying opinions as to what type of government Croatia should have, if it ever gained its independence from the Serbian-controlled Yugoslav state. A minority of Croatians favoured the Fascist *Ustaše* Party, which had been established in 1929 by Dr Ante Pavelić. A good portion of the country, however, were inclined to support the Croatian Peasant Party, which in the spring of 1941 was led by Vladko Maček. There were other Croatians who supported the establishment of a communist state, like Josef Broz Tito. The Communist Party had been banned from Yugoslav politics, so those Croatians who wanted a state like the Soviet Union had to operate surreptitiously. The Croatian Peasant Party had also been banned during its lifetime, notably in 1929, when King Alexander I declared his dictatorship. There were some Croatians who wanted to be led by a Croatian king, and those who wanted democracy to flourish in Croatia.

In effect, just before the war, there was no general consensus among the Croatian people as to what type of government an independent Croatian state should have. What they all agreed on was the desire for independence. The largest percentage of Croatians supported Maček's Peasant Party, but if a plebiscite were to have been held then, to see which government would be established in an independent Croatia, no political party would have won by an overwhelming majority. Yet, while Yugoslavia was a whole entity and still dominated by the Serbians, Croatian independence was not possible. The only thing that Croatians could do was to hope that the future might bring them freedom. That opportunity presented itself with the Axis invasion of Yugoslavia on 6 April 1941. The Axis military campaign against the Yugoslav government would create the conditions for the establishment of a Croatian state.

As the Italian, German, Hungarian, and Bulgarian military forces advanced into the Yugoslav countryside, many men who were in the Yugoslav Army simply dropped their weapons and either surrendered or walked home. Some never showed up at the various mobilization points around the country. The truth was that there were many people that made up the state of Yugoslavia who did not wish to be part of it. Yugoslavia had been and was an artificially-created state. It had been established by the Entente powers, who favoured Serbia because it had sided with France, Russia and the United Kingdom against the Central Powers. The Croatians, Slovenians, Bosnian Muslims, Macedonians, and Montenegrins had never been asked if they wished to join such a nation. The Yugoslav Kingdom was imposed on millions of people by force. Was it a surprise then, that when the country was invaded, Croatian, Slovenian, Macedonian and Bosnian Muslim conscripts simply did not wish to fight for Yugoslavia?

This is why, when Yugoslavia was invaded on 6 April 1941, many people that made up this multi-cultural hodgepodge nation turned their backs on the Serbian-dominated government, and simply walked away. Had the Serbians not insisted on dominating the country in such a lopsided fashion, perhaps many more people in the country might have fought to preserve the state. Some however, went a step further than merely refusing to fight, and took up arms and sided with the Axis invaders. One ethnic group that overwhelmingly supported the fall of Yugoslavia were the Croatians. When German forces marched into Zagreb, the future capital of the Croatian state, they were greeted by enthusiastic throngs of cheering Croatians. German soldiers were thrown flowers, and Croatian girls rushed the marching troops, bestowing many with flowers, hugs and kisses. The German troops marching into the city were beaming. The propaganda unit which normally escorted German advance forces had a field day, creating rolls upon rolls of film and photographs of the entire spectacle. It was on that same day that an old *Ustaše* adherent, Slavko Kvaternik, announced the creation of a Croatian government. Who would lead this new nation had been a question that had not been answered until then. The Germans, who wanted to establish a Croatian state that would be a stable ally of Nazi Germany, wished that Vladko Maček would lead the new Croatian government. The Italians, however, were adamant that Dr Ante Pavelić, the leader of the fascist *Ustaše* Party, assume the post. Pavelić had been condemned to death in absentia by a Yugoslav court. He had lived as an exile the last 12 years in Italy, under the protection of fellow fascist Benito Mussolini. There was a reason why very quickly, Ante Pavelić was chosen to lead the new Croatian state. It wasn't simply because the Italians were intransigent when it came to who would lead Croatia, as much as the fact that Vladko Maček turned down the German offer. The Germans had actually approached Maček before the war began. They were surprised at his refusal to be the leader of an independent Croatian state.

In point of fact, he was given the offer to lead the Croatian nation twice, and twice he turned it down. The final, second proposal, came through *SS Standartenführer* Edmund Veesenmayer, who contacted Maček (in civilian attire) through the German embassy in Belgrade.[1] This second offer was made just before the actual German invasion of the country. So, from the start, the Germans and Italians were at odds as to what type of government the Croatian people should have. Why did Maček refuse the German offer? This is a question that many academics have many opinions, but no clear-cut answer. The most likely scenario is that Maček did not want to be associated with either Hitler or Mussolini. He was not a fascist or a racist who would have liked Hitler's dictatorship. He also understood that whatever Croatian state would be established, would not be free of outside influence. Germany and Italy's long shadow would hover over the nation for the time that Croatia was a state.

This proved to be true. The Italians got their way, when the Croatian government was organized under the nominal rule of the absentee Italian Duke of Spoleto, Prince Aimone, who was made 'king' of the Croatians. He was given the official name of 'Tomislav II'. This farce officially lasted from 18 May 1941 to 31 July 1943. Count Galeazzo Ciano, Mussolini's son-in-law and an Italian diplomat, assessed the duke's role in Croatian affairs, when he said: 'The Duke doesn't give a damn about Croatia and wants only money, money and more money.'[2] So, in effect, Ante Pavelić was the *de facto* ruler on the country. This did not prevent Italy and Germany from interfering in Croatian affairs. Maček's fears that any Croatian state would not be free from outside influence and meddling proved to be prescient. By avoiding any involvement with the Germans and Italians, as well as the new, fascist Croatian state, Maček dodged being implicated in war crimes that would be linked to them.

Actual authority then, rested in Dr Ante Pavelić, the *Poglavnik* (supreme leader), although his title in the government was prime minister. Pavelić began his administration with the ruthless persecution of the Serbian minority within the borders of the new Croatian state – thus guaranteeing the rise of Chetnik resistance and a guerrilla war between Serbians and Croatians. Hatred begets hatred. Terror begets terror. Pavelić also began a campaign to 'clean house' by arresting any who might, in any way, oppose his rule. In October 1941, Maček and his family were arrested by the Pavelić regime, and sent to the infamous Jasenovac concentration camp. The leader of the Croatian Peasant Party had not been conspiring against Pavelić, but the *Ustaše führer* had him arrested anyway. He was released in 1942 and placed under house arrest. After the war, he requested, and was given asylum in the United States. He died of a heart attack in 1964. Throughout his time in exile, he was approached by many Croatian exile groups, who asked him to be their leader, but he refused them all. In the end, his decision not to join a Croatian government proved to be a wise one. As he predicted, the Independent State of Croatia was a brief intermission in the history of the eventual breakup of Yugoslavia. It only lasted approximately 47 months, or about three and a half years. It would not be until 1991 that Croatia would finally gain its independence. That independence would not come free. The Serbians made sure to punish the Croatians for seeking freedom. The struggle was costly and painful, but in the end, Croatia freed itself from the shackles of Serbian dominance.

The invasion of Yugoslavia

The only resistance that the Axis forces encountered when they invaded Yugoslavia, came mostly from Serbian-dominated formations of the Yugoslav Army. Thousands of soldiers ignored the mobilization order. Many who were already positioned, simply deserted. An example of one of these desertions was Major Vladimir Kren, who was a Croatian officer in the Royal Yugoslav Air Force. Kren actually defected to the Germans three days before the invasion. He gave the Germans the Royal Yugoslav Air Force codes, indicated where the air squadrons were positioned, and even pointed out significant military sites, that the *Luftwaffe* would later target. Some Croatian units within the Yugoslav Army even switched sides and welcomed the invaders. All of this reflected a nation that, if one were to be brutally frank, should never have been established. Yugoslavia was a transnational state, containing many ethnic and religious groups, but it was not the same as the transnational Austro-Hungarian Empire.

Yugoslavia was an artificial entity that had been created to favour the Serbians. The dream of establishing a 'Greater Serbia' was the principal driving force behind the creation of the Kingdom of the Serbs, Croats and Slovenes. Because the Serbs had been on the winning side of the First World War, the Entente powers granted them their wish for a larger state. But the various ethnic and religious groups in this new nation had few things in common with one another. While the Austro-Hungarian Empire existed, most of the people that made up the dual monarchy felt that they had more things in common than they had differences. This was not the case with Yugoslavia. Enmities and animosity were in abundance, with the various peoples that had been thrown together, having less in common with each other. However, one unifying factor among Slovenians, Croatians, and Bosnian Muslims was the hatred they felt for the Serbian-dominated central government. Anyone who understood this knew that sooner or later, Yugoslavia would one day break apart, as it did, starting in 1991. At its birth, the lands which had been allocated for the Independent State of Croatia had an estimated 6,195,000 people.[3]

Of this number, 3,300,000 were Croatians, 150,000 were *Volksdeutsche* (ethnic Germans), 750,000 were Bosnian Muslims, with the Serbians being the largest minority in the country, having 1,845,000 people living inside NDH territory. Serbs therefore, constituted about 30 per cent of the population of the NDH in 1941. Croatian Jews made up the smallest minority in the new state, numbering just under 39,000. Of that figure, the *Ustaše* and the Nazis would end up murdering about 30,000. The Roma people living in NDH territory numbered around 25,000.[4] The number of Roma who would later be killed in the infamous Jasenovac concentration camp was 16,173, or about 69 per cent of the pre-war Roma population that had been living in Croatia. Jews and Roma were also murdered by the *Ustaše* and the Germans throughout the countryside, so the number of Roma that were killed is higher. The remaining 86,000 people that comprised the NDH state were ethnic Slovenians, Italians, Hungarians, and Austrians. Thus, when the Croatian state was established in 1941, roughly 55 per cent of the total population was Croatian. This percentage includes the 39,000 Croatian Jews. While most Croatians were Catholic, the Serbians were overwhelmingly Eastern Orthodox Christians. The terror campaign that was unleashed in the summer of 1941 on Croatian territory, principally by *Ustaše* fanatics, and at the direction of the *Poglavnik* killed thousands of people. The Serbians retaliated by raising Chetnik bands. Soon, these Chetnik groups were also killing Croatians, and Bosnian Muslims, wherever they encountered them.

The Serbs were paying back the Croatian cruelty with equal barbarity and brutality. Most people living in the Balkans tend to have long memories, especially when they believe that an injustice has been perpetrated against them.

To give an example of this, today in Serbia, there is a right-wing youth group, recognized by the Serbian Orthodox Church, called the '1389 Movement'. This group seeks a return of Kosovo to Serbia, and references its title from the Ottoman defeat of the Serbs at the Battle of Kosovo in 1389. After this Muslim victory over the Serbs, the Ottomans killed every single noble family, down to the children. In effect, this massacre left the Serbian people temporarily leaderless, which of course was the brutal point. The Serbians never forgot nor forgave the Ottoman Muslims for this. But I digress. It became common practice beginning in 1941, for both the Chetniks and *Ustaše,* to enter a village, and murder everyone. Often the adults in the village would claim that they were Serbian, if the Chetniks had come, or Croatian if the *Ustaše* entered the village. In either case, women and children were not spared. A Chetnik or an *Ustaše* would approach a child and ask, 'do you believe in God, or are you a communist?' If the child was old enough, or their parents had warned them, the youngster knew that Serbian Chetniks and Croatian *Ustaše* would kill any communist that they encountered, so they would invariably answer, 'I believe in God'. Then the next thing that would be said to them would be, 'well, if you believe in God, show me how you make the sign of the cross on which Jesus was crucified'. The child, believing that he/she was now safe, would make the sign of the cross as they usually did in church. But that was the trap, because Catholics make the sign of the cross from left to right, while Orthodox Christians make the sign of the cross from right to left. That had been the intention all along – to get the youngster to make the sign of the cross, so they could tell if the child was either Serbian or Croatian. Both sides practiced this perverted, sick trick on children, who would then be murdered.

The rebirth of the Croatian Army

Prior to the Second World War, Croatia had a long history of military contributions. During the reign of the Austro-Hungarian Empire, for example, after the Austrian and Hungarian military, Croatia was the third largest supplier of troops for the dual monarchy. The largest contributor to the German war effort in the Balkans, aside from the militarily unreliable Italians, was the Croatian Armed Forces (*Hrvatsko domobranstvo*), which was established shortly after the declaration of the formation of the Independent State of Croatia (*Nesavina Drzava*

Hrvatska) on 10 April 1941. This rising was a spontaneous and enthusiastic event that occurred all across Croatia and expressed the will and desire by most Croatians who wanted to live in an independent state. The Croatian Army of the Second World War would exist from 10 April 1941 to 11 May 1945. At its height, it would boast of having a strength of 220,000 ground troops, not including a small navy and air force.

When the NDH state was declared on 10 April 1941, little time was wasted in organizing the first units of the Croatian Home Army. Pavelić himself had arrived in Zagreb on 15 April, with a contingent of *Ustaše* troops, and began organizing the new government and army. He did this with the help of Slavko Kvaternik, who was appointed the head of this new Croatian army. Almost immediately, the first volunteer units began to be organized. At birth, the Croatian military would number around 55,000 men.[5] Initially 16 infantry battalions (each with about 600 riflemen and 16 machine guns) were created. Additionally, two cavalry battalions, with perhaps two to three squadrons apiece, were put together. Later still, four engineer and ten artillery battalions were also raised. The artillery 'battalions' were in actuality only two weak artillery batteries instead of the then standard three to four artillery batteries. Artillery pieces would always be lacking in the Croatian Army. It would be a contributing factor to the army's lack of efficiency. In fact, all types of arms and equipment were always in short supply. Even uniforms were hard to acquire.

While the political *Ustaše* troops were better clothed and armed (basically with Italian arms and uniforms), the regular initial NDH army units were clothed in a hodgepodge of French Army uniforms and helmets and old First World War Austrian attire. The initial Croatian Army was organized into 'divisional' commands and corps staffs in the summer and autumn of 1941. The original sixteen infantry battalions were enlarged to fifteen infantry regiments of two battalions apiece between May and June 1941. This was accomplished by the induction of new volunteers called to the colours. Every male between the ages of 18 and 55 were obliged to serve in the Croatian armed forces, whether it was the standing army, small air force, the navy, or the Home Guard. Service in the *Ustaše,* the political troops, was not made mandatory until 1943. The age groups were separated into three distinct categories, with the standing army getting the younger, more physically fit men, while the older age groups were relegated to the Home Guard. Initially the staging and forming bases for the new Croatian Army was as follows:

Sava Divisional Region – Zagreb, with:
- 1. Infantry Regiment – Bjelovar
- 2. Infantry Regiment – Zagreb
- 3. Infantry Regiment – Karlovac

Osijek Divisional Region – Osijek, with:
- 4. Infantry Regiment – Osijek
- 5. Infantry Regiment – Pozega
- 6. Infantry Regiment – Vinkovci

Bosnia Divisional Region – Sarajevo, with:
- 7. Infantry Regiment – Sarajevo
- 8. Infantry Regiment – Tuzla
- 9. Infantry Regiment – Travnik

Vrbas Divisional Region – Banja Luka, with:
- 10. Infantry Regiment – Banja Luka
- 11. Infantry Regiment – Sisak
- 12. Infantry Regiment – Otocac

Jadran Divisional Region – Mostar, with:
- 13. Infantry Regiment – Mostar
- 14. Infantry Regiment – Trebinje
- 15. Infantry Regiment – Knin

The following units were independent and out of 'divisional' control:

Standing Army Units:
- *Zagreb* Cavalry Regiment – Zagreb
  - I. Cavalry Battalion / *Zagreb* Cavalry Regiment – Zagreb
  - II. Cavalry Battalion / *Zagreb* Cavalry Regiment – Virovitica
- Independent Cavalry Battalion – Sarajevo
- 1. Motorized Infantry Battalion – Zagreb
- 2. Motorized Infantry Battalion – Sarajevo

Home Guard Units:
- Home Guard Staff Headquarters – Sarajevo
- Home Guard (Static) Infantry Battalion: Bijeljina
- Home Guard (Static) Infantry Battalion: Drinjaka
- Home Guard (Static) Infantry Battalion: Srebrenica
- Home Guard (Static) Infantry Battalion: Sarajevo
- Home Guard (Static) Infantry Battalion: Bjelovar

Ustaše Units:
Ustaše Life Guard Battalion – Zagreb
Ustaše Cavalry Squadron – Zagreb
1. *Ustaše* Infantry Regiment (three battalions)
2. *Ustaše* Infantry Regiment (three battalions)
3. *Ustaše* Infantry Regiment (three battalions)

Additional units were ordered during the summer and autumn of 1941. The 'Sava' Divisional Region was redesignated as 1. (Corps) Territorial Command, while the 2. (Corps) Territorial Command was formed in Brod from the Vrbas Divisional Region stationed in Banja Luka. Later still, 3. (Corps) Territorial Command was organized from the Bosnia Divisional Region in Sarajevo. These 'Territorial' commands were the equivalent of corps-sized headquarters, and were redesignated as such. The 1. Corps was named in the summer of 1943, the 2. Corps in the autumn of that same year, and the 3. Corps in the spring of 1944. In the autumn of 1941, the newly-organized Croatian Army underwent another reorganization. A further additional number of troops was created in the summer and autumn of 1941:

The 4. *Ustaše* Infantry Regiment was formed.
The 5. *Ustaše* Infantry Regiment was formed.
The *Ustaše* Life Guard Battalion in Zagreb was expanded to a regiment in size.
The NDH state created the 1. Railway Security Battalion.
The NDH state created the 2. Railway Security Battalion.

The infantry regiments were now reorganized into brigade-sized units, and allocated on the basis of two infantry regiments (four battalions) per brigade, with around 6,000 men per brigade, at full strength. Each brigade had perhaps between 1–2 artillery 'battalions' (remember that these so called battalions contained only two weak artillery batteries) per brigade. In this manner, the 1., 2., 3., 4., and 5. Croatian Infantry Brigades were formed. The factor of insufficient heavy weapons would plague the NDH forces throughout their brief lifespan. In fact, aside from about 100,000 Italian and German rifles, some French uniforms and helmets, the Italian government had made no real effort to equip the Croat state's forces with any heavy weapons. The Germans had tried to supply the Croatians with some artillery captured from the Yugoslav army, but it was all sub-standard, as was evidenced by the comments of *Generalmajor* Hellmuth Reinhardt in a US Army pamphlet published after the war dealing with the use of captured materials by the Axis forces. The 37mm Skoda anti-tank guns captured in Yugoslavia were retained by the Croatian Armed Forces. The largest part of the captured Yugoslav guns was placed at the disposal of Croatia to build up her army. A few modern 150mm Skoda guns were later used in coastal defence. Italian meddling in the affairs of the Croatian state did not end after the government was established. For example, in those areas of NDH territory where the Italian Army had occupation troops, the recruitment of men into the Croatian Armed Forces was strictly forbidden by the Italians. The guerrilla war which began in the late summer of 1941, had meanwhile increased, especially in the province of Bosnia-Herzegovina. To meet this crisis the Croatian High Command dispatched the following units to that region between July and August 1941:

1. One battalion of the 1. Infantry Regiment to Bosanski Petrovak.
2. One battalion of the 2. Infantry Regiment to the Una Valley.
3. One battalion of the 3. Infantry Regiment, also to the Una Valley.
4. One newly organized infantry battalion in Osijek for duty in Bosanski Petrovak.
5. One battalion of the 10. Infantry Regiment for the Sana Valley.
6. Two battalions of the 11. Infantry Regiment for the Una Valley.
7. Another newly mobilized infantry battalion for the Una Valley.
8. One artillery battery each from Zagreb, Osijek, and Banja Luka for duty in Bosanski Petrovak.
9. The 'Zagreb' Cavalry Regiment for duty in Gracac (Lika).

The German and Italian occupation zones

The decision by Adolf Hitler to invade Greece and Yugoslavia was made on military and political grounds. The immediate reason for the German invasion was to save the floundering campaign of the Italian army which, following Mussolini's order, had launched an ill-advised attack against Greece in October 1940. The relationship between Hitler and Italy's fascist leader Benito Mussolini, proved to be stormy and mercurial. This strained alliance set the tone for future dealings between both totalitarian regimes. The tensions which existed between these cobelligerents was confirmed by the difficulty which both dictators found in trying to cooperate.. An example of this complicated union were the numerous occupation troubles which the Germans and Italians experienced after they conquered Greece and Yugoslavia. Both Hitler and Mussolini were often at odds as to how to rule these conquered nations. The artificially-created occupation zones, fashioned to delineate Italian and German spheres of control, produced a bureaucratic nightmare that only benefited the enemy.

Figure 3. The Italian occupation zones, and the various annexed territories after the conquest of Yugoslavia. These were a constant obstruction to the proper running of the NDH state. Croatian troops chasing Chetnik forces were often prohibited from crossing a zone. As a result, the Chetniks would escape. The Germans provided Croatia with weapons, but recruited large numbers of Croatian men. The drain in manpower guaranteed that NDH forces were always short of personnel, and could not expand on a larger scale than they did. (*Author's line drawing*)

These problems gave rise to tensions between the Axis powers. There was already animosity between *Il Duce* and the *Führer*. Hitler's plans in Europe called for Italy to remain neutral in the war. The reason why Hitler desired this, was not because he wanted to prevent Italy from obtaining territory through the spoils of war, but because he needed to keep the British from threatening what was termed the 'soft underbelly' of Europe. When Mussolini declared war on the French and British on 10 June 1940, hoping to gain some territory from what was clearly going to be a French defeat, he opened the entire Mediterranean region to the conflict. Instantly, this region of the world became a battle zone. He would eventually lose Italian East Africa (including Italian

Somaliland), and later still, his Libyan colony. The war would come to Mussolini's doorstep when in July 1943 the Allies would invade Sicily.

Now the Italian colonies in East Africa and Libya would be ripe for British conquest. East Africa would be conquered by Allied forces in November 1941. In Libya, Mussolini had ordered Marshall Graziani to invade British Egypt with a force of 115,000 Italian soldiers. The 63,000 British and Commonwealth troops in Egypt not only stopped the Italian invasion, but destroyed the Italian 10. Army, capturing all of Cyrenaica (eastern Libya) in the process. Faced with the coming Italian defeat in North Africa, Hitler had to send three German divisions, the famous *Afrika Korps,* to save the Italians from losing Libya as well. Count Galeazzo Ciano stated that Mussolini's decision to invade Greece while simultaneously trying to capture Egypt, was made simply to try and one-up the German dictator. Ciano recounted how Mussolini had complained to him, 'Hitler always faces me with a *fait accompli*. This time I am going to pay him back in his own coin. He will find out from the newspapers that I have occupied Greece.'[6]

This alliance between Nazi Germany and Fascist Italy therefore, was a strained relationship from the start. This feeling was not just felt at high levels, but filtered down to the lower ranks. Mistrust grew to dislike between the Germans and Italians, which eventually turned into contempt. These feelings eventually worked against being able to obtain full cooperation between the Axis partners, which in turn only aided the enemy. This is a perfect paradigm for the relationship that developed between Hitler and Mussolini during the war. Their military union was therefore more a form of expediency, rather than an actual coalition.

The initial German garrison in Yugoslavia

The gap created by the departure of German divisions earmarked for the invasion of the Soviet Union was only partly filled by the recently created German LXV Corps, which was immediately stationed in Belgrade. This German corps headquarters contained the following German divisions:

704. Infanterie Division
714. Infanterie Division
717. Infanterie Division

These divisions were spread out to cover Serbia. A fourth German division, the *718. Infanterie Division,* was stationed in the German zone of interest in Croatia, with its headquarters located in Banja

Luka. In contrast to the troops they replaced, more than one-half of the personnel of these divisions, particularly the platoon leaders and non-commissioned officers, were over age for infantry service. The combat experience of most of the company and higher commanders was limited to the First World War, and the divisions lacked their full complement of motor vehicles and logistical services. Training had been interrupted by the assignment to occupation duty to the extent that one division had only completed battalion exercises and had performed no regimental or divisional manoeuvres at all. German strength in the Balkans remained at approximately at this level until mid-September 1941, the only change being that in mid-August, the elite German *6. Gebirgs Division* left. The *713. Infanterie Division* of the same type as the divisions attached to the *LXV. Armeekorps,* moved into the Balkans shortly before the departure of the mountain division.

The guerrilla war begins

The guerrilla war as was experienced by the new Croatian state was led by two distinctly different groups whose aims were the same: the destruction of the fledgling Croat state. These two groups were the Tito Partisans who advocated a united Yugoslav Communist state along the Soviet model. The second guerrilla group was led by the Serbian ex-Yugoslav Army staff officer Draza Mihailovich. Mihailovich's guerrillas were called the *Chetniki* or Chetniks. The Chetniks wanted to reestablish the old system of a Serbian king ruling all of Yugoslavia, and in this way, Serbian dominion and control of Yugoslavia would return. The Chetniks began their campaign against the newly created Independent State of Croatia as early as 13–16 April, when they raided the villages of Ilici and Cim. There the Chetniks committed atrocities on the local Croatian population, sparing neither women nor children. It should be noted that these Serbian attacks came significantly before the fanatical *Ustaše* began their terror campaign against the Serbian population living in Croatia. In June 1941 the localities of Avtovac, Ljubinje, and Nevesinje were also attacked by Chetnik bands. In the summer of 1941 Chetnik guerrilla units were operating in the Pljesivica Mountains and the regions southwest of Bihac and in the Krbava and Lika Valley.

The Tito Partisans for their part, initially remained in their mountain camps and did not wage war on the German occupation forces. This was because Stalin and Hitler had a truce, albeit a temporary one, that all communists everywhere had to obey. This however, did not stop Tito's partisan forces from attacking Italian, Hungarian, and Bulgarian occupation troops. Only after Nazi Germany invaded the Soviet Union was Tito given a free hand to operate. Tito's units made the first attack against German interests in Bosnia in July 1941, when they attacked the town of Drvar with about 2,000 men and concentrated their forces there. Soon, about 3,000 more men joined the partisan ranks so that by the end of August 1941, Tito had a force of about 5,000 men. These new recruits had come mainly from Serbians fleeing the *Ustaše* terror spree that was sweeping all across Croatia. Between 1936–8 Stalin conducted the 'Great Purge',[7] where high ranking, as well as low ranking political and military leaders were removed from office and either sent to a Siberian Gulag or executed outright. This purge also occurred in the Communist Party leadership outside of the Soviet Union. The purge in Croatia eliminated all of the top Croatian Communist Party leaders. The only one to survive was Josip Broz Tito. Tito himself was a Croatian, but his political ideology trumped any allegiance that he may have held for the establishment of a Croatian state.

The fact that he survived the Great Purge indicates that he was, if not trusted completely, at least deemed sufficiently loyal to Stalin and the Soviet Union to remain alive. The forced conversion of Eastern Orthodox Serbians to Catholicism (the main Croatian religion), plus the *Ustaše* atrocities only damaged the fledgling Croatian state. The excesses of the Pavelić regime created the right conditions for a guerrilla war to erupt (as it did), and gave the Tito Partisans and the Serbian Chetnik guerrillas thousands of angry and embittered volunteers, thirsting for revenge. Atrocities now caused counter-atrocities and the old Balkan cruelties and hatreds were once again resurfaced.

Petrovak, which lies about 20 miles northwest of Drvar, was also attacked by the Tito Partisans. Other areas where the communists struck were Banja Luka, Knin, Gospic, Vrtace, and Krnjeuse. Petrovak itself was taken by units of Tito's Partisans twice during the summer of 1941. By the beginning of the autumn of 1941, Tito had amassed about 10,000 men in and around Drvar and had established a partisan republic. The Croatian army command was in a state of transition, as was its field army.

This and other factors only helped the guerrillas and paralyzed the quickness of action which would normally be an important factor in fighting a partisan war, especially a war that included two large and equally determined enemies (i.e. the Communists and Chetniks). For example, the standing army was under the control of the Croatian Defence Ministry (*Ministrastvo Hrvatskog Domobransiva*), while the *Ustaše* units were under the control of the Croatian Interior Ministry.

Thus, for example, Colonel Stozernik, the *Ustaše* leader in Banja Luka had better communications with, say, Dr Gutic, the *Ustaše* leader in Sanski Most, than with NDH Army headquarters in Zagreb.

Command and control problems developed which took a long time to resolve. This on top of having to work with hand-me-down equipment, and not much of it at that.

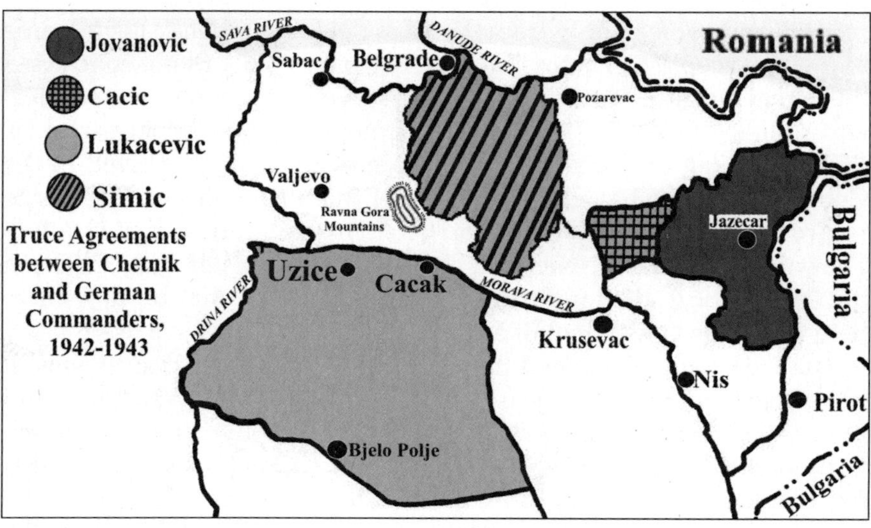

Figure 4. Temporary armistice agreements between the Germans and some Chetnik guerrilla bands, 1942–3.

At least the guerrillas were just as badly equipped until 1943, when the Italian collapse gave them unprecedented quantities of arms and munitions. Problems within the ranks also arose. The older class of soldiers (the officers and senior NCOs) who had seen service in the old Austro-Hungarian Army, had a different way of looking at things than, say, the younger officers and enlisted men, whose term of service had been with the Royal Yugoslav Army. A rift arose between those two separate military worlds. Add to this the need to keep newly-formed, underequipped and poorly-trained units under constant combat for weeks on end, and you began to see the complete collapse of some units, or the refusal in other formations of the men to follow the orders of the officers.

The so-called occupation zones formed by the Italians in Yugoslavia had the effect of paralyzing anti-guerrilla efforts by the Germans and their Croatian allies. The escaping guerrillas would simply cross this imaginary border and the Germans and Croatians would be forced to give up the chase. In theory the Italians were supposed to work with the Germans, taking over the chase when the guerrillas entered their region, but in reality, the planning and execution of an Italian drive was often days late and the partisans would be long gone by the time the first Italian units would arrive.

The anti-Croatian attitude of the Italians grew as the war dragged on. Unresolved differences, over time, usually turn into resentment. Resentment, over time, turns to dislike and even contempt. This unresolved issue of Italian influence over Croatian territory, encouraged the Italians to 'arrive late' when 'chasing' a Chetnik unit, which had just made an incursion into NDH lands. This led the Italians to collaborate further with the Chetniks, by way of supplying them with weapons, munitions, and other supplies. They had begun to do this because the Chetniks were attacking communist forces. No thought was taken by the Italians, that the Chetniks were also attacking Croatians. The Italians covered up this undermining of the NDH state by assigning these Chetnik bands the blanket title of 'Auxiliary Anti-Communist Militia'.

Now Chetnik officers were seen walking side by side with Italian officers in Bihac and Mostar. Additionally, the occupation zones allowed not only Chetnik guerrilla units to escape German and Croatian traps, but Tito's communist partisans also used them to their advantage. Croatian and Italian relations deteriorated, even after the fascist Italian Socialist Republic was set up in northern Italy in the autumn of 1943. Mussolini didn't even bother to send an ambassador to Zagreb, since he continued to have claims against Istria, some of the Dalmatian region, plus other areas which belonged to Croatia. In German-occupied Serbia, the Tito Partisans were seen as both a threat to the Germans and the Chetniks. This eventually led to a temporary truce being made with some leaders of Chetnik bands in Serbia. The Germans only deemed this a temporary expediency, until sufficient forces could be brought into the region to deal not only with the Tito Partisans, but Mikhailovich's Chetnik guerrillas as well. British intelligence eventually got wind of these armistice deals with some of the Chetnik bands through the Tito communists, who painted the entire Mikhailovich organization as collaborationist. This was done in order to convince the British to stop supplying the Chetniks with weaponry and supplies and to limit the distribution of such military support for Tito's forces. Draza Mikhailovich soon realized the danger and ordered those Chetnik commanders who had signed these temporary truces to abrogate them, but by the it was too late. By June 1943 the British were no longer supplying weapons and supplies to the Chetniks. More importantly, they were now convinced that the entire Serbian Chetnik guerrilla movement was a collaborationist organization. Tito had won a tremendous political victory.

Deteriorating Axis Relations

In the summer of 1942, relations between the two Axis countries were still good enough that a Croatian Legion, sponsored by the Italians, was raised and organized for employment under Italian control. The Germans had done the same thing almost a year earlier, in July 1941 when they raised a Croatian Legion for employment on the Eastern Front. This reinforced regiment (designated the 369th) was led by Colonel Viktor Pavecic (who later died in Stalingrad). The number of men which eventually served in this German sponsored Legion was about 5,000 though the reinforced regiment contained 3,000–3,800 men. One source states that this regiment contained a replacement battalion (stationed in Döllersheim) with a strength of around 700–800 men. More than likely the above mentioned second figure of 3,800 included this replacement battalion in the count, even though it was a rear-echelon unit and only supplied men for the regiment.

Later still, about 1,300 Croatians went from the Döllersheim Training Camp to Stockerau Training Camp near Vienna in November 1941. This was in anticipation of their being used as the core of a replacement and training brigade for the projected German-Croatian Legion divisions:

369. (kroatische) Infanterie Division
373. (kroatische) Infanterie Division
392. (kroatische) Infanterie Division

The *369. (deutsche-kroatische) Infanterie Regiment* met its end in Stalingrad. Approximately 1,000 wounded Croatian soldiers were flown out of the beleaguered *6. Armee* pocket before its surrender in early February 1943. As stated earlier, the Italians had formed a Croatian Legion in 1942. They also raised a 2,000-man transport unit which was employed under 8. Italian Army in southern Russia. The transport unit, like many rear area formations, were sent to the front, given the successful Red Army breakthroughs made during their winter 1942/43 offensive. The unit was destroyed in December 1942, fighting along the Don River. The 1,300-man Croatian Legion was never sent to fight on the Russian Front. It was employed by the Italians along the Dalmatian coast in their Third Operational Zone. The three Italian operational zones were garrisoned by about 200 battalions at any one time. At their height in strength, Zone I had 80 Italian battalions, Zone II had 100, and Zone III had only 20.

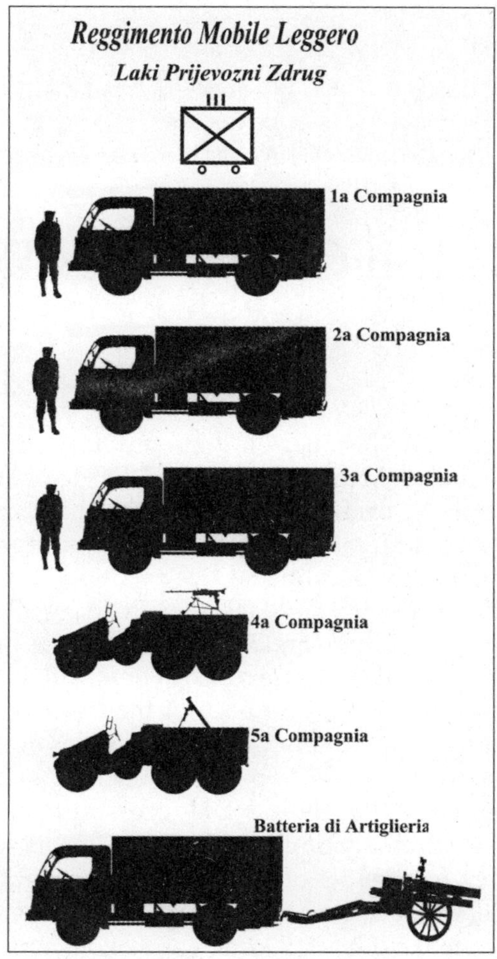

Figure 5. When Mussolini discovered that the Croatians had sent Germany a regiment to fight on the Russian Front, *369 (kroatische) Infanterie Regiment*, he became jealous. Soon, the Fascist dictator coerced Ante Pavelić to send the 8th Italian Army fighting in Russia a Croatian volunteer legion. The regiment was formed using 1,100 men, 70 NCOs and 45 officers – 1,215 in total. These were divided into three motorized infantry companies, one machine-gun company, one 81mm mortar company and one 65mm 65/17 artillery battery. The commanding officer was Lieutenant-Colonel Egon Zitnik. This Croatian legion was destroyed in combat in early 1943.

Chapter 4

REINFORCEMENTS

By the end of 1941, the number of *Ustaše* military units numbered a total of fifteen combat battalions and two service battalions with a combined strength of around 10,000 men. At this time, the number of troops in the regular Croatian Army has been estimated at perhaps 32,000–33,000 men, although one source mentions a figure of 42,000. Perhaps this difference of 9,000–10,000 men includes all of the auxiliary units such as the Home Guard and Railway Security, plus such support battalions like the one medical, one construction, and three replacement battalions which were formed for each of the five divisional districts. This doesn't even include the numbers of men involved in all of the headquarters' staffs, plus additional units such as local militias. The combat capabilities of all of these NDH forces in 1941 would have to be categorized as extremely limited. This was due, as stated earlier, to a great deficiency in all sorts of military items, especially in artillery pieces, mortars and tanks. Transportation was also severely lacking as most units had to make due with horses and oxen to pull their wagons or heavy weapons. This was the reason the Croatian Army formed mobile units: because of the limited motor transport that was available. The army now pooled together trucks, motorcycles, automobiles, and what few tanks were available in order to raise motorized units that could be employed as a type of fire brigade, shuffling from one critical spot to another.

It's no small wonder then, given the poor state of the Croatian Armed Forces, that the Chetniks and Tito communists accomplished as much as they did in 1941. The Tito Partisans could boast of holding an area about 80 square miles with the following borders: the entire Grmec mountain range, extending from the elbow of the Una River, near Bihac and Banja Luka, about 90 miles from Bihac to the southeast near Varcar Vakuf about 80 miles from Bihac. Besides these groups, other rebel groups were formed, especially in the Kozara Mountains and in eastern Bosnian. In November 1941 Tito's guerrillas conquered Uzice and it was there that Tito proclaimed his first red republic. Although the NDH forces had managed to clear out the area south of Prijedor during the summer of 1941, guerrilla bands had continued their attempt to cross the Drina River between Bijeljina and Zvornik in August of that year. These were the Chetnik units which were especially troublesome southeast of Sarajevo. In September 1941, Chetnik attacks began to concentrate on interrupting the railway activity west of Zvornik and on the Tuzla-Doboj Road.

Soon, the area northeast and east of Sarajevo in the Javor and Romanija Mountain regions were also infested with Chetnik guerrillas. In October 1941 the Chetnik guerrillas received reinforcements from Serbia and attacked Zvornik. The Croatian garrisons of Visegrad and Rogatica in southern Bosnia were then surrounded. It was not until 19 October that the NDH forces were able to drive off, with great difficulty, the estimated 6,000 Chetniks from Zvornik. Two days later however, the town of Rogatica fell when it was stormed by a large Chetnik force. Already German assistance to the Croatian State had been forthcoming. In October alone, the Germans had sent five *Landesschützen* (regional defence) battalions, which were made up of older-age German reservists to Croatia. Though this wasn't much, it was all that the German command could spare at the time. These battalions were allocated as follows:

Sarajevo – *447. Landesschützen Bataillon*
Zagreb – *925. Landesschützen Bataillon*
Banja Luka – *823. Landesschützen Bataillon*
Sisak – *923. Landesschützen Bataillon*
Doboj – *924. Landesschützen Bataillon*

The *923. Landesschützen Bataillon* and *924. Landesschützen Bataillon* were specifically assigned to protect the railway line in their respective area of operations. The morale of the NDH forces had, on the whole, decreased dramatically from the very beginning. There were many reasons for this. As stated before, aside from about 100,000 rifles and some ex-Yugoslav Army artillery pieces, the supplies of modern weaponry and equipment had been wholly inadequate. The Army was outfitted with captured stocks which the Germans had mainly donated. Some Croatian units were clothed in French uniforms with captured French helmets, while others were still wearing the Yugoslav

Army field blouse, with added pockets and buttons sewn on; quite comparable to the Austrian-style field blouse dating back to the First World War. Others wore Austrian uniforms from the First World War and the outdated M16 Austrian helmet. Czech Army helmets were also used by the Croatian Army. The Yugoslav Army '*Sajkace*' soft caps were likewise also used, but later on they were replaced by the Austrian First World War Alpine cap with two buttons and the NDH emblem on the front of the cover. The *Ustaše* were initially dressed in Italian style Light Blue tropical uniforms although there were exemptions to this, like Jure Frantecic's 'Black Legion' which wore, as its name implies, an all-black uniform. Thus, for the most part, the old Austro-Hungarian Empire uniform influenced the early version of the Croatian Army uniform. This was reinforced by the induction of former Austro-Hungarian officers from the provinces of Croatia, Bosnia, etc. into the Croatian Army. The ex-Yugoslav Army blouses were somewhat changed by reducing the high collars and adding NDH insignia. Muslim troops from Bosnia, inducted into the NDH forces, were made to wear a red fez with the NDH insignia in the front.

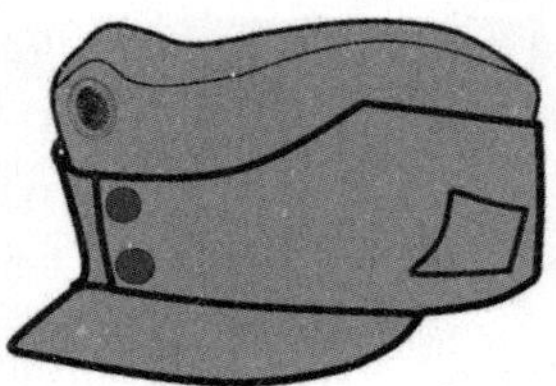

Figure 6. Author's line drawing of the softcover alpine cap used by the Austrian Army in the First World War, and the Croatian Army in the Second World War.

These red fezzes had been worn before by Bosnian Muslims serving in the old Austro-Hungarian Army. The military trousers varied as well, though many were rather broad at the ankle, which had also been worn by the Austrian *Bosniaks* (Bosnians) in the First World War. Not only did a lack of proper clothing, equipment, and arms play a role in lowering the morale of Croatian army troops, but a conflict arose between those old, former Austro-Hungarian army officers and senior NCOs being called to the colours, and those younger officers and lower ranking NCOs who had served in the defunct Royal Yugoslav Army.

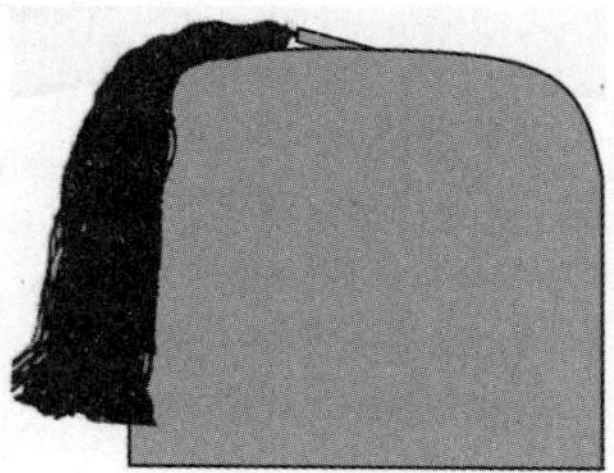

Figure 7. Author's line drawing of the red fez cover worn by Muslim members of the Army of the Independent State of Croatia from 1941–5.

The latter had a *laissez-faire* attitude and tended to shy away from hard training, while the former Austro-Hungarian trained officers and NCOs considered themselves superior to the younger men and had an old-fashioned idea of how an army should be run. It was like mixing oil and vinegar – the blend was good initially but was bound to split and lose its effectiveness under stress, and as has already been described, the Chetniks and the communists were not about to give the fledgling Croatian state any respite. General von Glaise Horstenau wrote a very concise and succinct evaluation regarding the newly created Croatian Army and explains what happened in the first formative year:

> It is part of the tragedy of this young state which is scarcely able to function in its present hybrid composition, that it was not allowed to create more than a militia of the most modest pretensions from the excellent military material, which had won fame for centuries on the battlefields of Europe. With little or no training and some hardly adequate Yugoslav experience, the units were opposed months ago to a clever and resolute enemy. They marched and fought, only seldom being relieved, in the Bosnian Mountains, and were now very tired. Certainly a few units have fought with distinction, such as the few companies which held Visegrad for 70 days. But in general, the attack and resistance capacity of the Croatian soldier fell from week to week. Offensive operations remained static as a rule after the first attack, defensive battles ended in panic. Military discipline also left much to be desired. Insubordination, mutiny, and desertion increased. All this reflected weariness and lack of training, but also the refusal to engage in a struggle regarded, in wide circles of the Croatian people, as a civil war whose outbreak and expansion was blamed on the fury of the hated *Ustaše*.[1]

If we add the weight of Italian demands, one of which was that the Croatian state could not recruit its own men in areas under Italian control, their blatant assistance to the Chetnik guerrillas and absurd occupation zone policies, plus two resolute and very determined guerrilla movements bent on the destruction of the young Croatian state, we arrive at the situation that faced the NDH government in the autumn of 1941. It was a military nightmare. It was with a clear understanding of the ever-worsening Croatian military situation that the Germans promised more help – this in spite of the fact that they were busy trying to quell a Chetnik uprising in Serbia at this time. The NDH planned to enlarge its army in the beginning of 1942 by the addition of a reinforced division which would be specialized in mountain warfare. The necessary mountain equipment would come primarily from the Germans, and in the winter of 1941/42 this new Croatian division, which would number about 17,000 men at its peak strength, began to take shape. Four mountain brigades, each of three to four battalions were formed and stationed initially in the following towns and surrounding area:

1. Mountain Brigade – Zagreb
2. Mountain Brigade – Bjelovar
3. Mountain Brigade – Slavonski Pozegi
4. Mountain Brigade – Brod

In addition, the mountain division would also have supporting units. Meanwhile the insurgents in Bosnia had to be checked, so the German *718. Infanterie Division* was sent to the Zagreb and Banja Luka areas to help defend these two important cities. Towards the end of December 1941, *718. Infanterie Division* was transferred to southeast Bosnia and told to concentrate on the areas in and around Sarajevo, Doboj, and Tuzla. This force amounted to only about 7,000 German troops of the older age group. The division also possessed limited artillery and mobility, given the fact that this division was what was termed a line-of-communication division. The division's task was to secure the industrial and mining facilities in the greater Sarajevo–Tuzla–Zenica area as well as to protect the important railway lines: Zagreb–Belgrade–Bosanski Brod–Sarajevo. To this force was added the first initial batch of five German *Landesschützen* battalions. From 9–15 January 1942, this division took part in *Unternehmen Südostkroatien* (Operation Southeast Croatia). While *718. Infanterie Division* deployed one regiment each from Tuzla and Sarajevo, the *342. Infanterie Division* (*LXV. Armeekorps z.b.V./12. Armee*) crossed the Serbian-Croatian border near Zvornik in a comprehensive movement towards Vlasenica.

Later still, four more of these regional defence battalions arrived and were relegated to railway security. The Croatians already had two of their guard battalions on full-time railway security duty. Now these two Croatian battalions came under German guidance. The battles fought during the winter of 1941/42 were difficult and hard ones for the Croatian Army. The Romanija Mountains (about 15 miles east of Sarajevo) had to be cleared of guerrillas more than once. First by the Zagreb Cavalry Regiment in December 1941, and then by the *Ustaše* Black Legion (two battalions initially) under Major Jure Frantecic in February 1942.[2] This *Ustaše* regiment was again in action in April 1942 – this time in the region north of the Rogatica-Drina River bend, as far as Drinjaca and Vlasenica. On 8 April, the Black Legion engaged some Chetniks in Drinjaca. Assigned to block off the northern area near Han Njesak, in an operation against Chetnik units in Rogatica, the *Ustaše* commander (Frantecic) decided to press on with an attack of his own from Drinjaca on 9 April 1942. Advancing south, his regiment took Brotunak on 10 April, and Srebrenica on 11 April. At this point German reports stated that Chetnik guerrilla units were beginning to withdraw from the area of Rogatica towards the south and southeast, while still pressing their assault on Rogatica. The Germans, taking advantage of the situation, ordered that several units of *718. Infanterie Division* undertake an encircling manoeuvre. On 20 April 1942, the division moved against guerrilla units in the region of Podloznik – Sokolac – Han Pijesak. The regiment under Francetić (who had now been promoted to Lieutenant-Colonel) was ordered to reach the Han Pijesak – Podzeplje area by the same date. For this operation, the *III. Bataillon* of *737. Infanterie Regiment* and an engineer company of *717. Infanterie Division* were employed. The Italians were to employ several divisions for this operation, but they were not ready and had not even arrived by 25 April 1942, the start date for the operation. This caused the action to be postponed. Additionally, Jure Francetić's *Ustaše Crna legija* (Black Legion) had once again disobeyed orders, and had run headlong against Chetnik units stationed in Vlasnica. The *Ustaše* advance however, ended in a military reversal for the Black Legion, when the Chetniks received additional support from Serbia in the form of Major Jezdimir Dangic's Chetnik brigade. This freshly arrived Chetnik force was now directed primarily against Frantecic's *Ustaše* and the Muslim civilian population. The result was a withdrawal of the Black Legion after having taken heavy losses.

An earlier attempt had been made in January 1942 to clear eastern Bosnia of guerrillas. With this in mind, the German *718. Infanterie Division* had been moved in December 1941 to southeast Bosnia. Parts of the division reached Tuzla, while other parts entered Doboj, Zavidovici, and Vares. The Germans were now keeping their promise to support the NDH state. In the coming offensive in eastern Bosnia, the 4. and 5. Croatian Infantry Brigades were to provide units for the anti-guerrilla sweep. Later, after the operation was completed, one regiment of the *718. Infanterie Division* was to remain permanently stationed in Tuzla and another in Sarajevo. The German *342. Infanterie Division,* earmarked for service in the Soviet Union, was used in January 1942 in southeastern Croatia before it was moved to Russia. The fighting in the summer and autumn of 1941 had indicated that the newly-created Independent State of Croatia would face stiff military opposition. The winter and spring battles of 1942 affirmed this. Defending this new nation was not going to be a cakewalk. On 2 May 1942 *718. Infanterie Division* took part in *Unternehmen Trio II.* This operation to clear the area around Sarajevo – Gorazde – Foca – Kalinovik of Partisan units and put the Partisans to flight depended heavily on the Italian divisions *Taurinense, Cacciatori delle Alpi,* and *Pusteria* divisions. However, due to the late arrival of the *Cacciatori delle Alpi* division, the Partisans were able to escape south.

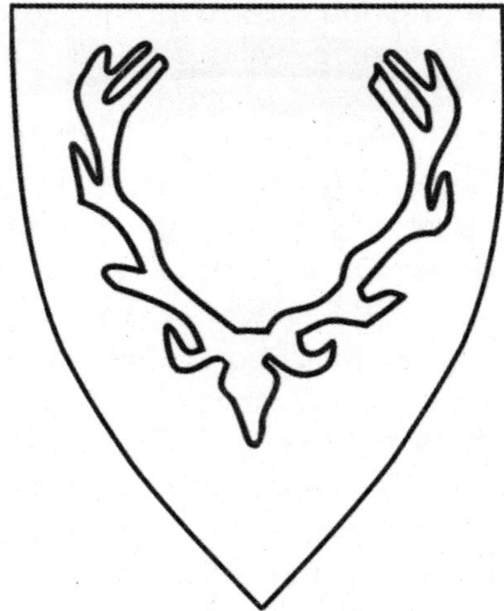

Figure 8. Author's line drawing of the divisional shield for *718. Infanterie Division* – the head and antlers of an elk.

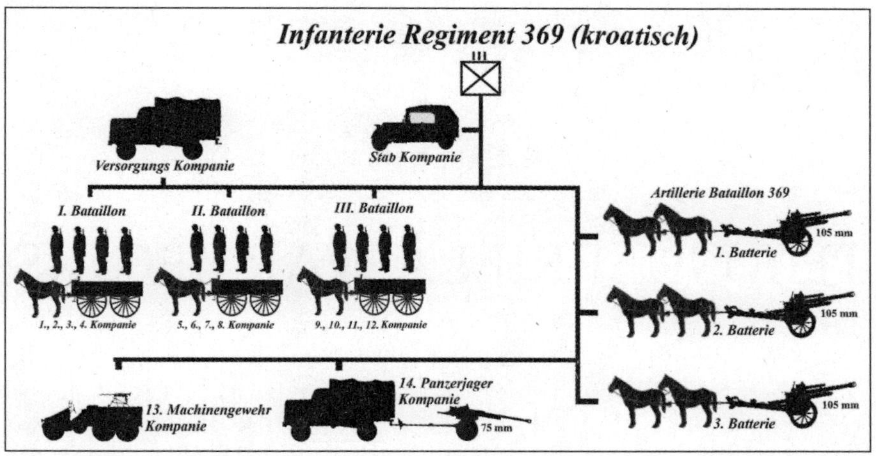

Figure 9. Schematic diagram of the reinforced 369th Croatian Infantry Regiment. This volunteer formation fought in the southern regions of the USSR under the German *100. Jäger Division*. Employed at Stalingrad, it was destroyed during the battle after the German surrender in early 1943. At peak strength, the regiment was magnificently armed and equipped. It began the Russian campaign with 5,000 officers, NCOs and enlisted men. This was basically a brigade in size, so each of the three infantry battalions had the strength of a small regiment each.

Chapter 5

THE GUERRILLA WAR BEGINS

On 15 January 1942 the operation in southeastern Croatia got underway. The specific area in question was the Ozren Mountain range located in eastern Bosnia. By 21 January the operation, which also included several *Ustaše* battalions and one Italian *Alpini* battalion, netted 50 dead guerrillas and 200 taken prisoner. The operation to drive the guerrillas into a pocket in the area of the Javor Mountains by elements of the *342. Infanterie Division* and *718. Infanterie Division* ended towards the end of January with the guerrillas losing 521 dead and 1,400 captured. In addition, substantial weapons were captured. During these operations in January, the NDH forces accounted for about eight to ten battalions – all drawn from the Croatian 4. and 5. Infantry Brigade. Additionally, perhaps somewhere around two to four *Ustaše* battalions also participated.

With the Germans withdrawing another division from Yugoslavia for use in the USSR (i.e. *342. Infanterie Division*), the Italians were approached formally, and asked if they would discuss the possibility of having their 2. Army, then the highest Italian command in Yugoslavia, to assume more responsibilities in their Third Operational Zone. The Italians immediately declared their willingness to allow troops of their 2. Army to increase their presence there, which caused much concern and trepidation on the part of the Croatian command. Already, in the Italian Second Operational Zone, territory which also technically belonged to Croatia, the Italians had allowed the NDH forces to garrison some towns but they were forbidden to construct fortifications or defensive positions of any kind. To the Croatians, this was like fighting a war with one hand tied behind your back. The Croatians were afraid that if they consented to the arrival of more Italian units into NDH territory, they would never be rid of them. Indeed, the Italians were already requesting that if such a move was to be approved, they wanted

Sarajevo as a base and garrison city. This worry weighed heavily on Croatian Marshal Kvaternik and his Chief of Staff, General Laxa. The Germans themselves also had their misgivings over whether the Italians could keep order. Back in December 1941 Lieutenant-Colonel von Funk, the Chief of Staff to the German Command in Zagreb, had telegraphed the German Armed Forces Commander Southeast with the following report:

> The Italian 2. Army could scarcely guarantee the suppression of the revolt in Bosnia. It is occupied with the strong unrest in Gatta, Foca, and along the Split-Karlovac railway line. The Italian methods up until now have fanned rather than suppressed the revolt. If the Italian 2. Army was to be responsible for the whole of Croatia, a spreading of the revolt is to be feared among the Croatian population. It appears necessary to leave the German 718. Infanterie Division in Croatia, in order to maintain the security area and thereby the demarcation line, and to let German power in this area remain independent of the Italian 2. Army. I would prefer this situation to the obvious extremely serious political and economic consequences which would accompany an occupation of Croatia by the Italian 2. Army.[1]

With these warnings, the German command toned down their requests to the Italians, and instead began to negotiate with the Italians and Croatians throughout the months of January and February 1942 over the establishment of a joint command which would control employment of all Axis forces against regions of guerrilla activity. This was especially needed after the withdrawal of two of the five German regional defence battalions from NDH territory to Serbia and Salonika. The *447. Landesschützen Bataillon* went to Salonika, while the *923. Landesschützen Bataillon* was sent to Serbia. Additionally, the *342. Infanterie Division* was leaving Serbia, on its way to Russia. Also leaving for the Russian Front was *113. Infanterie Division,* which had arrived in Serbia on 1 November 1941 to rest and recuperate after having taken heavy losses in Zhitomir and Korosten, then took more casualties because it was the first German division to force the Dnieper River by Kiev during the summer of 1941. Both divisions left for Russia in January 1942. To make matters worse, while the German forces were being reduced in Yugoslavia, Tito's Partisan forces were growing in strength. On 2 February 1942, at Cajnice, he formed the 2nd Proletarian Brigade. Later in that same region, he formed the 3rd Sandzak Storm Brigade. In Montenegro he also raised the 4th and 5th Proletarian Brigades. The meeting between the Axis military leaders finally occurred in the town of Rijeka (Fiume) located on the Dalmatian coast. There the following officers of the various Axis military commands met to agree upon future joint operations:

a) Croatian Chief of Staff General Vladimir Laxa.
b) Commander in Chief of the Italian 2. Army General Mario Roatta.
c) General Vittorio Ambrosio, Chief of the Italian General Staff.
d) General of Engineers Kuntze, the *Wehrmacht* Commander Southeast.
e) General von Glaise Horstenau, the German Plenipotentiary General to the Independent State of Croatia in Zagreb.
f) General of the Artillery Bader, the Plenipotentiary Commanding General in Serbia.
g) General Antonio Gandini of the Italian Army High Command.
h) Major General Rintelen, the liaison officer at the Italian Army Armed Forces Headquarters.

The decision reached at the conference was to use the following troops for the projected, initial combined operation:

Croatian Forces:
In Rogatica: Two battalions of troops.
In Bale: One battalion of troops.
In Mokre: Two battalions of troops and one artillery battery.
In Sokolac: Two battalions of troops and one artillery battery.
In Zvornik-Carpati: Three battalions of troops and one artillery battery.
In Bijeljina: Two battalions of ethnic German Croatians who were to hold their positions.
In Tuzla: Three battalions of troops plus the staff of the 3. Croatian Infantry Division.
In Doboj: Four battalions of troops plus the staff of the 4. Croatian Infantry Division.
Italian Forces:
Three divisions, as well as strong aerial forces.
German Forces:
718. Infanterie Division.

There was a total of four German divisions in Serbia in the spring of 1942. In addition, there were other smaller formations, but all were required to maintain a minimum garrison of Serbia. The exact list of German forces in Serbia, as of 21 March 1942, was as follows:

704. Infanterie Division
714. Infanterie Division
717. Infanterie Division
718. Infanterie Division[2]
562. Landesschützen Bataillon
592. Landesschützen Bataillon
920. Landesschützen Bataillon
Feldkommandantur 599., 610., 809., 816., 725.
Kreiskommandantur I/823., 861., 867., II/378

At the start of 1942 there were three main centres of Partisan activity in Croatia:

1. Between the Bosna and Drina Rivers.

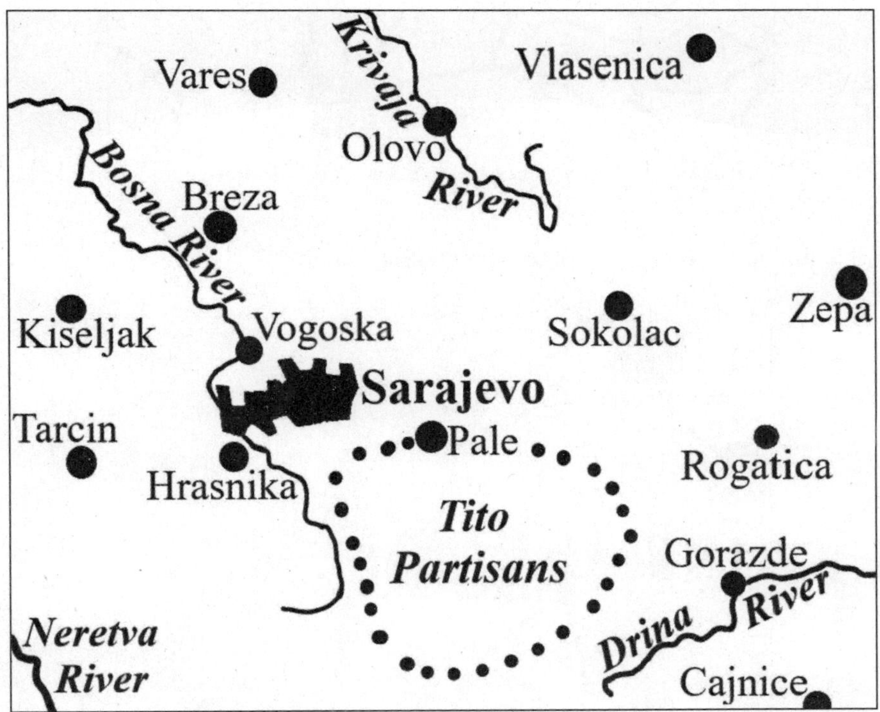

Figure 10. Partisan concentrations south of Sarajevo, January 1942.

2. Near Banja Luka, around the Kozara Mountains.

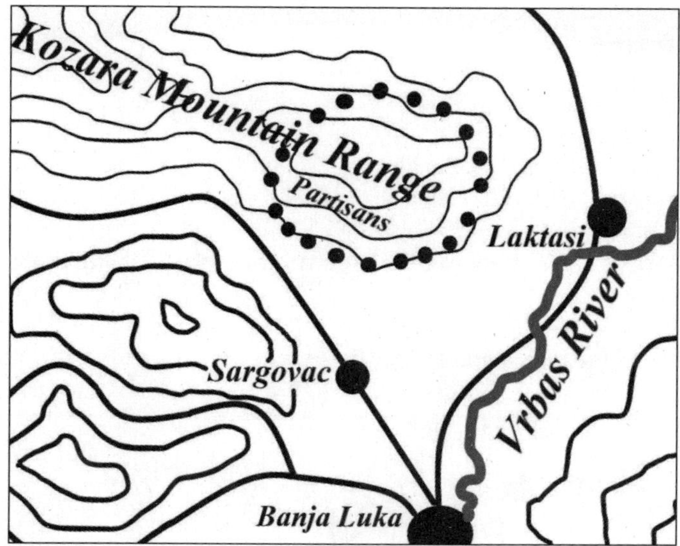

Figure 11. Partisans in the region of the Kozara Mountain Range and Banja Luka, January 1942.

3. In the Petrova Gora Mountains south of Karlovac.

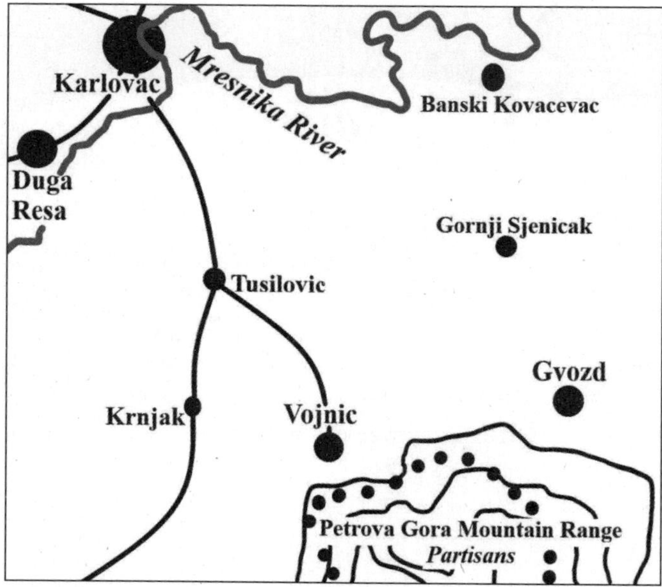

Figure 12. Partisan concentration in the Petrova Mountains, January 1942.

The first two areas were considered large centres of the revolt so were set aside for offensive operations for later on in the year. Meanwhile, the Petrova Gora Mountains would be swept by Croatian forces. The Croatian units at the end of 1941 have been estimated at various sizes. The regular army for example, has been quoted as having anywhere from 32,000–42,000 men, while we are fairly sure that the *Ustaše* had 10,000 men by the end of 1941. One other source gives a figure of 70,000 Croatian *Domobrans* (regular Croatian soldiers), 15,000 *Ustaše*, and 8,000 *Gendarmerie*. In addition to the four mountain brigades formed during the winter of 1941/42, an additional brigade, named the Petrinja Brigade, it comprised five poorly armed and lightly equipped battalions of *Gendarmerie* (Rural Police). Formed in Brod, it was employed initially in the region of Zumberok between Zagreb and Karlovac. The 1. Croatian Mountain Brigade was sent to the Zumberok area, like the Petrinja Brigade, while the 2. Croatian Mountain Brigade was sent to Mostar.

The 3. Croatian Mountain Brigade was sent to the region of the Kozara Mountains in order to protect the mine installations at Ljubija, though it was not moved there until June and July 1942. The 4. Croatian Mountain Brigade was also sent to the Zumberok area. In March 1942 a combined force of *Ustaše*, Home Guard, Croatian *Domobrans*, and *Gendarmerie* units undertook an operation in the Petrova Mountains south of Karlovac. The Communist forces there did not give battle, but instead opted to withdraw south. The Croatian Army's plans for 1942 envisioned forming five mountain infantry brigades, complete with all mountain equipment such as rock-climbing gear, mountain artillery guns, special equipment etc. In reality, all that could be formed were four weak mountain infantry brigades which had limited (though acceptable) mountain warfare capability, and the *Gendarmerie* Petrinja Brigade, whose offensive capability was strictly limited at best. The agreement hammered out on 3 March 1942 had twelve main points which included:

> The purpose of the joint Italian-German-Croatian operation to be carried out in the spring of 1942 was the 'final mopping up of the insurgents in Croatia'. The enemy situation was described as follows: In Serbia there are no strong enemy groups. In Croatia northeast of the demarcation line, in addition to smaller enemy groups, there are two strong centres of unrest between the Bosna and Drina Rivers, in the area of Banja Luka and Petrova Gora. In addition, there are groups of insurgents southwest of the demarcation line. General Roatta, the commanding officer of the Italian 2nd Army, is intended for the unified command of the operations. General Roatta will take over the command of the operations when

> the units reach the starting off points. General operational plan: The available troops will be committed first in East Bosnia, Later the operation will extend in a northwesterly direction. The operational plan will be agreed upon by the Commander in Chief of the Italian 2. Army and with General Bader: General Bader will be subordinated to the High Command of the Italian 2. Army, and lead the operation himself. For this purpose, the Italian, German, and Croatian army units intended for the operation are subordinate to him. The operation must be carried out as speedily as possible. 15 April 1942 is fixed for the commencement of the operation. The administration (civilian powers) in the occupied territories, after the pacification of the individual zones will be the responsibility of the Croatian civilian authorities, who will be appointed for administration according to the decision of the Commander in Chief of the Italian 2. Army. During the operation and the following pacification, the demarcation line cannot be regarded as such. The signatories of the treaty pledge themselves not to negotiate either with the Chetniks or with the Tito communists. This point regulates the equal treatment of the rebels and the population. The signatories of the pact pledge themselves to exchange their information on the enemy.[3]

The above twelve points were agreed upon, but towards the end of March 1942 the Italians had managed to convince the Germans and Croatians of the value of eliminating one enemy first, instead of going after both Chetnik and Communist guerrilla groups at once. The proposed jumping-off date for the operation had to be eventually extended due to the fact that the Italian divisions earmarked for the operation could not arrive on time. To make matters even more complicated, Lieutenant-Colonel Frantecic and his *Ustaše* Black Legion had advanced on Vlasnica against orders, towards the third week in April, only to be repulsed in front of the town by Chetnik formations that had arrived to reinforce the town's defences. Eventually, the planned operation involving the employment of Italian units alongside German and Croatian formations never materialized. In their place the Germans added the *III. Bataillon* of the *737. Infanterie Regiment,* from *717. Infanterie Division* in Serbia. They also employed the *714. Pionier Kompanie* of the *714. Infanterie Division,* which was also located in Serbia.

The plan now encompassed the use of the *Ustaše* Black Legion in the area of Han Pijesak–Podzeplje by 20 April 1942, while the *II. Bataillon/737. Infanterie Regiment* was to take over security duties on the Drina River around the town of Visegrad all the way to the Zepa Estuary. The Croatian forces employed would come from the 4. Croatian Mountain Brigade and 5. Croatian Mountain Brigade. The German *718.*

Infanterie Division, plus these two Croatian mountain brigades, were to immediately advance on the town of Rogatica and relieve the trapped Croatian Army units there. In addition, the enemy units in the area were to be surrounded and destroyed. The assembly points were to be the area of Praca–Sokolac–Han Pijesak Estuary of the Zepa region. The assembly date was set as 22 April 1942. The conclusion of the operation was to end with the sealing up of the frontier around the Drina River bend. The Croatian government had also agreed to curtail *Ustaše* atrocities in order to pacify the fears of what remained of the Serbian population of Bosnia-Herzegovina.

The operation in East Bosnia ended with the expulsion of the Chetnik forces there. No sooner had this operation concluded, that the Germans and Croatians once again turned their attention to eastern Bosnia, this time to the estimated 6,000–10,000 Tito Partisans who had 'sat out' the earlier Axis anti-partisan drive against the Chetniks in the same general area, waiting for the outcome. The bulk of these Communist forces were concentrated in the Kozara Mountain range and according to Croatian army reports, the Communists controlled the areas of Bos, Gradisca–Sava–Una–Kostajnica–Bos, Novi–Prijedor, and west of Banja Luka. Indeed, the Communists had their hands on the localities of Kijuc and Sanski Most. On 16 May 1942 they conquered Prijedor, where two Croatian Home Guard battalions made a gallant though futile two-day defence of the town before being overwhelmed by superior numbers. For the projected operation against these Tito forces, the Croatian Army had allocated the 1., 2., and 3. Mountain Brigade. The situation of the enemy units and the assembly of the NDH forces were described as follows:

> The main insurgent centre was apparently in the wild rugged and wooded mountains of the Kozara range. Croatian security was at the moment in the east of the insurgent territory, in the line – Bos Gradisca to the west of Banja Luka, then in the south in and around Sanski Most. Communist forces were also in the west, on the Una River from Bos Novi as far as the confluence of the Una and the Sava Rivers. Between Banja Luka and the Croatian group in Sanski Most, as well as between Kostajnica and Bos Novi, there was no Croatian security. The bridgeheads of Bos Dubica–Kostajnica–Dobrlin and Bos Novi were in the possession of the Croatians. To the north of the insurgent territory the Sava plain was inundated, in parts up to a width of 8 kilometres.[4]

Some of the Croatian mountain brigades had already arrived. Others were being disembarked. The 1. and the 2. Croatian Mountain Brigade in the area of Bos Novi–Kostajnica, the 3. Croatian Mountain Brigade near Banja Luka. Additional Croatian forces in Banja Luka included an *Ustaše* battalion and a newly raised volunteer battalion. In the spring of 1942, the Croatian Army volunteer units had been formed to supplement the regular Croatian army, with local volunteers. Initially, the following volunteer units were raised:

1. Muslim Volunteer Regiment *Efendic Hadzi* in Tuzla.
2. Volunteer Battalion *Kotorisce* in the Vrbanja Valley.
3. Volunteer Battalion *Banja Luka* in Banja Luka.

The *Ustaše* had also been expanding their organization – raising the 6. and 7. *Ustaše* Regiment in that spring, and expanding the Life Guard Regiment, which was charged with protecting the *Ustaše* leader, Dr Ante Pavelić, to a brigade-sized unit. This occurred beginning 10 May 1942. The majority of the *Ustaše* units had already proven that they could hold their own against the insurgents, but the newly-created 'volunteer militia' which were neither volunteers nor well-armed, for the most part, performed lamentably poorly. German forces earmarked for the operation against the Tito guerrillas in eastern Bosnia amounted to three battalions of infantry with artillery support. These battalions had come from *714. Infanterie Division,* and were organized into a combat group under the control of *Generalmajor* Friedrich Stahl, the commander of *714. Infanterie Division*. Meanwhile, the *718. Infanterie Division* was assigned to garrison duty in eastern Bosnia. On 15 June 1942 the guerrillas attempted to breakout from the area before the Axis troops could launch an attack. The Croatian units, described by the Germans as still suffering from a lack of tactical ability and experience, suffered a reverse when their 2. Croatian Mountain Brigade, which had been committed on the left flank of the 1. Croatian Mountain Division, its parent unit, withdrew from the field under the pressure of superior Partisan forces across the Prijedor and Bos Dubica highway.

The German regimental combat team attempted to strengthen the positions and morale of the NDH forces, but on 21 June, the 2. Croatian Mountain Brigade was severely trounced by Tito's Partisans, who had continued to apply pressure to the brigade. The Partisans used their knowledge of the local countryside to exact a heavy toll on the 2. Croatian Mountain Brigade. On 22 June 1942, even the 1. Croatian Mountain Brigade, considered the best of the four mountain brigades, was defeated, when the communists attacked the northern flank of the encirclement, in a surprise move which forced the 1. Croatian Mountain Brigade across the same stretch of highway between Bos Dubica and

Prijedor. German reports stated that the men of the 1. Croatian Mountain Brigade 'were seized by panic, and were streaming back.' Two entire Croatian battalions lost all of their machine guns, ammunition, and heavy equipment. The Tito Partisans were only too thankful for the NDH brigade to provide them with further weapons. The operation continued into July and, though it proved costly for the Croatian forces, was judged a fair success by the Germans. The Croatians of course, had a much different opinion. Their losses between 18–25 July alone were counted at 235 dead, 182 wounded, 521 missing, 108 horses, 53 machine guns, 15 heavy machine guns, 15 mortars and 3 mountain artillery guns from the 1. and 2. Croatian Mountain Brigade. The communist partisans in the Kozara Mountains were able to flee the trap set for them and the Axis offensive can be judged at having been a partial failure since the Germans and their allies failed to encircle and destroy the guerrilla force. Still, they did manage to expel these Partisan forces from the area, but that only meant that some other territory would now be infested with these guerrilla forces. Forces that were now better armed and equipped than before the offensive began. It was at this time that the Italian command decided to withdraw numerous Italian garrisons from along the Italian-German demarcation line. This gave the Tito Partisans an area where their authority was not contested by any Axis force. It was decided that the German *714. Infanterie Division* would remain in western Bosnia in order to help the Croatian Army forces to help maintain control of the region. The 3. Croatian Mountain Brigade remained in the Kozara Mountains to protect the mine installations at Ljubija, while the 2. Croatian Mountain Brigade was sent to Mostar to regroup, re-equip, and recuperate. The 1. Croatian Mountain Brigade and the newly formed 4. Croatian Mountain Brigade were now sent to the Zumberak area, between Zagreb and Karlovac and the Papuk Mountains of Slavonia.

Croatian Gendarmerie Forces

Under Major-General Milan Miesler, the Croatian *Gendarmerie* was established as rural police on 30 April 1941. Seven regional units held 18,000 troops by September 1943. Twenty-three companies were formed out of these – that is, one for each county plus one additional one for the capital, Zagreb. There were 142 district platoons, each with multiple postings, formed from the division of the companies. For anti-Partisan operations in Slavonia, a three-battalion Combined Gendarmerie Regiment was formed in early 1942; it was renamed the Petrinja Brigade in July. In 1945, the Croatian Gendarmerie Division was established by twelve autonomous Police Volunteer Battalions. The Croatian Gendarmerie Division was only composed of infantry and had no divisional support units whatsoever, thus making the title 'division' superfluous. Along with the rest of the Croatian Army, it surrendered.

Figure 13. The Croatian *Gendarmerie* cap badge. The Croatian white and red chequerboard shield with the round red-white-blue cap badge emblem above, surrounded by a bronze knot, with oakleaves on both sides of the national shield on a red cloth background. (*Author's collection*)

Chapter 6

RECRUITMENT AND FURTHER OPERATIONS

Faced with a growing partisan menace that included two distinct guerrilla groups, the leadership council of the State of Croatia advised the state's leader, Ante Pavelić, to increase recruitment within the population. As 1942 rolled onwards, there was a clear feeling in Zagreb that the Croatian government was in a race, not so much with Draza Mikhailovich's Chetniks, but with Tito's Partisans. This race involved the recruitment of all able-bodied men into either the communist guerrilla army or the NDH forces. The Croatian Army understood that if they did not obtain these men, they would fall prey to guerrilla recruiters. Everywhere that Tito's communist bands travelled, they actively recruited men. Volunteers came forward to join the communists, but press gangs were also common. If anyone refused, they would invariably be accused of being a Fascist supporter. Those who did not volunteer outright, and evaded the recruitment drive, were branded traitors and collaborators, and faced a difficult time. Most often they were taken out at night from their homes on the excuse of an interrogation, and their families would never see them again. If the families inquired, they were told that the individual was shot while trying to escape. Employing such tactics and methods, Tito's Partisan army began to grow exponentially.

Some Croatians found such methods reprehensible, but effective. The Croatian Army was likewise capable of press gangs, but in their case not as often. In any event, the NDH did begin to grow in number, if not in effectiveness, during the summer of 1942. Several more volunteer units were raised for the NDH, in support of the regular forces. Most of these were small, company-sized formations raised principally in Bosnia and Herzegovina. The *Ustaše* raised their 8. and 9. *Ustaše* Regiments during that same summer. It was also in the summer of 1942 that the Croatian Labour

Service began to grow, forming work companies that were supposed to build fortifications, and conduct road and bridge repairs due to guerrilla attacks, etc. These companies were few in number. Indeed, according to the English author Nigel Thomas, only 6,000 men were in the Croatian Labour Service by September 1943. The Croatian police forces which numbered around 5,000 men for the City Police and 6,000 *Gendarmerie*, or Rural Police, were transferred over to the control of the *Ustaše* command in June 1942.

This association lasted until January 1943 when the German *Ordnungspolizei* (Order Police – the uniformed street police) took over control of the Croatian police and expanded it greatly. The *Ustaše* Defence Battalion, which had been raised in 1941 to run the concentration camps at Jasenovac, Laborgrad, Pag Island, and later still at Stara-Gradisca and Gredjani, was expanded to a full brigade in the summer of 1942. The organization of this brigade resembled the German *Gestapo* (Secret State Police) and *Sicherheitsdienst* (SS Security Service) apparatus. By 1943 this camp brigade had a strength of some 15,000 guards, officials, bureaucrats and officers in its system. *Ustaše* field numbers increased sharply in 1942, partly due to the formation of two more regiments in the spring, two in the summer and one more in the autumn. The unit raised in the autumn was the 10. *Ustaše* Regiment. Another reason for its rise in numbers was the formation of cadre battalions which were established to recruit and to train the men who were being inducted into the *Ustaše* combat units. A total of ten *Ustaše* recruit battalions were formed in 1942. These recruit battalions were also referred to as preparatory battalions. The total number of *Ustaše* combat and recruit battalions formed for the entire year of 1942 were fifteen combat and ten recruit battalions. The above numbers do not include the *Ustaše* 'Life Guard' Brigade of one infantry, one motorized, and one cavalry battalion. In addition, there were five *Ustaše* regiments, numbered 1., 2., 3., 4., and 5., containing three battalions each (altogether fifteen battalions).

To the above-mentioned figure, we can add about eight battalions of the *Ustaše* railway defence force, which were organized into two railway brigades, the 1. *Ustaše* Railway Defence Brigade and 2. *Ustaše* Railway Defence Brigade. While the voluntary militia grew to some twenty-one battalions by 1944, there were but perhaps eight to ten militia battalions raised in the whole of 1942. The Muslim population of Bosnia-Herzegovina was also recruited for the Croatian Army and *Ustaše,* though initially they served in the militia units which numbered around 4,000–5,000 men in 1942 and later increased to some 7,500 militiamen in 1943. Eventually these Muslims were absorbed into the regular army in 1944. However, there were Muslim volunteers in the *Ustaše* as early as 1942. In addition to the above

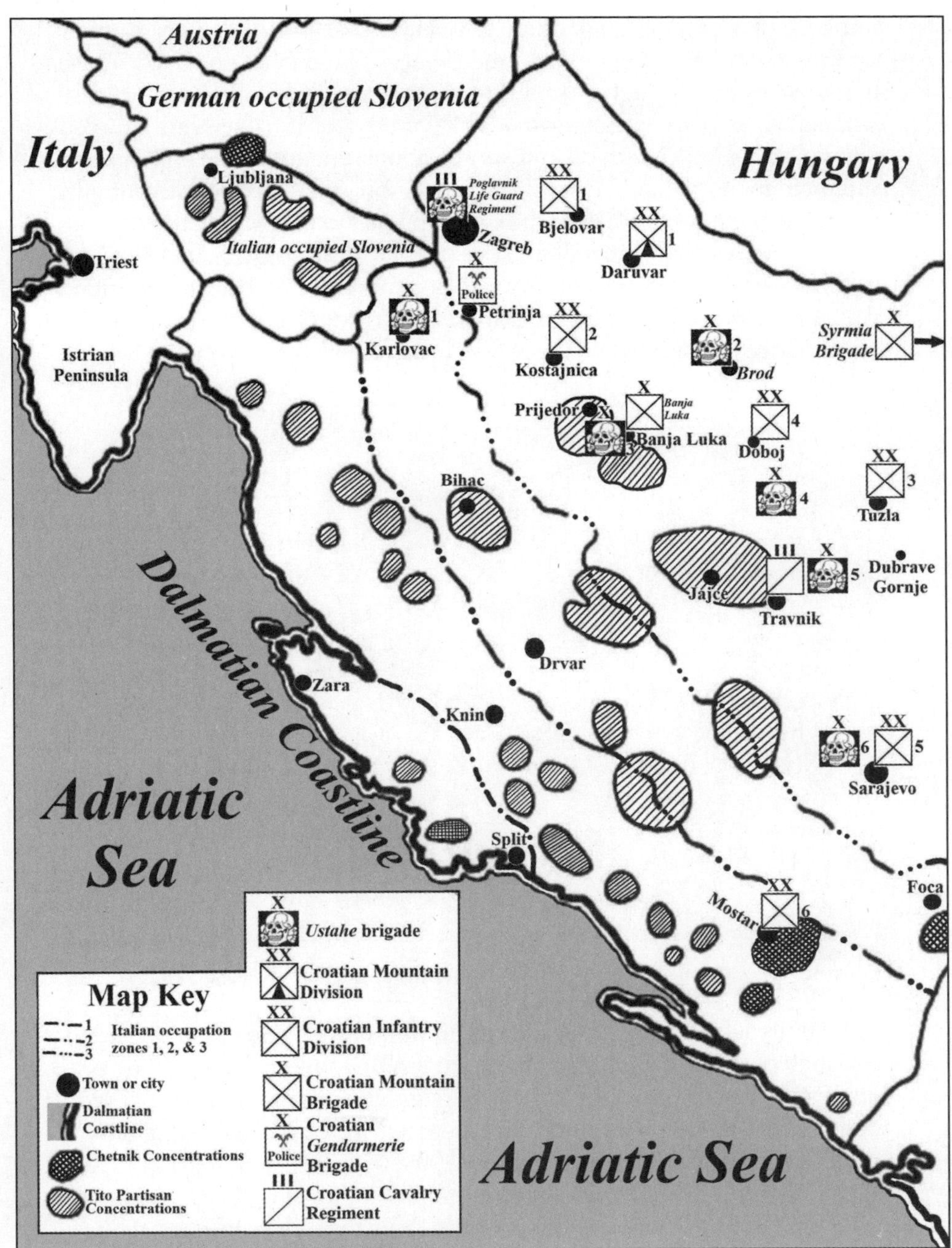

Figure 14. Location of the major Croatian military units in January 1943.

numbers of troops, the Croatian government also raised eight railway security battalions from older, middle-aged personnel in 1942. These men were lightly armed and had no heavy weapons at all. Each of these battalions had perhaps between 600–800 men apiece. They were charged with guarding important rail junctions, stations, and also rode military and civilian trains as needed, depending on the local guerrilla threat. Eventually, they were made subordinate to the German *Eisenbahnsicherungsstab Kroatien* (Railway Security Staff Croatia), whose main headquarters in 1943, was based in the town of Brod. Following the operation in the Kozara mountain region, the Croatians and their German allies next fixed their eye sights on the Samarica region, lying west of the Kostajnica–Bos Novi line.

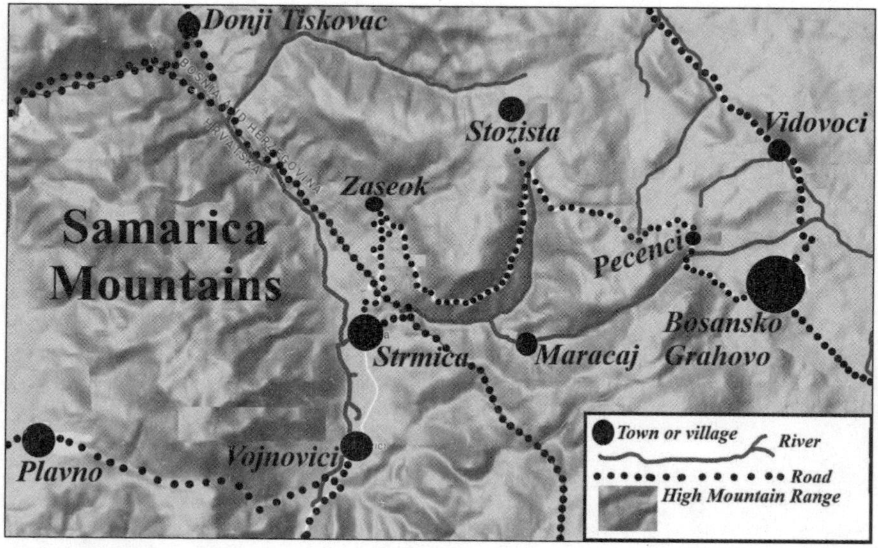

Figure 15. Operations in the Samarica mountain range, July–August 1942.

The units which were allocated for this anti-partisan operation included 4,500 men of the 1. and 2. Croatian Mountain Brigade, plus about four rifle battalions from the 1. (Sisak) Corps Territorial Command. This included another 2,000 troops. German units assigned included two battalions of the *721. Infanterie Regiment* (1,100 men), the *734. Infanterie Regiment*, two companies of the *202. Panzer Bataillon*, employing captured French Somua S-35 tanks, four to five artillery batteries, and two companies of the *659. Pionier Bataillon (motorziert)*, with another 300 men. The operation against the guerrilla force in the Samarica area did not begin until July 1942 since the 1. Croatian Mountain Division's brigades needed a period of rest and refitting before being committed once more. Once the offensive began, it lasted until 24 August 1942. The following losses were taken by the participants:

Table 1. Axis and Partisan Losses in July–August 1942 by the Samarica Mountain Range.

Losses	German Forces	Croatian Forces	Partisan Forces
Dead	2	77	1,031
Wounded	12	108	27
Missing	1	362	Unknown
Taken Prisoner			260 Partisans
Shot in Reprisal			212 Civilians

Meanwhile the main Partisan force under Tito was not standing idly by. Though they had won a temporary breathing space in mid-April 1942 the pressure on the communist forces in and around the city of Foca was growing. There was a lull in the fighting around Foca until 4 May, when a force of some 12,000+ Chetniks – all under Italian direction, began to converge in the area with German support. Unfortunately for the Axis and luckily for the Partisans, the Italians had chosen to withdraw their forces from the Third Operational Zone. This allowed the Tito units to withdraw northwards with relative impunity. On 10 May 1942, Foca was abandoned by the communists who now headed north to try and cross the Neretva River and reach the relative safety of the northwest Bosnian mountain range. In the Drvar-Petrovak area the left-wing group of Tito's invasion force linked up with a local communist force of some 1,500–2,000 men which had been operating in this region since the summer of 1942. They next began to move on Bihac, which they conquered on 5 November 1942. Around this time, specifically on 3 November, the strengths of the German divisions were listed as follows:

Table 2. Strength of German Occupation Divisions, 1942.

Division	Bayonet Strength	Number of Men	% Fighting
704. Infanterie Division	5,909	9,765	61
714. Infanterie Division	5,703	8,947	63
717. Infanterie Division	5,083	7,221	70
718. Infanterie Division	5,153	7,505	68

Faced with this Partisan invasion which could not apparently be stopped by Croatian Army units, Ante Pavelič decided to dismiss Field Marshal Kvaternik in October 1942, and appoint himself as commander of all Croatian forces. He chose as his Chief of Staff Lieutenant-Colonel Ivan Prpic. As for Kvaternik, he and his son Dido took refuge in Slovakia, where they remained until the end of the war.

In order to cover up the dispute between Pavelič and Slavko Kvaternik and his son, Dido, the newspapers were told to say that Field Marshal Kvaternik had retired on 4 January 1943. After the war, Dido Kvaternik, as well as his wife, three children, and his sister, Olga, were able to escape to Argentina. Slavko Kvaternik was not so lucky. He was caught by the United States Army and handed over to the new Tito-led communist government. He was tried as a war criminal, and hanged in the central square of Zagreb on 7 June 1947. Meanwhile, the Germans had also been very alarmed at the ease in which the Tito Partisans had penetrated deep into NDH territory. The German command decided that a permanent *Wehrmacht* presence had to be established on Croatian territory, in order to secure these areas from further guerrilla conquest. With this in mind, the Germans too, went about setting up a new command in October 1942.

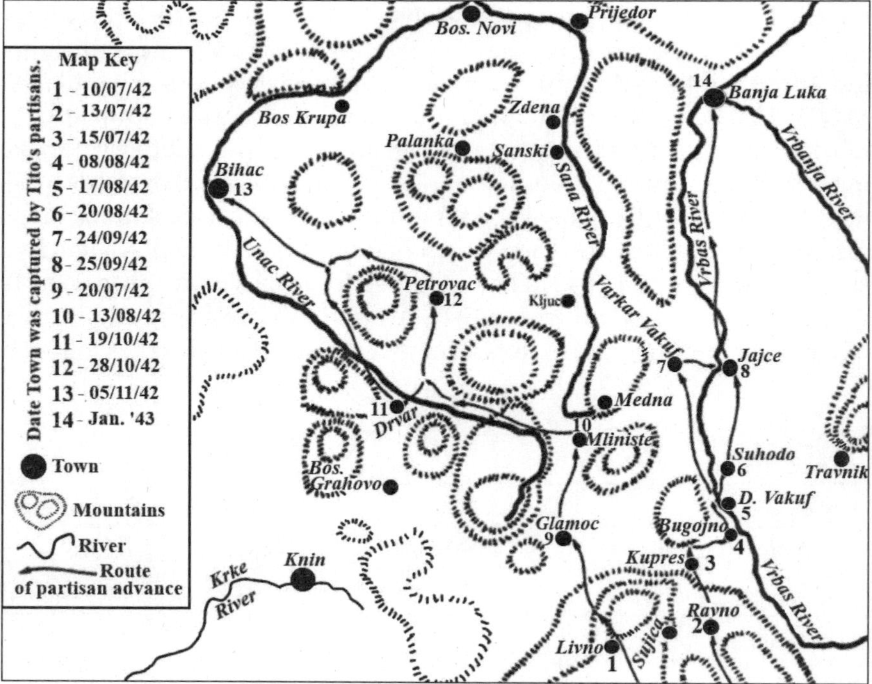

Figure 16. Beginning in July 1942, 12,000 Tito Partisans invaded the region bordering Bihac-Knin-Ravno-Banja Luka. This map traces the movement of Tito's forces through the region. Half of the town of Banja Luka was captured by the Partisans in early January 1943.

The headquarters formed was based in the capital of Zagreb and was to control German units operating in NDH territory. The German officer charged with this new command was *Generalmajor* Rudolf Lüters.[1] However due to organizational problems, this new German HQ's command and control staff was not fully operational until the beginning of 1943. The delay in setting up the headquarters of the *Kommandeur der deutschen Truppen in Kroatien* (Commander of German Troops in Croatia) did not prevent the Germans from reinforcing the Croatian Army.[2]

In leaving the city of Foca on 10 May, Tito moved out with about 12,000–13,000 guerrillas and headed north towards Bosnia. By 8 July these forces stormed Konjice and were in Livno that same day. His 'army' now divided into two groups – a right-wing force and a left-wing force. The right-wing group moved towards Jajce, overwhelming the small Croatian garrisons of Ravno, Kupres, Bugojno, D. Vakuf and Suhodo as they advanced north. From 18–24 August, the town of Varkar Vakuf was attacked and fell to the partisans. This town was located just west of Jajce, which was conquered almost exactly a month later, on 25 September, after a two-pronged partisan assault. Meanwhile, the left-wing group had not remained idle. After conquering Livno, this group moved on Glamoc and then took Mliniste. It joined up with a smaller guerrilla force there. They next turned westward towards Drvar and Petrovak, following the Unac River as they went. Banja Luka was attacked on 31 December 1942, and captured half of the town before being driven out by a motorized regiment of the German *Brandenburg* commando force. Jajce was lost to the Germans in January 1943. The German *187. Reserve Division* arrived in Zagreb and set up its headquarters there in December 1943. Its divisional components were spread out as follows:

Divisionshauptquartier – Zagreb.
Reserve Grenadier Regiment 45 – Zagreb.
Reserve Grenadier Regiment 130 – Petrinja.
Reserve Grenadier Regiment 462 – Bjelovar.
Reserve Artillerie Bataillon 96 – Zagreb.
Reserve Pionier Bataillon 86 – Melk.

Other reinforcements which arrived in September 1943 were the units under the *III. (germanische) SS Panzerkorps,* and included *SS Freiwilligen Panzergrenadier Brigade Nederland* and *SS Freiwilligen Panzergrenadier Division Nordland* plus smaller corps support units. This SS corps and its formations remained on Croatian territory until December 1943, when it was transferred by rail to the Leningrad sector in the Soviet

Union, and placed on the western fringes of the so-called Oranienbaum Pocket (west of Leningrad). Additional German reinforcements for Croatia included the arrival of the bulk of the *Brandenburg* commando formation. Initially only the *Jäger Regiment 1 Brandenburg* (*motoriziert*) had arrived, but just in the nick of time to relieve the Axis forces which were holding on for dear life in Banja Luka. As stated earlier, this town had been under attack by Tito's right-wing forces since 31 December 1942. The garrison had already lost half of the town to the guerrillas. With this German help, the NDH units managed to regain the other half of the town and expel the partisans. The Croatian Army achieved some success in the beginning of January 1943 when one of its Home Guard Volunteer regiments, supported by elements of the 1. *Ustaše* Brigade and 3. Croatian Cavalry Battalion, retook the town of Jajce from the Tito Partisans.

The German Security Apparatus

With the increasing partisan activity in Croatia, and the fact that the Croatian armed forces were unable to stop partisan incursions, German police forces were also ordered to reinforce Croatia. They entered the country initially with a staff of the *SS Beaufträger der Reichsführer-SS*. By the spring of 1943, this staff and its sub-units consisted of a total of 196 officers and 1,690 NCOs and enlisted men of the *Ordnungspolizei* (German Order Police). In January 1943 the Croatian police and railway units came under the control of the German police force, which began to expand the organization. All of the German SS and police apparatus were brought into the country. The *SIPO* (*Sicherheitspolizei*), or State Secret Police, came in and established *KdS* stations, or *Kommandeur der Sicherheitspolizei* in numerous cities and towns. Similarly, the German *ORPOI* or *Ordnungspolizei* (Order Police, the German uniformed street police) set up *KdOs* (*Kommandeur der Ordnungspolizei*). The *KdO* stations were controlled by higher echelon commands called *Befehlshäber der Ordnungspolizei*, or *BdO* for short. Similarly, the *KdO* stations were controlled by *BdS* (*Befehlshäber der Sicherheitspolizei*). The *Sicherheitspolizei* had two sub-groups: (1) the *Kripo* (short for 'Criminal Police') and (2) the *Gestapo* (*Geheimstaatspolizei*), or State Secret Police. The first thing which the German SS & police command did was to begin the recruiting of Croatian volunteers for the *SIPO* and *ORPO*.

The first unit formed was titled *Polizei Gendarmerie Bataillon* (Rural Police Battalion), formed in the spring of 1943. By 16 March 1943, it contained 749 men. By May (two months later) it had been expanded into a full regiment of 1,886 men. In February 1943 a *Polizei Wach Bataillon Kroatien* (Police Guard Battalion Croatia) was also established.

A large proportion of these volunteers were ethnic German Croatians, and it seems that every effort was made to recruit these *volksdeutsch,* though ordinary Croatians could also volunteer. So effective was the German recruiting drive that by July 1943 around 25,000 men were in the *ORPO* and *SIPO* units. The initial strength of the seven *ORPO* battalions and about ten *SIPO* companies would eventually be increased further still.

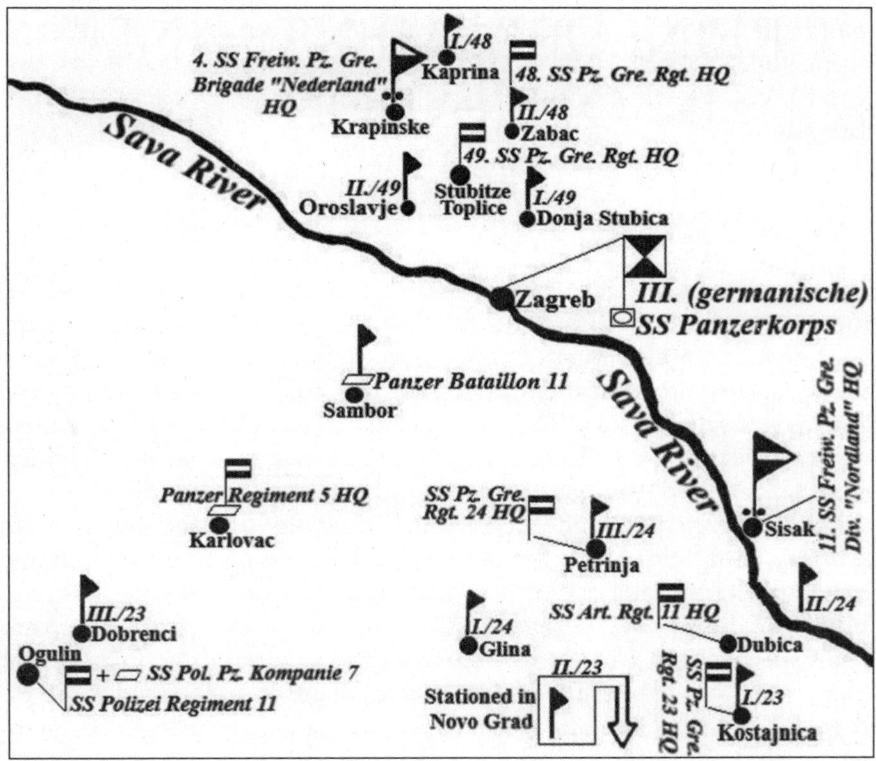

Figure 17. Location of the *III. (germanische) SS Panzerkorps* in Croatia, September 1943.

Chapter 7

CROAT-GERMAN REINFORCEMENTS AND OPERATIONS

The Croatian Army also had plans for further expansion in 1943. A total of five additional mountain brigades were to be formed in that year, but again as had previously occurred, a lack of sufficient and proper arms and equipment hindered the Croatian state from having their wishes met. The 6., 7., 8., 9., and 10. Croatian Mountain Brigades were thus cancelled and plans were set in motion to organize so-called *Jäger* brigades that in essence were light infantry formations. These brigades were to be made up of four rifle battalions and one or two artillery battalions. We must remember that these artillery battalions had, at best, perhaps one or two artillery batteries each. One positive aspect of these *Jäger* brigades was that they were formed from younger men and from reservists from the original fifteen *Domobran* infantry regiments, which began to be disbanded in the beginning of 1943. As a result, the stamina of these healthier, physically fit men meant that the *Jäger* brigades would have the best manpower that was available in Croatia. The Croatian Armed Forces as they stood in January 1943 were spread out too thinly over the Independent State of Croatia. This fact was not overlooked by both Tito's Partisans and Draza Mihailovich's Chetniks.

Poor tactics and low morale

Historians believe that sometime between 475 and 221 AD, *The Art of War,* was written by the Chinese scholar and general, Sun Tzu. In this work, Sun Tzu stressed many tactics and strategies that could help a kingdom win a war. One of the tenets of the book was that 'he who defends everything, defends nothing'. Meaning, that if you divided your military so thinly to guard every single piece of land, your army would be weak everywhere. You would then not be able to defend any territory or anything. The strategy of attempting to control every bit of NDH territory, was a mistake that the Croatian military never corrected. In fairness to the Croatian Army High Command, that decision had been made by the *Poglavnik,* and not by the generals. Another poor tactic employed by the Croatian Army was the concept of placing a small garrison of troops, stationed in a fortified village and town. The Croatian Army High Command did this in order to comply with the wishes of Ante Pavelić, who ordered that all NDH territory must be defended. The Tito Partisans exploited this weakness, by surrounding a town or village with overwhelming force and destroying the Croatian garrison. This tactic was employed by the Partisans again and again, throughout the war.

You did not have to be a great military tactician to realize that creating stationary strongpoints was like placing an open invitation for the guerrillas to attack and destroy that strongpoint. And yet, the French would employ this failed strategy in Indochina (Vietnam) in the early 1950s. It proved to be a major reason why they lost the war. The Partisan tactic of attacking these fortified localities was simple, as it was deadly. First, they would isolate the town by severing the telephone lines and cutting off all of the roads leading in and out of it. If a rail line existed and led anywhere near the town, the tracks were blown up before the town was surrounded. This prevented the arrival of reinforcements and a possible retreat by the garrison troops. Next, the Partisans would ask for the surrender of the NDH forces and if that failed, attack in overwhelming numbers and storm the town. The destruction of these NDH garrisons, one by one, had a detrimental effect on the morale of NDH troops. It also caused a steady loss of troops and weaponry. The loss of troops was bad enough, but losing military equipment that the Partisans would capture was just as equally detrimental to the Croatian war effort. The lack of proper and sufficient weapons and equipment, was a major factor that contributed to the low morale of most NDH units.

Continued losses in the field, coupled with poor leadership at the top, also added to this low morale. These garrisons became a focal point of Croatian losses on a day-to-day basis. With each defeat, the guerrillas became stronger and bolder, and the Croatian Army smaller and weaker. Benito Mussolini put it best when he said: 'A regime, of whatever kind, collapses only under the weight of defeat.' Dr Ante Pavelić was not a military tactician. He was a lawyer by training and a politician by design. Yet, beginning in the summer of 1942, he was personally leading the Croatian Armed Forces to their inevitable defeat, by insisting that every bit of ground be held. Those in the Croatian command understood this all too well, but his decisions, however detrimental to the war effort, had to be carried out. It does not appear that this tactic of leaving small forces in fortified towns or villages, was ever stopped. In the end, this policy only aided the partisans. The location of the various Croatian units, as listed in the Croatian order of battle of January 1943, aptly proves this tactic of the Croatian Army attempt to hold onto all territories of the NDH state, even if that meant that dispersed forces would therefore be sufficiently weak to be attacked piecemeal fashion by the Tito Partisans and Mikhailovich's Chetniks:

1. Territorial Corps Command – located in Sisak.
   1. Croatian Infantry Division – Bjelovar
   2. Croatian Infantry Division – Kostajnica
   Petrinja Brigade – Petrinja
2. Territorial Corps Command – located in Brod.
   3. Croatian Infantry Division – Tuzla
   4. Croatian Infantry Division – Doboj
   Banja Luka Brigade – Banja Luka
   Syrmia Brigade – Ruma
   Zagreb Cavalry Brigade – Travnik
3. Territorial Corps Command – located in Sarajevo [the commander was General Mihailo Lukic]
   5. Croatian Infantry Division – Sarajevo
   6. Croatian Infantry Division – Mostar
   Independent of Territorial Command, with:
1. Croatian Mountain Division – HQ at Daruvar, with:
   Croatian Mountain Brigade – Zumberak region (Zagreb to Karlovac)
   Croatian Mountain Brigade – Prijedor
   Croatian Mountain Brigade – Prijedor area
   Croatian Mountain Brigade – Zumberak region.

Ustaše Brigade – Prijedor *Ustaše* Life Guard Regiment – Zagreb.
   2. *Ustaše* Brigade – Broda
   3. *Ustaše* Brigade – Banja Luka
   4. *Ustaše* Brigade – Doboj / Tuzla
   5. *Ustaše* Brigade – Travnik area
   6. *Ustaše* Brigade – Sarajevo

Muslim Home Guard Volunteer Regiment Efendic Hadzi – Tuzla
Home Guard Volunteer Battalion Kotorisce – in the Vrbanja Valley.

Home Guard Volunteer Battalion Gracanica – Gracanica.
Home Guard Volunteer Battalion Banja Luka – Banja Luka.
Home Guard Volunteer Battalion Kladanj – Kladanj.
Home Guard Volunteer Battalion Derventa – Derventa.
Home Guard Volunteer Battalion Teslic – Teslic.
1., 2., 3., 4., 5., 6., 7., 8., 9., 10., 11., and 12. Croatian Railway Security Battalion – dispersed throughout the Croatian rail line system.

With regard to the effectiveness of the railway troops, it was limited, given that the approximately 147-mile Lika to Knin-hub line (M604), ran through many isolated forests and mountains that were the perfect location for a partisan ambush, or for a demolition team to blow up the tracks. In March 1943 the Tito Partisans effectively cut this rail line for the rest of the war, when the viaduct, which was built over a steep ravine, was blown up by the First Partisan Corps. The Zagreb to Rijeka line, which connected to the M604, remained active, but under constant Partisan attack. There was one armoured train that the NDH forces employed between Zagreb and Rijeka. It was armed with two Hotchkiss H38 / 39 tank turrets. In addition, two open wagons, protected by sandbags, carried troops and machine guns. The other two armoured trains employed by the NDH were located elsewhere in the country. In addition to these troops, there were approximately 15,000 *Ustaše* personnel who ran the concentration camps at Jasenovac, Laborgrad, Stara Gradisca, Gredjani, and Pag Island. By the beginning of 1943, these men were split up into two 'camp' brigades, though one of these brigade headquarters would be disbanded in December of that same year. Eventually some men were siphoned off from the concentration camp system to form or replenish *Ustaše* combat units. This went on from 1943 so that by 1944, about 10,000 *Ustaše* personnel were working in the concentration camp system.

Their fate will be dealt with later on, but a justifiable comparison should be made here, of these *Ustaše* personnel, with the Death's Head units that ran the Nazi concentration camp system. The camps run by the *Ustaše* were places, like the Nazi concentration camps, where people died on a daily basis. It is also true that, just like these German *Totenkopfstandarte* members often switched from working in the death camps, to serving in SS combat units; so too did these *Ustaše* men work in many instances, as camp guards and later, as *Ustaše* soldiers. Their war guilt is undeniable.

Figure 18. Areas under Partisan control in September 1943. (*Author's line drawing*)

A major reinforcement to the German and Croatian forces in NDH territory arrived in January 1943, when the first of three German-raised Croatian Legion divisions, the *369. (deutsch-kroatische) Infanterie Division Teufel,* made its appearance. The Croatians called it *Vražja Divizija* – the Devil's division. This unit had an initial strength of some 14,000 well-trained men who had been trained and organized at *Truppenubungslager Stockerau* (Troop Training Camp Stockerau). Its major units included:

369. Infanterie Division Hauptquartier
- *Division Stab Kompanie*
- *Feldgendarmerie Zug*
- *Feldpost Amt*

369. Kroatische Legion Infanterie Regiment

I. Infanterie Bataillon
- *1. Infanterie Kompanie*
- *2. Infanterie Kompanie*
- *3. Infanterie Kompanie*
- *4. Infanterie Kompanie*

II. Infanterie Bataillon
- *5. Infanterie Kompanie*
- *6. Infanterie Kompanie*

7. Infanterie Kompanie
8. Infanterie Kompanie
III. Infanterie Bataillon
9. Infanterie Kompanie
10. Infanterie Kompanie
11. Infanterie Kompanie
12. Infanterie Kompanie
13. Mörser Kompanie
14. Panzerjäger Kompanie
15. Pionier Kompanie.
370. Kroatische Legion Infanterie Regiment
I. Infanterie Bataillon
1. Infanterie Kompanie
2. Infanterie Kompanie
3. Infanterie Kompanie
4. Infanterie Kompanie
II. Infanterie Bataillon
5. Infanterie Kompanie
6. Infanterie Kompanie
7. Infanterie Kompanie
8. Infanterie Kompanie
III. Infanterie Bataillon
9. Infanterie Kompanie
10. Infanterie Kompanie
11. Infanterie Kompanie
12. Infanterie Kompanie
13. Mörser Kompanie
14. Panzerjäger Kompanie
15. Pionier Kompanie.
369. Kroatische Legion Aufklärungs Abteilung
1. Reiter Schwadron
2. Reiter Schwadron
369. Kroatische Legion Artillerie Regiment
I. Artillerie Bataillon (105mm Fh.18)
1. Artillerie Batterie
2. Artillerie Batterie
3. Artillerie Batterie
II. Artillerie Bataillon (105mm Fh.18)
4. Artillerie Batterie
5. Artillerie Batterie
6. Artillerie Batterie
III. Artillerie Bataillon (150mm s.Fh.18)
7. Artillerie Batterie
8. Artillerie Batterie
9. Artillerie Batterie

369. Kroatische Legion Panzerjäger Bataillon
- *1. Panzerjäger Kompanie (50mm PAK 38) (motoriziert)*
- *2. Panzerjäger Kompanie (75mm PAK 40) (motoriziert)*

369. Kroatische Legion Pionier Bataillon
- *1. Pionier Kompanie*
- *2. Pionier Kompanie*
- *3. Pionier Kompanie*

369. Kroatische Legion Signals Bataillon
- *1. Signals Kompanie*
- *2. Funk Kompanie*

369. Kroatische Legion Feldersatz Bataillon
- *1. Ausbildungs und Ersatz Kompanie*
- *2. Ausbildungs und Ersatz Kompanie*
- *3. Ausbildungs und Ersatz Kompanie*
- *4. Ausbildungs und Ersatz Kompanie*
- *5. Ausbildungs und Ersatz Kompanie*

All of these new forces were quickly used by *Generalmajor* Rudolf Lüters, the commander of German troops in Croatia, who proposed to Pavelić that a joint operation be launched in January 1943 against the Partisan concentrations in northern Bosnia. The name of this operation was titled *Weiss* (White) by the Germans. It was organized into three phases, *Weiss-I, Weiss-II,* and *Weiss-III*. The first phase was to last from 20 January to 18 February 1943. The second phase ran from 19 February to 20 March, while the third phase was to begin on 21 March and was to be completely an Italian endeavour. This last phase of the operation, *Weiss-III,* would turn out to be totally unsuccessful. The Italians were to initially employ their 5. Corps comprising the 57. Infantry Division *Lombardia,* 13. Infantry Division *Re,* and 12. Infantry Division *Sassari.* The Germans were to employ the *714., 717.,* and *718. Infanterie Division,* plus the recently arrived *369. (deutsch-kroatische) Infanterie Division Teufel* (Devil).[1] The *Waffen SS* was to supply their ethnic-German *SS Freiwilligen Gebirgs Division Prinz Eugen.* This SS Mountain Division had a core of German officers and NCOs, but was primarily composed of ethnic Germans from the Banat region of Yugoslavia. Additional German units included the *130. Reserve Grenadier Regiment* of *187. Reserve Infanterie Division,* and the *202. Panzer Bataillon,* which had been formed using captured stocks of French tanks. The Croatian contribution to the operation would include the 2. and 3. Croatian Mountain Brigade, and the 1. *Ustaše* Brigade.

The 3. *Ustaše* Brigade and elements of the German *Jäger Regiment 1 Brandenburg* (both in the area of Banja Luka), would lend their support as blocking troops. The Italian *Lombardia* Infantry Division was to move from the region of Plaski, in the direction of Slunj, while the *Re* Infantry Division was to leave the areas of Vrbovine and Lovinac, with the objective of taking Bihac and Korenica. The *Sassari* Infantry Division, was to advance partly on Bihac and partly against Drvar and Petrovac. They would then link up with the German units coming from the north and east at Varkar Vakuf.

The Germans were to employ their *714.*, *717.*, and *718. Infanterie Division* from the east in a north to south pattern from the area of Banja Luka all the way down to just south of Travnik. These divisions would act as a screening force and would also advance against the enemy when the opportunity presented itself. The *SS Freiwilligen Gebirgs Division Prinz Eugen,* which was in the region of Karlovac, was to advance in the direction of Slunj and Bihac, while the *369.* (*deutsch-kroatische*) *Infanterie Division Teufel,* coming from the area of Sisak-Kostajnica, would attack south over Prijedor towards Bos. Petrovac and link up with the left-wing group of *7. SS Freiwilligen Gebirgs Division Prinz Eugen*. The *202. Panzer Bataillon* and the *130. Reserve Grenadier Regiment* would support both units by filling in between them, acting as the anchor for both divisions. The *717. Infanterie Division,* in the region of Banja Luka and Mrkonjicgrad, was to attack in the direction of Kluj; while the *714. Infanterie Division* was to move against partisan forces in Sanski Most. Croatian troops were to be concentrated into one area: the region in and around the town of Prijedor.

The 2. and 3. Croatian Mountain Brigade and the 1. *Ustaše* Brigade were to advance on the towns of Bos Novi and Zdena. Partisan strength in this area of operations was estimated to be the following: the 1. Bosnian Partisan Corps, comprising the 4. Partisan Division (three brigades), 5. Partisan Division (four brigades), plus two independent brigades and three separate detachments. In total, this force numbered nineteen brigades and six detachments. The operation began as planned and conceived by the German command, but instead of allowing themselves to be drawn into a fight, Tito's Partisans were ordered to withdraw southwards, towards Herzegovina and Montenegro. This move probably saved the 1. Bosnian Partisan Corps, as it would have surely been caught in a deadly crossfire from Axis forces that were advancing from three separate directions. The Germans did their utmost to pursue the fleeing guerrillas, while the Italian 6. Army Corps and their Chetnik allies were to block the partisan escape route on the Neretva River. This proved impossible, as the Italians and the Chetniks could not hold the Partisans. As a result, the bulk of Tito's forces escaped the Axis trap. German losses were 335 dead and 101 missing.

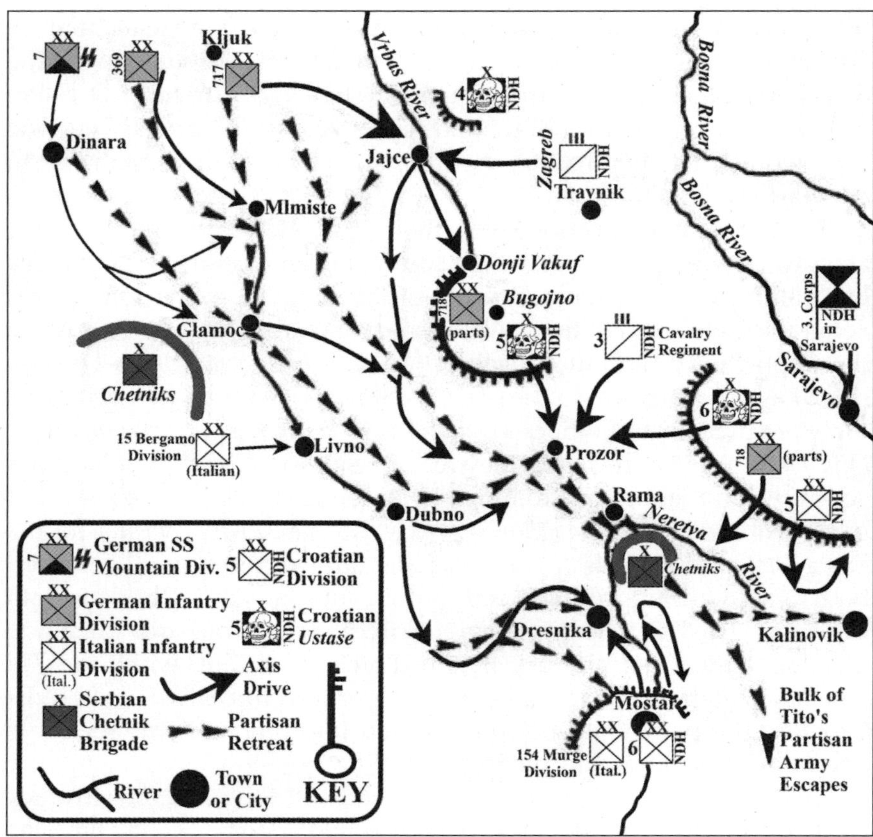

Figure 19. Detail of *Unternehmen Weiss* (Operation White). In spite of numerous attempts, the bulk of Tito's partisan army was able to break through the trap set by the Axis forces. (*Author's line drawing*)

Croatian losses were estimated to be around 500 dead and missing, while the Italians suffered terribly at the hands of the Partisans. About 2,000 Italians were taken prisoner by Tito's guerrilla forces during the entire operation. Italian losses in dead, missing and wounded were horrendous. The official Italian history of the battle claims their units were hardest hit, losing some 2,000 soldiers taken prisoner by the Partisans. The *Re* Division lost 115 dead, 420 wounded, and 42 missing. The *Sassari* Division fared worse, with a total of over 1,000 dead, while the *Lombardia* Division lost about 500 killed.

The Partisans lost around 8,500 dead and 2,010 captured during the whole anti-partisan operation. Although the guerrillas had lost over 10,000 men, their army had escaped relatively intact. The Axis had won a tactical victory but Tito had exacted a strategic victory from the Axis because his guerrilla army survived to continue the struggle. The large numbers of Italian prisoners taken by the Partisans also showed that the ordinary Italian soldier was not willing to die for the Fascist cause. The Germans were fuming. The Italian inability to prevent the Partisans from escaping only worsened the shaky military alliance between Nazi Germany and Fascist Italy. The relationship between Hitler and Italy's Fascist leader, Benito Mussolini, had been difficult and unpredictable from the very start of the war. This strained coalition would set the tone for future cooperation between the armed forces of both countries. The tensions which existed between these co-belligerents was affirmed by the stress which both dictators found in trying to collaborate with one another. An example was the various occupation troubles which the Italians and Germans experienced after they occupied Yugoslavia and Greece.

Another example was the inability of both German and Italian forces to work effectively for a common goal. Hitler and Mussolini were often at odds with one another, as to how best to control these conquered Balkan territories. Artificial occupation zones created to delineate Italian and German spheres of influence created an administrative nightmare that only benefited the guerrillas. These issues gave rise to more and more tension between the Germans and Italians. Mistrust grew to dislike between both military forces, which eventually turned into contempt. This is a perfect paradigm for the relationship that developed between the German dictator and the Italian *Duce* during the war. Their military union proved to be more a form of expediency rather than an actual military coalition. But I digress. The second part of Operation 'White' ran from 18 February through 20 March 1943, and saw the withdrawal of the communist guerrilla forces in a southeasterly direction. The Partisan 8. and 12. Brigades, facing the *7. SS Freiwilligen Gebirgs Division Prinz Eugen* and *369. (deutsch-kroatische) Infanterie Division Teufel,* withdrew under pressure but their retreat was orderly. Similarly, the 4., 7., and 9. Partisan Brigade facing the German *717. Infanterie Division* also withdrew.

The 10. Partisan Brigade covered the left flank in the area between Drvar and Bos. Grahovo, south of Drvar. The 2. Partisan Brigade faced elements of the German *718. Infanterie Division* and 5. *Ustaše* Brigade at Bugojno, and covered the right flank of the guerrilla withdrawal. The partisans were carrying with them an estimated 4,000 wounded fighters. From the west the Italians and their Chetnik allies were pressing home their attacks towards Livno, Duvno, and Dresnica. Fortunately for the Partisans, the Chetnik force sent to block their retreat at the bend of the Neretva River was too weak to prevent their escape from the trap. The Italian command had made the decision to employ only this Chetnik force there, so the failure to prevent the Partisans from escaping was the fault of the Italians. Heavy fighting marked the opening of *Unternehmen Weiss-II* (Operation White II). Additional troops of the Italian 6. Army Corps in Montenegro arrived to bolster the Italian force, but substantial numbers of Partisans managed to break through the Italian line and escape south and southeast into the wilder mountain regions of Herzegovina, Montenegro, and eastern Bosnia. Dispersing into almost inaccessible areas, the Partisan command group and numerous individuals managed to elude their pursuers. *Unternehmen Weiss III* (Operation White III), the Italian part of the operation, was completely unsuccessful.

Throughout the year the Germans had been demanding that the Italian Army cease arming and supplying the Chetniks. The Italians were supporting them because of the Chetniks were fighting Tito's partisans. The problem was that the Chetniks were mostly hostile to the Germans and especially to the Croatian state. Before the next major anti-partisan operation was launched – *Unternehmen Schwarz* (Operation Black), Mussolini finally acquiesced and instructed the Italian Army to stop supplying the Chetniks with arms and munitions. The Germans had already received orders to arrest any Chetnik troops that they encountered, even if they claimed to be allies of the Italians. As the war in Yugoslavia entered its almost two-year mark, the military situation, it was clear, was growing progressively difficult for the Axis.

Chapter 8

EXPANSION OF NDH AND GERMAN FORCES

After this first full-scale anti-guerrilla operation, both sides set about regrouping and reorganizing their forces. While Tito and his men were up in the hills licking their wounds, the Germans began to reorganize four of their divisions and re-designate them. In this way the *704., 714., 717.,* and *718. Infanterie Division* were re-designated as *Jäger* divisions, and renumbered as the *104., 114., 117.,* and *118. Jäger Division*. In this instance, the word '*Jäger*' stands for 'light infantry', denoting that these divisions were less powerfully organized as the regular infantry formations, but better suited for movement through rugged terrain, which covered most of the Balkans. Renewed German recruitment of the Croatian and ethnic German Croatian population yielded further units. In April 1943 they raised the *Polizei Gendarmerie Bataillon*. The *Ustaše* also organized their 11. and 12. *Ustaše* Regiment, while the Croatian Army railway security battalions came under the control of the German *Eisenbahnsicherungsstab Kroatien* (Railway Security Staff Croatia), who increased their number from twelve *Eisenbahnsicherheitsbataillone* (railway security battalions) to eighteen battalions and located them in the following areas across Croatian territory:

1. *Kroatische Eisenbahnsicherheitsbataillon* – Zagreb
2. *Kroatische Eisenbahnsicherheitsbataillon* – Nova Gradisca
3. *Kroatische Eisenbahnsicherheitsbataillon* – Ruma
4. *Kroatische Eisenbahnsicherheitsbataillon* – Karlovac
5. *Kroatische Eisenbahnsicherheitsbataillon* – Zapresic
6. *Kroatische Eisenbahnsicherheitsbataillon* – Bred
7. *Kroatische Eisenbahnsicherheitsbataillon* – Doboj
8. *Kroatische Eisenbahnsicherheitsbataillon* – Ogulin
9. *Kroatische Eisenbahnsicherheitsbataillon* – Dugoselo

10.*Kroatische Eisenbahnsicherheitsbataillon* – Sunja
11.*Kroatische Eisenbahnsicherheitsbataillon* – Vrpolje
12.*Kroatische Eisenbahnsicherheitsbataillon* – Zemca
13.*Kroatische Eisenbahnsicherheitsbataillon* – Krizevci
14.*Kroatische Eisenbahnsicherheitsbataillon* – Ivanic Grad
15.*Kroatische Eisenbahnsicherheitsbataillon* – Vinkovci
16.*Kroatische Eisenbahnsicherheitsbataillon* – Sarajevo
17.*Kroatische Eisenbahnsicherheitsbataillon* – Novska
18.*Kroatische Eisenbahnsicherheitsbataillon* – Sid

The Croatian infantry divisions, with the exception of the 6. Infantry Division (led by General Vladimir Metikoš), located in the Italian sphere of influence in Mostar, were now ordered to disband on 1 May 1943. The regiments were to merge with the existing Croatian 1. Mountain Division, and out of them would be formed the four new *Jäger* brigades. The four mountain brigades of the 1. Mountain Division would be left basically unchanged, except that they would be fleshed out and refreshed. Some men from the original fifteen regiments were used to replenish the mountain brigades. The regimental and brigade organization now looked like this:

1. Croatian Mountain Brigade – Banova Jaruge, Kutina, Kriz, with:
    1. Croatian Mountain Infantry Regiment.
    5. Croatian Mountain Infantry Regiment.
2. Croatian Mountain Brigade – Konjic, with:
    2. Croatian Mountain Infantry Regiment.
    9. Croatian Mountain Infantry Regiment.
3. Croatian Mountain Brigade – Petrinja, Kordun Banija, with:
    3. Croatian Mountain Infantry Regiment.
    11. Croatian Mountain Infantry Regiment.
4. Croatian Mountain Brigade – Daruvar, Pakrac, Lipik, with:
    4. Croatian Mountain Infantry Regiment.
    8. Croatian Mountain Infantry Regiment.
1. Croatian *Jäger* Brigade – Doboj, Derventa, Teslic, with:
    4. Croatian *Jäger* Regiment.
    6. Croatian *Jäger* Regiment.
2. Croatian *Jäger* Brigade – Unac Valley, Bosanski Novi, Bosanski Krupa, Otokac, with:
    1. Croatian *Jäger* Regiment.
    10. Croatian *Jäger* Regiment.
3. Croatian *Jäger* Brigade Brcko, with:
    5. Croatian *Jäger* Regiment.
    8. Croatian *Jäger* Regiment.
4. Croatian *Jäger* Brigade – Banja Luka, with:
    7. Croatian *Jäger* Regiment.
    13. Croatian *Jäger* Regiment[1]

In May 1943 the Croatian Army Order of Battle looked like this:

1. (Corps) Territorial Command – Zagreb
    1. Croatian Mountain Brigade –
        1. Croatian Mountain Infantry Regiment
        5. Croatian Mountain Infantry Regiment
        11. Croatian Artillery Battalion
        1 engineer platoon
    3. Croatian Mountain Brigade –
        3. Croatian Mountain Infantry Regiment
        11. Croatian Mountain Infantry Regiment
        3. Croatian Artillery Battalion
        1 engineer platoon
    4. Croatian Mountain Brigade –
        4. Croatian Mountain Infantry Regiment
        8. Croatian Mountain Infantry Regiment
        1. Croatian Artillery Battalion
        12. Croatian Artillery Battalion
        1 engineer platoon
    2. Croatian *Jäger* Brigade –
        1. Croatian *Jäger* Regiment
        10. Croatian *Jäger* Regiment
        4. Croatian Artillery Battalion
        8. Croatian Artillery Battalion
Independent (1. Corps) units:
        2. Croatian Infantry Regiment – Zagreb
        12. Croatian Infantry Regiment – Gospic
        15. Croatian Infantry Regiment – Knin, Sinj, Gospic
        2. Croatian *Jäger* Battalion – Gospic
        1. Croatian Bicycle Battalion – Korpivnica
2. (Corps) Territorial Command – Brod
Croatian *Jäger* Brigade –
        4. Croatian *Jäger* Regiment
        6. Croatian *Jäger* Regiment
        5. Croatian Artillery Battalion
Croatian *Jäger* Brigade –
        5. Croatian *Jäger* Regiment
        8. Croatian *Jäger* Regiment
        7. Croatian Artillery Battalion
4. Croatian *Jäger* Brigade –
        7. Croatian *Jäger* Regiment
        13. Croatian *Jäger* Regiment
        6. Croatian Artillery Battalion
Syrmia Rifle Brigade – Ruma
        1. Volunteer Rifle Battalion
        2. Volunteer Rifle Battalion
        3. Volunteer Rifle Battalion

Independent (2. Corps) Units:
3. Croatian Infantry Regiment – Zvornik
Muslim Volunteer Regiment Efendic Hadzi – Tuzla
4. Croatian Assault Brigade – Bred
    Home Guard Volunteer Battalion Kladanj – Kladanj
    Home Guard Volunteer Battalion Banja Luka – Banja Luka
    Home Guard Volunteer Battalion Kotorisce – Kotorisce
Home Guard Volunteer Battalion Teslic – Teslic
Home Guard Volunteer Battalion Derventa – Derventa
Home Guard Volunteer Battalion Gracanica – Gracanica
(Corps) Territorial Command – Sarajevo
5. Croatian Mountain Brigade –
    2. Croatian Mountain Regiment
    9. Croatian Mountain Regiment
    9. Croatian Artillery Battalion
  6. Croatian Infantry Division –
    1. Volunteer Infantry Regiment
    14. Infantry Regiment
Independent (3. Corps) Units:
Zagreb Cavalry Regiment – Travnik:
    1. Cavalry Battalion
    2. Cavalry Battalion
    3. Cavalry Battalion
    Home Guard Volunteer Battalion Kula Faziagic
    Home Guard Volunteer Battalion Kupres – Kupres

At the end of April 1943, the second German-raised Croatian Legion division, the *373. (deutsche-kroatische) Infanterie Division*, made its appearance in Croatia, after training in Germany. It was initially stationed west and northwest of Mostar, Bosnia with its 15,000+ men. It was initially tasked with defending the area west and northwest of Mostar. Its organization was as follows:

373. Infanterie Division Hauptquartier
Division Stab Kompanie
    Feldgendarmerie Zug
    Feldpost Amt
Grenadier Infanterie Regiment 383
I. Infanterie Bataillon
    1. Infanterie Kompanie
    2. Infanterie Kompanie
    3. Infanterie Kompanie
    4. Infanterie Kompanie
II. Infanterie Bataillon
    5. Infanterie Kompanie
    6. Infanterie Kompanie

7. Infanterie Kompanie
8. Infanterie Kompanie
III. Infanterie Bataillon
9. Infanterie Kompanie
10. Infanterie Kompanie
11. Infanterie Kompanie
12. Infanterie Kompanie
13. Mörser Kompanie
14. Panzerjäger Kompanie
15. Pionier Kompanie.
Grenadier Infanterie Regiment 384
I. Infanterie Bataillon
1. Infanterie Kompanie
2. Infanterie Kompanie
3. Infanterie Kompanie
4. Infanterie Kompanie
II. Infanterie Bataillon
5. Infanterie Kompanie
6. Infanterie Kompanie
7. Infanterie Kompanie
8. Infanterie Kompanie
III. Infanterie Bataillon
9. Infanterie Kompanie
10. Infanterie Kompanie
11. Infanterie Kompanie
12. Infanterie Kompanie
13. Mörser Kompanie
14. Panzerjäger Kompanie
15. Pionier Kompanie.
373. Kroatische Legion Artillerie Regiment
I. Artillerie Bataillon (105mm Fh.18)
1. Artillerie Batterie
2. Artillerie Batterie
3. Artillerie Batterie
II. Artillerie Bataillon (105mm Fh.18)
4. Artillerie Batterie
5. Artillerie Batterie
6. Artillerie Batterie
III. Artillerie Bataillon (150mm s.Fh.18)
7. Artillerie Batterie
8. Artillerie Batterie
9. Artillerie Batterie
373. Kroatische Legion Aufklärungs Abteilung
1. Radfahr Kompanie
2. Radfahr Kompanie
373. Kroatische Legion Panzerjäger Bataillon
3. Panzerjäger Kompanie
4. Panzerjäger Kompanie

373. Kroatische Legion Pionier Bataillon
- *1. Pionier Kompanie*
- *2. Pionier Kompanie*
- *3. Pionier Kompanie*

373. Kroatische Legion Signals Bataillon
- *1. Signals Kompanie*
- *2. Funk Kompanie*[2]

Figure 20. Author's line drawing of the *Heer* signals arm patch.

Figure 21. Above, from left to right, the three arm patches of the *369., 373.,* and *392. (deutsche-kroatische) Infanterie Division*. The arm patches were worn on the upper right sleeve of the field blouse. The *369. Infanterie Division* was nicknamed the '*Teufel*' (Devil) division, while the *373. Infanterie Division* was called the 'Tiger' division. The *392. Infanterie Division* was called the *Blau* (Blue) Division. The arm patches all featured a red- and-white chequered shield. In the case of the *369. Infanterie Division,* the word '*Hrvatska*' (Croatia) was placed on top with red lettering on a black background. The first shield was also very elaborate, while the shields for the *373.* and *392. Infanterie Division* were simpler in design.

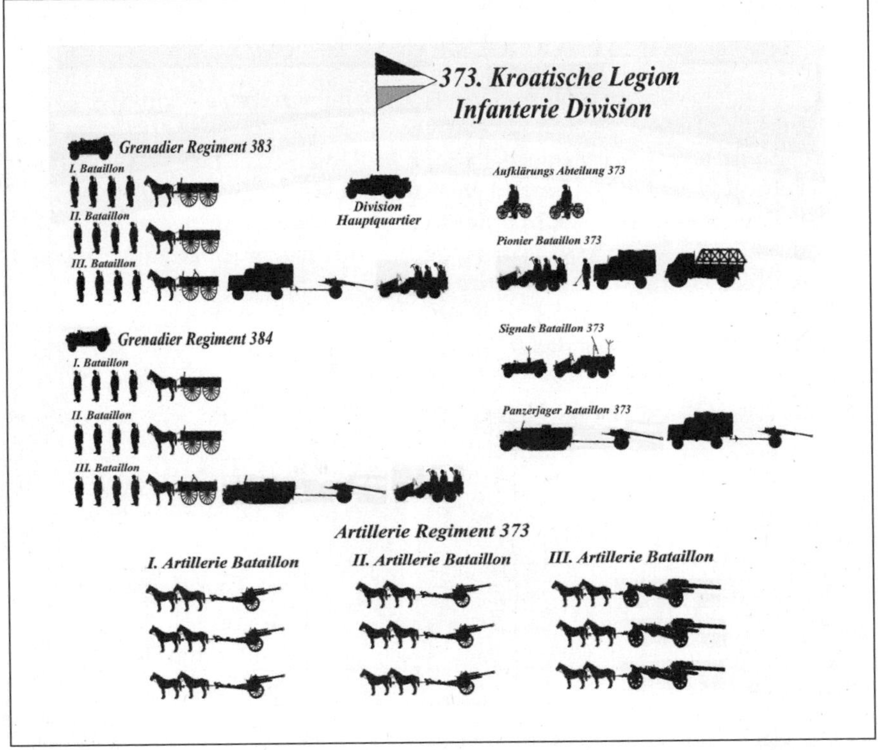

Figure 22. Schematic diagram showing the order of battle for the Croatian-German 373rd Infantry Division. (*Author's line drawing*)

During the summer of 1943 this new *373. Kroatische Legion Infanterie Division* would undertake operations mainly in the Banja Luka and Bihac regions. For example, by 5. July 1943, it was operating against Tito's Partisans located between Bugojno and Travnik. The *369. Kroatische Legion Infanterie Division* however, would operate further south, mainly in the Sarajevo and Mostar areas. German assistance to the Croatian state continued throughout the summer of 1943. In particular, the police forces and security formations of the NDH were expanded greatly. The German police system was introduced, whereby several *Kommandeur der Ordnungspolizei* (*KdO* – Commander of the Order Police) headquarters were established on Croatian soil. These in turn, controlled several *Gendarmerie* stations in several key towns. Overall control of the *KdO*s was administered by the *Befehlshaber der Ordnungspolizei* (*BdO* – Higher Commanding Officer of the Order Police). The first *BdO* was stationed in Osijek in May 1943. This command post was later transferred to Zagreb on 28 June 1943. The *KdO*s in Croatian territory were as follows:

KdO Zagreb – with police stations in Zagreb, Bjelovar, and Varazdin.
KdO Osijek – with police stations in Osijek, Brod, Nova Gradiska, Vukovar, and Ruma.
KdO Sarajevo – with police stations in Sarajevo, Tuzla, Travnik, and Mostar.
KdO Banja Luka – with police stations in Banja Luka, Jajce, Bihac, and Petrinja. This *KdO* command was later transferred from Banja Luka to Knin in February 1945. In order to properly train, equip, and process the new Croatian police men, two recruit training battalions were established during the summer of 1943 in Osijek:
Polizei-Ausbildungs-Bataillon
Polizei-Ausbildungs-Bataillon II[3]

Table 3. Area of Operations and Higher Commands for the German-Croat Divisions.

Year	Month	Army Group	Army or Corps	Area of Operations	Unit
1943	January	SE[4]	*BddTK*[5]	Sisak-Petrinja-Sunja	369
1943	February	SE	′	Cazin	369
1943	February	SE	′	Bos. Petrovac-Kluj	369
1943	February	SE	′	West of Ribnik-Mliniste	369
1943	March	SE	′	Glamoc-Malovan	369
1943	March	SE	′	Duvno-Scit-Prozor-Rama-Jablanica	369
1943	April	SE	′	Glavaticevo-Kalinovik-Pale-Podgrab	369
1943	April	SE	′	W & NW of Mostar	373
1943	May	SE	′	Cajnice & NW of Plevlja	369
1943	May	SE	′	S of Jajca, 48km S of Banja Luka	373
1943	June	SE	′	NW of Balinovac and up to Rataj	369
1943	June	SE	′	Travnik area	373
1943	July	SE	′	Travnik-Sanski Most	373
1943	July	SE	′	Vlasenica-Tuzla-Lukavac-Petro. Selo	369
1943	August	SE	′	Kotor Varos	373
1943	August	SE	*BddTK*	Sarajevo region	369
1943	September	F/2. *Panzerarmee*[6]	*XV. Gebirgsarmeekorps*[7]	Banja Luka region	373

Year	Month	Army Group	Army or Corps	Area of Operations	Unit
1943	September	F/2. *Panzerarmee*	,	Sarajevo region	369
1943	October	F/2. *Panzerarmee*	,	Banja Luka region	373
1943	October	F/2. *Panzerarmee*	,	Sarajevo region	369
1943	November	F/2. *Panzerarmee*	,	Banja Luka region	373
1943	November	F/2. *Panzerarmee*	,	Sarajevo region	369
1943	December	F/2. *Panzerarmee*	*XV. Gebirgsarmeekorps*	Banja Luka region	373
1943	December	F/2. *Panzerarmee*	*V. SS Gebirgsarmeekorps*	Sarajevo region	369
1944	January-March	-	*BdE in Kroatien*	Zagreb region	392
1944	January-May	F/2. *Panzerarmee*	*XV. Gebirgsarmeekorps*	Banja Luka region	373
1944	January-November	F/2. *Panzerarmee*	*V. SS Gebirgsarmeekorps*	Mostar region	369
1944	June-July	F/2. Pz. A.	*LXIX. Armeekorps*	Drvar-Grahovo	373
1944	April-December	F/2. *Panzerarmee*	*XV. Gebirgsarmeekorps*	Senj, Rab & Pag Islands, Knin	392
1944	December	F/E[8]	*V. SS Gebirgsarmeekorps*	Mostar region	369
1944	August-December	F/2. *Panzerarmee*	*XV. Gebirgsarmeekorps*	Knin region	373
1945	January -March	F/E	*XV. Gebirgsarmeekorps*	Bihac region	392
1945	January	F/E	*XCI. Armeekorps*	Sarajevo region	369
1945	January-February	F/E	*XV. Gebirgsarmeekorps*	Bihac region	373
1945	February -March	F/E	*XXI. Gebirgsarmeekorps*	Sarajevo region	369
1945	April	E[9]	*XV. Gebirgsarmeekorps*	Dalmatian coast region	392
1945	April	E	*XV. Gebirgsarmeekorps*	Sisak region	373

Year	Month	Army Group	Army or Corps	Area of Operations	Unit
1945	April	E	*XXI. Gebirgsarmeekorps*	Brod and Cilli regions	369
1945	May	SE	*XCVII. Armeekorps*	Fiume (Rijeka) region	392

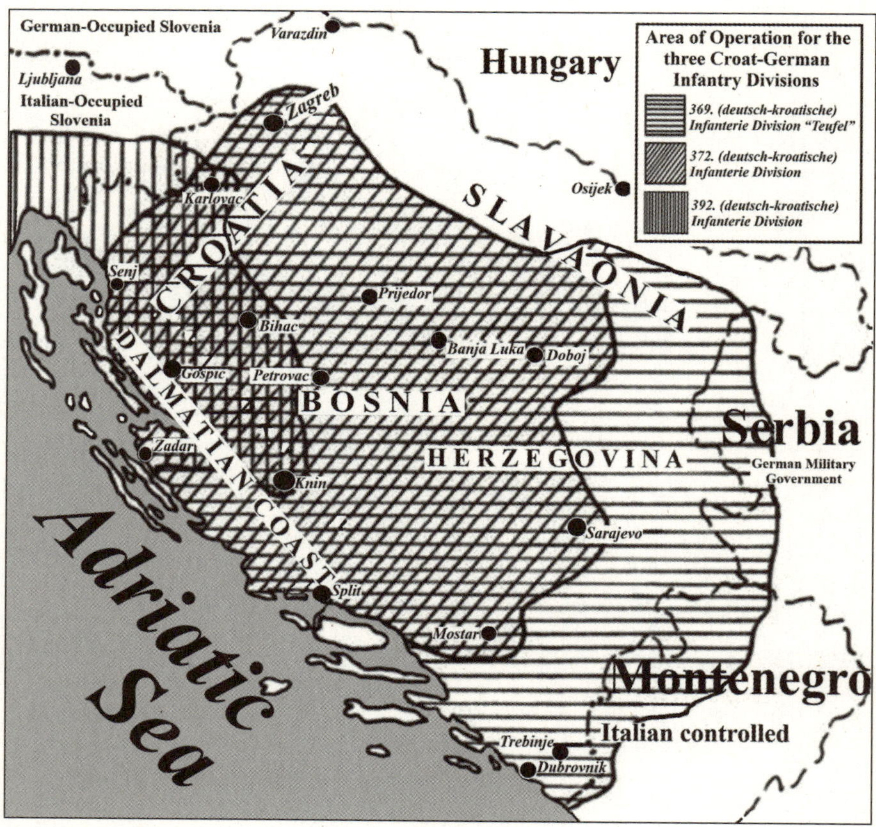

Figure 23. Area of operations for the Croat-German infantry divisions. The *392. (Deutsch-Kroatische) Infanterie Division* operated mostly in western Croatia, northwest Bosnia, the northern section of the Dalmatian coastline, as well as southern Slovenia. Not shown on the map are operations on the Istrian Peninsula.

There was justification for the ironic joke made by the Germans, that the Croatian Army was the replacement depot for the Tito Partisans. There were several instances when the NDH forces deserted in large numbers.

1. **Desertions During Partisan Gains in 1943:** In the summer and autumn of 1943, especially after the Italian Armistice in September, Croatian troops stationed along the Adriatic coast began deserting in larger numbers. Italian soldiers defected, and NDH forces in the region also faced growing pressure from Partisans, prompting numerous desertions.
2. **Lika and Kordun Desertions (1943):** The Lika and Kordun areas, which had significant Partisan activity, saw frequent desertions by *Domobrans* throughout 1943. As the Partisans increasingly controlled the countryside, some entire Croatian units abandoned their posts and joined Tito's forces.
3. **4th Croatian Infantry Division in Eastern Bosnia (Late 1943):** Units within the 4th Croatian Infantry Division in Eastern Bosnia experienced high desertion rates to the Partisans by late 1943. This area was heavily influenced by Partisan successes, and morale among Croatian forces was low, making desertion appealing for soldiers disillusioned with the NDH regime.
4. **Mass Desertions after the Fall of Italy (September 1943):** With Italy's surrender, the Partisans capitalized on new supplies and equipment, which made their forces more appealing to those within the Croatian Army who were uncertain of the Axis' future. This period marked a spike in desertions from NDH forces, as many saw the Partisans as a better alternative.
5. **Desertions within *Ustaše* Units:** Although less common than with *Domobrans*, some *Ustaše* members (the NDH's more elite paramilitary force) also defected to the Partisans, especially as the war turned decisively against the Axis powers. The *Ustaše* were generally more ideologically committed, but war-weariness and fear of post-war repercussions led some to join the Partisans.
6. **1944 Desertions in Dalmatia:** As Partisan control strengthened in Dalmatia, many Croatian soldiers defected in groups. The Partisans often encouraged these desertions by guaranteeing protection and even offering rank or status in their own forces.
7. **Desertions of Forced Conscripts in Late 1944 and Early 1945:** The NDH forcibly conscripted young men into its army, but as the Partisans gained control over most of Yugoslavia, many conscripts escaped to the Partisan side to avoid fighting in a war they no longer believed the NDH could win.

During an operation around Varos, 1,200 Croatian *Domobrans* and about 800 Croatian Home Guard volunteer militiamen were completely routed by a brigade of Tito Partisans, though few desertions were noted in this incident, the operation had to be called off on 7 November 1943. In Virovitica, 20 officers, 22 NCOs and 500 enlisted men of the Croatian *Domobrans* surrendered to the Partisans without a fight. Reports stated that the Tito Partisans had threatened the unit with mass execution if they resisted the guerrilla force. The psychological effect was instantaneous: the Croatian troops surrendered on 15 November 1943. Near Cacin, five officers, 21 NCOs, and 280 men deserted with all weapons, ammunition, and equipment. In fact, total desertions in the Croatian Army between June and October 1943 stood as follows, in regards to major units affected:

a) *Bataillon / 2. Jäger* Brigade (786 men).
b) Part of 4. *Jäger* Brigade (1,097 men).
c) Bulk of 3. *Jäger* Brigade (2,217 men).
d) Approximately two companies from the 373. Croatian Legion Division (334 men).
e) Around three companies from the 369. Croatian Legion Division (489 men).

In December 1943 the *11.* , *12.*, and *13. Kroatische Eisenbahnsicherheitsbataillone* were transferred from the German *Eisenbahnsicherungsstab* (Railway Security Staff) into the *Ordnungspolizei*. These three Croatian railway security battalions were to eventually form the *3. Kroatische Polizeiregiment* (3rd Croatian Police Regiment) under German auspices. The other remaining railway security battalions remained under the German Railway Security Staff. On 21 April 1943 the German-Croatian police forces in NDH territory stood at around 20,000 men. This number would increase to about 32,000 men by the following year. The number of ethnic German Croatians in uniform at the end of 1943 included the following:

13,500 in the *Waffen SS*
3,500 in German Order Police units
1,050 in the German Army
2,000 in the Croatian Army, 700 in work programs (not under arms).

The initial batch of ten *SIPO* (*Sicherheitspolizei,* or State Secret Police) companies formed from the ethnic German Croatian population, plus some purely Croatian volunteers, were allocated as follows by mid-1943:

KdS Kompanie in Zagreb
KdS Kompanie in Knin
KdS Kompanie in Tuzla
KdS Kompanie in Bjelovar
KdS Kompanie in Osijek
KdS Kompanie in Bihac

KdS Kompanie in Sarajevo
KdS Kompanie in Doboj
KdS Kompanie in Karlovac
KdS Kompanie in Banja Luka

Later still, the following KdS commands were formed after the Italian surrender:

KdS Kompanie in Zadar
KdS Kompanie in Mostar
KdS Kompanie in Split
KdS Kompanie in Rijeka (Fiume)
KdS Kompanie in Dubrovnik

Each *KdS* command had perhaps somewhere between 150–300 SD men. This included the Croatian-born and German-born personnel. Officers were German, with the NCOs being predominantly German, with some Croatians thrown in. The enlisted personnel were almost entirely made up of ethnic German Croatians or pure Croatian personnel. The reorganization of the Croatian Army continued throughout the spring, summer, and autumn of 1943. As mentioned earlier, the divisional system was abandoned, with the exception of the 6. Croatian Infantry Division in Mostar, and a brigade system was initiated. The 1. Mountain Regiment of the newly reformed 1. Mountain Brigade had come from the remnants of the old 1. Mountain Brigade, while the 5. Mountain Regiment, which was also in the new 1. Mountain Division, had been raised from the remains of the old 5. Infantry Brigade.

To raise the new 2. Mountain Brigade, elements of the old 2. Mountain Brigade and the 9. Infantry Regiment were used; the former, from the old 2. Mountain Brigade, became the 2. Mountain Regiment, while the latter became the 9. Mountain Regiment. The old 3. Mountain Brigade became the nucleus of the 3. Mountain Regiment of the new 3. Mountain Brigade, while the former 11. Infantry Regiment was redesignated as the 11. Mountain Regiment, and merged in the new 3. Mountain Brigade. The formation of the new 4. Mountain Brigade was a bit more elaborate. It was to contain the 4. and 8. Mountain Regiments. The 4. was formed by using the 11. *Ustaše* Battalion and two battalions from the old 4. Mountain Brigade. The 8. was formed by using two more battalions from the old 4. Mountain Brigade, plus the 37. *Ustaše* Battalion.

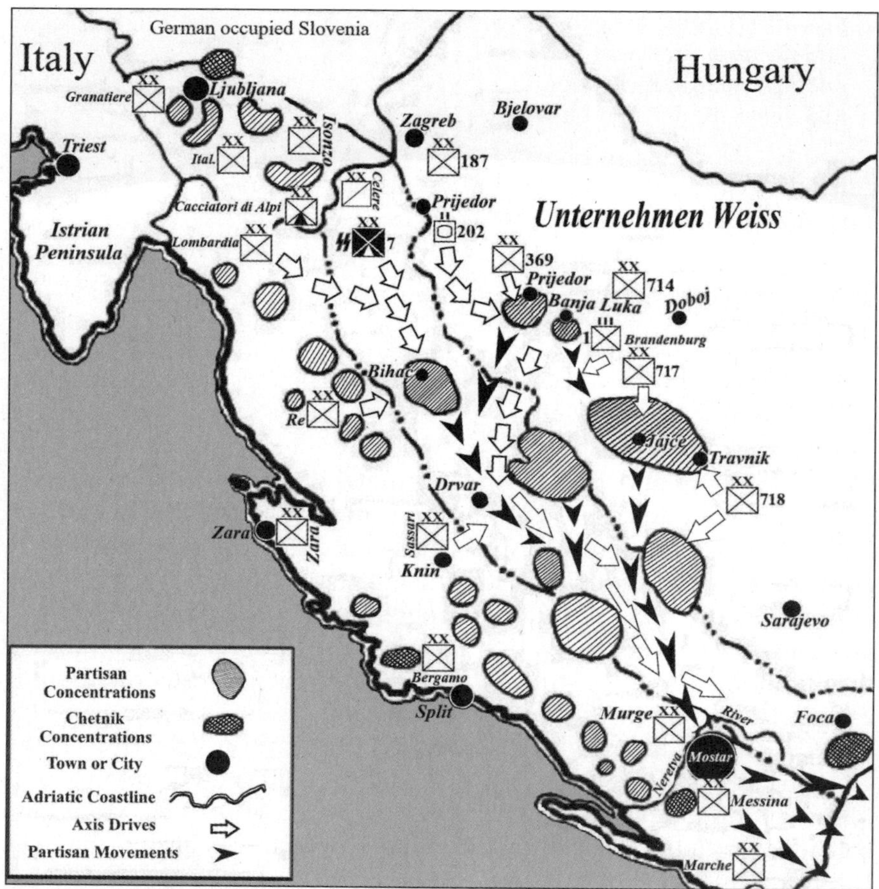

Figure 24. *Unternehmen Weiss* (Operation White), March–April 1943. (*Author's line drawing*)

The new 1. *Jäger* Brigade contained the old 4. & 5. Infantry Regiments, which remained numbered the same. The same thing occurred with the 2. *Jäger* Brigade and its two regiments (the 1. & 10.). Similarly, the 3. *Jäger* Brigade with its 5. and 8. Infantry Regiments was formed likewise, as was the 4. *Jäger* Brigade. The old divisional headquarters were now all disbanded. That included the infantry divisional headquarters and the divisional headquarters of the 1. Mountain Division. Although the NDH forces were in the process of reorganizing, operations against the Partisans had to continue unabated. It was thus that after the conclusion of *Unternehmen Weiss* (Operation White) in March/April 1943, the Germans began to relocate their forces for another anti-partisan drive, this one titled *Schwarz* (Black). It soon became obvious that the situation would not be improved by such measures as the expansion of the demoralized Croatian police and military forces. Large concentrations of Chetniks, including those supported by the Italians, formed a constant threat to German forces in the event of an Allied landing, and the Commander-in-Chief Southeast directed that *Unternehmen Schwarz* (Operation Black) under the Commander of German Troops in Croatia, be undertaken in May and June to destroy the Chetniks in Herzegovina and Montenegro. The German forces were able to deploy strong units, bringing up a reinforced regimental combat team of the *104. Jäger Division* (i.e. the old *704. Infanterie Division* redesignated) from the German forces in Serbia.

The German Commander of Troops in Croatia received the elite and battle-hardened *1. Gebirgs Division,* recently arrived from the rigors of the Russian front. Other German units included the *369. (deutsche-kroatische) Infanterie Division, 7. SS Freiwilligen Gebirgs Division Prinz Eugen , 118. Jäger Division* (i.e. the old *718. Infanterie Division*), plus the *Jäger Regiment 1 Brandenburg (motoriziert)*. The Italians employed the 1. Alpine Division *Taurinense,* 23. Infantry Division *Ferrara,* and the 19. Mountain Infantry Division *Venezia.* Yugoslav records also state that the Bulgarian 61. and 63. Infantry Regiment also participated in setting up blocking positions during the operation. The Croatian contribution to this anti-partisan drive was negligible: only the 4. *Jäger* Brigade was made available for the operation, but given the poor state of condition of the NDH forces, and the vast reorganization that was going on, it's a wonder that they were able to contribute any forces at all.

Chapter 9

GERMAN INFLUENCE INCREASES IN NDH TERRITORY

As the anti-partisan war expanded in Yugoslavia, the Germans voiced concern, and cast a worried look at their Italian allies. It seemed to the Germans that the closer that the Allies got to Italian soil, the Italians Army was becoming increasingly uncooperative, and even hostile, to German intentions to continue the war against the Tito Partisans and the Chetniks. The Italians had not done the Croatians any favours, by protecting several Chetnik partisan bands. These Serbian forces would raid Croatian towns and villages, and would quickly withdraw into the Italian zone, where NDH units could not follow them. The Germans were no fools. In early July, they began to slowly move divisions into Italy, ostensibly to help repel an Allied landing on the Italian mainland. That was one mission that the German Army had in Italy. The second was to position units at critical points throughout the nation and prepare for a possible Italian surrender. In Yugoslavia and Greece, the main German concern was that once the Italian Army in these two countries surrendered, that they would give their weapons and munitions to the Partisans. Some officers spoke contemptuously of the Italians and most likely many would switch sides. Their fears were not unfounded, and proved to be correct. In 1943, the German police system was introduced in Croatia. Several *KdO* headquarters were established on Croatian soil. These in turn, controlled several *Gendarmerie* stations in several key towns. Overall control of the *KdO*s was administered by the *BdO* (*Befehlshaber der Ordnungspolizei*), or Higher Commanding Officer of the Order Police. The first *BdO* was stationed in Osijek in May 1943. This command post was later transferred to Zagreb on 28 June 1943. The *KdO*s in Croatian territory were as follows:

KdO Zagreb – with police stations in Zagreb, Bjelovar, and Varazdin.
KdO Osijek – with police stations in Osijek, Brod, Nova Gradiska, Vukovar, and Rum (Ruma).
KdO Sarajevo – with police stations in Sarajevo, Tuzla, Travnik, and Mostar.
KdO Banja Luka – with police stations in Banja Luka, Jajce, Bihac, and Petrinja. This *KdO* command was later transferred from Banja Luka to Knin in February 1945.

In order to properly train, equip, and process the new Croatian policemen, two recruit training battalions were established during the summer of 1943 in Osijek:

(kroatische) Polizei Ausbildungs Bataillon I
(kroatische) Polizei Ausbildungs Bataillon II[1]

On 15 July 1943 an agreement was finally signed between the Germans and the Croatians establishing this new *Gendarmerie* and Order Police force. Initially one police regiment, made up of two battalions, was raised, but that total would increase greatly. Additionally, numerous independent police battalions would be formed. By 1944 in fact, the total strength of the German-raised Croatian police forces was estimated to be about 10,000 *Gendarmerie* troops. By 1945 the number of Croatians serving in the police regiments and battalions formed by the Germans were around 32,000 men. It was from this pool of manpower that twelve police battalions were then grouped together in 1945 to form the Croatian *Gendarmerie* Division. The commander of this new joint German/Croatian police force was *SS Gruppenführer und Generalleutnant der Polizei* Konstantine Kammerhofer, who was Himmler's direct representative in Croatia. Kammerhofer was in charge of the *Höhere SS und Polizeiführer Kroatien* command. In this capacity, he had various missions to perform. One was to induce ethnic-German Croatians to join the *Waffen SS*. The initial commander of the *BdO* in Osijek, which was later transferred to Zagreb, was *Oberst der Gendarmerie* Rudolf Handl. Kammerhofer's sub-commands in the SS structure in Croatia included three SS & Police Leader command headquarters, which were situated as follows:

SS & Police Leader – Zagreb, led by *SS Brigadeführer und Generalmajor der Schutzpolizei* Willi Brandner.
SS & Police Leader – Banja Luka & Osijek, led by *SS Standartenführer* Paul Dahm.
SS & Police Leader – Sarajevo, led by *SS Oberführer* Werner Fromm.[2]

The Croatian equivalent to Colonel Rudolf Handl was Colonel Vilijko Pecnikar, who had formed the first Croatian *Gendarmerie* units in August 1941. The initial batch of *Gendarmerie* battalions amounted to seven, though this number would increase. Each battalion consisted of four rifle companies, which had two German officers and ten German NCOs per Croatian company. Recruitment of troops into the Croatian Army continued throughout 1943. By the end of the year, the Croatian state had called to the colours the 1920–1922 classes. In each of the three corps-sized territorial commands, one armoured car battalion was formed in 1943. The 1. & 2. Bicycle Battalions were also absorbed into a new brigade whose principal unit was the Zagreb Cavalry Regiment. This new mobile brigade was organized in the autumn of 1943. The railway security battalions were also increased by the addition of three German-raised (ethnic-German Croatian) railway security battalions in December 1943: *11., 12.,* and *13. Kroatische Eisenbahnsicherheitsbataillone* (11th, 12th, and 13th Railway Security Battalions). In July 1943 the Croatians raised another volunteer force, the so-called *Husko Legion,* which eventually numbered around 3,000 men by the autumn of 1943. This unit was led by Husko Miljkovic. This individual defected to the Partisans in February 1944, taking with him his entire brigade. To this must be added the approximately 7,500 Muslims who served in the capacity of auxiliary militia to the *Gendarmerie.* A Tuzla Brigade was also established in that town, and consisted of seven infantry battalions when organized in May 1943.

In addition, the small Croatian Air Force Parachute Company, which had been formed in January 1942, was expanded to a full-strength battalion towards the end of 1942. For most of its history, this parachute battalion operated in and around the Croatian 1. Air Base just east of Zagreb. Though the NDH forces were growing in size, so was the number of desertions from its units. For example, on 7 August 1943 about 107 Croatian soldiers from the 13. Regiment deserted from D. Vakuf, about 25km southwest of Travnik. They took with them all of their arms and equipment and defected to the Tito Partisans. Soon after, a band of about 100 partisans, mostly dressed in Croatian Army uniforms, was spotted near Kotor Varos by a patrol of the *373. (deutsche-kroatische) Infanterie Division.* During the firefight that ensued, 80–100 of the guerrillas were killed. Whether this partisan group were the same men who deserted from the 13. Regiment was never definitely established, but is a typical example of the desertion problem that became endemic in the NDH forces. This was especially true in 1944, when everyone except the most fanatical or most naive knew that Germany was going to lose the war. Tito offered amnesty to Chetniks led by the monarchist guerrilla leader, Draza Mihailovich, and to Croatian Army forces who would surrender, beginning on 17 August 1944. As a result, tens of thousands of royalist Chetniks switched sides and joined the Tito Partisans. Many Croatian NDH troops took advantage of this amnesty, especially given that it was for a limited time only. After the end of the amnesty period, the Tito Partisans would consider those Chetniks and Croatians who did not switch sides to be irredeemable, and therefore would not be shown any mercy.

In fact, because of these constant and increasing desertions, the Germans came to regard the Croatian Army sarcastically, saying that it was the 'supply and replacement depot of Tito's partisans'. To a certain degree, the Germans had a point. As time went on, the reliability of the NDH forces waned even further, and Ante Pavelić was compelled to rely more and more on his loyal *Ustaše* units and German military support. The value of the *Ustaše* was diminished somewhat by the introduction of compulsory military service in the *Ustaše* forces in 1943. Now even unwilling Croatian men were being drafted into the dreaded *Ustaše* detachments. Still, the *Ustaše* units remained the most effective fighting force of the Independent State of Croatia. Their fanaticism for the Pavelic regime and fear of terrible retribution if they lost the war, is what kept most of these *Ustaše* units motivated. In November 1944 the Croatian Army and the *Ustaše* were finally merged together in an effort to improve the overall fighting effectiveness of the Croatian Army. The new force formed was named the *Hrvatske Oruzane Snage* (Croatian Armed Forces). The regular army forces of the NDH, because of high desertions, had been reduced to only about 70,000 men by the end of 1944. The *Ustaše* however, had grown to about 104,000 men by that same period. In April 1943 however, the regular Croatian Army units still amounted to a very sizable force that contained about 135 battalions:

70 infantry battalions.
10 artillery battalions.
3 cavalry battalions.
4 engineer battalions.
5 garrison battalions.

1 bicycle battalion.
18 railway security battalions.
21 home guard volunteer battalions.
1 railway technical battalion.
2 medical battalions.

Additional Croatian forces raised by the Germans included the three Croat-German Legion divisions (369., 373., & 392.) and Croatian SS & Police units. For example, by September 1943 the Germans had raised a total of seven Croatian police battalions, whose composition included a cadre of German officers and NCOs in each battalion, but the bulk of the enlisted were Croatians. These battalions were stationed in the following areas:

(*kroatische*) *Polizei Bataillon I* – Zagreb.
(*kroatische*) *Polizei Bataillon II* – Split.
(*kroatische*) *Polizei Bataillon III* – Banja Luka.
(*kroatische*) *Polizei Bataillon IV* – Sarajevo.
(*kroatische*) *Polizei Bataillon V* – Mostar.
(*kroatische*) *Polizei Bataillon VI* – Knin.
(*kroatische*) *Polizei Bataillon VII* – Zemun.

In addition, a (*kroatische*) *Polizei Ersatz Bataillon Esseg* (Croatian Police Reserve Battalion Osijek) was formed in the summer of 1943 to train additional recruits. The rail lines had been under constant attack ever since the start of the partisan war in late 1941. Destruction of these important transportation lines was hurting the Axis cause on a daily basis. It was therefore vital for not only the German, but also for the Croatian military to keep the rail lines well protected and intact. The railway security battalions were dispersed throughout the countryside as follows:

Table 4. Deployment of Railway Security Battalions

Railway Security Unit	Town/City
1. *Eisenbahnsicherheitsbataillone*	Zagreb
2. *Eisenbahnsicherheitsbataillone*	Makarska
3. *Eisenbahnsicherheitsbataillone*	Banja Luka
4. *Eisenbahnsicherheitsbataillone*	Sarajevo
5. *Eisenbahnsicherheitsbataillone*	Ivanic Grad/Dugoselo

6. *Eisenbahnsicherheitsbataillone*	V. Gorica / Caprag
7. *Eisenbahnsicherheitsbataillone*	Novska / Banova Jaruga
8. *Eisenbahnsicherheitsbataillone*	Vinkovci / Jankovci / Osijek / Borovo
9. *Eisenbahnsicherheitsbataillone*	Brod / Vinkovci
10. *Eisenbahnsicherheitsbataillone*	Sunja / Zivaja / Blinski Kut
11. *Eisenbahnsicherheitsbataillone*	Vinkovci / Jankovci / Otok
12. *Eisenbahnsicherheitsbataillone*	Mitrovika / Kukunjevci / Ruma Morovici
13. *Eisenbahnsicherheitsbataillone*	St. Pazova / Pavlovci / Putinoi
14. *Eisenbahnsicherheitsbataillone*	Doboj / Jobova / Usora / Derventa
15. *Eisenbahnsicherheitsbataillone*	Doboj / Suhopolje / Karanovac
16. *Eisenbahnsicherheitsbataillone*	Magla / Zepce / Begov Han / Zavidovici.
17. *Eisenbahnsicherheitsbataillone*	Zenica / Visoko / Semizovac / Lasva
18. *Eisenbahnsicherheitsbataillone*	Virovitica.

An additional four railway security battalions were formed by the end of 1943 and located in the following towns:

19. Eisenbahnsicherheitsbataillone – Djurdjenovac
20. Eisenbahnsicherheitsbataillone – Virovitica
21. Eisenbahnsicherheitsbataillone – Novska / Brod
22. Eisenbahnsicherheitsbataillone – Nova Gradisca

Unfortunately for the NDH cause, while the Germans were busy reinforcing their Croatian allies, the number of desertions within the Croatian Army continued to grow at an alarming rate. During a six-week period, for example, the number of desertions and surrenders within the NDH forces were as follows:

On 6 October 1943 – 500 Croatian *Domobrans* deserted in Kupres.
On 14 October 1943 – the entire 2. Battalion/Croatian 3. Infantry Regiment (10 officers, 30 NCOs, and 364 enlisted men), deserted to the Tito Partisans with all of their arms and ammunition.
On 21 October 1943 – in Sanski Most around 1,000 Croatian *Domobrans* deserted, taking with them all of their weapons, ammunition, and equipment.

Chapter 10

MAJOR GERMAN-CROATIAN ANTI-PARTISAN DRIVES

The next major operation, after *Unternehmen Weiss* (Operation White), was *Unternehmen Schwarz* (Operation Black). This would employ German, Croatian, Italian and Bulgarian units. About 200 Italian and 100 German aircraft also took part in the operation. The number of German troops taking part in this operation numbered somewhere around 60,000 men. The Croatian contribution was small; about 4,000 men of the 4. *Jäger* Brigade. The Italians contributed about 50,000 men, while the Bulgarian contribution was two regiments numbering about 3,000 men. This new operation not only hit the Chetnik forces in Montenegro and Herzegovina, but also affected Tito's Partisans, which were now concentrated between the Vrbas and Neretva River. The initial phase of the operation began on 2 May 1943, and was not concluded until 16 June. The first two weeks of the operation was concentrated at destroying the Chetnik forces.

This part of the operation eventually netted about 4,000 Chetniks killed and 1,500–2,000 captured. In spite of this success, a portion of the Chetnik bands were able to break through the blocking positions of *118. Jäger Division*. Those Chetniks that escaped headed east after crossing the Drina River near the Serbian border. Thereafter they entered Serbia, and headed for the Vršac Mountains, where they regrouped and reorganized. Thereafter the attention of the Axis forces was focused on Tito's Partisans, who had been watching the Axis drive against the Chetniks with glee. The initial drive against the communist guerrillas began on 15 May 1943 and did not end till the 20th. The encircled Partisan forces included:

6th Uzhodno-Bosniak-Majeviska Brigade
7th Banziska Division
1st Proletarian Division
2nd Proletarian Division
3rd Udarna Division
3rd Battalion of the 10th Herzegovina Partisan Brigade

As the German *1. Gebirgs Division* and *369.* (*deutsch-kroatische*) *Infanterie Division* began driving the Partisans east of the Vrbas River, between Jasenjani and Blagaj, the Partisans eventually crossed the Neretva River, whereupon most turned north. The guerrillas were able to make a breakthrough in two places: just southwest of Foca, where the 6. Vzhodno Bosniak Majeviska Brigade managed to get through the lines of *Jäger Regiment 750* (belonging to *118. Jäger Division*); and further southwest of Foca, where the main bulk of the guerrilla forces fought a running battle with the *7. SS Freiwilligen Gebirgs Division Prinz Eugen,* the Italian *Ferrara* Infantry Division, the German *1. Gebirgs Division,* and the 61. Bulgarian Infantry Regiment (which was tailing the rear echelon of the withdrawing guerrillas). The Italian *Taurinense* Division and the Croatian 4. *Jäger* Brigade had moved down the Drina River and positioned themselves on the right flank of the withdrawing Partisan forces. The bulk of the guerrilla army skirted its way in a west to northwesterly direction, fighting numerous flank attacks launched against it by the Axis forces chasing them. Between 3–15 June 1943, the major part of Tito's army (1st, 2nd, and 7th Division) moved through Vucevo, Suha, Tjentiste, Bare, Lucke Kolibe, Vrbnica, Balinovac, and finally Rataj, where they were able to spread out and disperse northwards. Just north of Balinovac the *369.* (*deutsch-kroatische*) *Infanterie Division* and 4. *Jäger* Brigade confronted the bulk of these three withdrawing partisan divisions. A fierce struggle ensued as the lone German division tried to block the escape route of three desperate and determined guerrilla divisions. The Croatian lines were broken in several places, and through these gaps poured the entire Partisan army.

In spite of this, the operation was judged a success by the Germans, who managed to take the pressure off of the Independent State of Croatia by destroying a large Chetnik power base in Montenegro, and forcing the bulk of Tito's forces into the hills. Though the bulk of the Partisan army escaped, the Axis counted a grand total of 5,697 communist dead left on the battlefield. Another 800–1,000 Partisans were wounded. Tito himself had been wounded during the breakout, but the Axis forces had also taken a beating. The *369.* (*deutsch-kroatische*) *Infanterie Division* suffered heavy losses at the hands of the Partisans north of Balinovac, as it attempted to contain the Partisan flood heading north. A passage from a book, written by a British military officer attached to Tito's guerrillas during this time, describes the ferocity and violence of the fighting between the guerrillas and the Croatian legionnaires:

> At dusk partisan patrols crossed the valley bed and stormed these German positions. A few moments later we passed, and there remained but the stripped bodies of their dead, and a broken pennant of the Devil's Division.[1]

Now temporarily free of any major Partisan or Chetnik intrusion into Croatian territory, the NDH forces were now given several months in which they were able to reorganize their forces in an attempt to improve their performance.

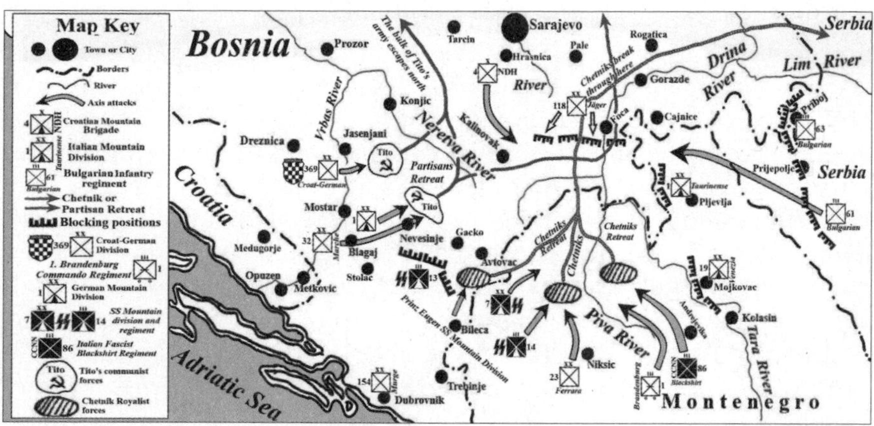

Figure 25. *Unternehmen Schwarz* (Operation Black), 2 May–15 June 1943. (*Author's line drawing*)

This reorganization, however, did not prove to be as helpful as they had hoped. Desertions from the Croatian Army continued to grow. This case was significantly lower in the German-raised and officered Croatian Legion divisions, but there too, desertions existed. For the most part, the Croatian military forces were confined to the larger centres of population, such as the towns and cities, while the domination of the countryside was left to the Germans, Chetniks, and Partisans to fight over. When the Croatian forces did come out into the countryside, it was always in strength, and usually as part of a combined German anti-partisan drive. German operations

Three members of the 369th Croatian Legion Infantry Division, sometime in 1943. (*Getty Images*)

A recruiting poster for the Croatian Army. The words read: '*sto bog da isreka Njemačka*' ('God says Germany'). (*Author's collection*)

Adolf Hitler greets Ante Pavelić, the Fascist leader of the Independent State of Croatia, at his Berghof home in Bavaria, Germany. Pavelić was there for a state visit, but also to discuss what Nazi Germany expected of the Croatian *Führer*. (*Getty Images*)

The Croatian Air Force Legion (*Hrvatska zrakoplovna legia*) was established in Zagreb in July 1941 with 360 officers, NCOs and men. The Legion was composed of the 4th Air Force Regiment. This unit contained the 4th and 5th Bomber Wings. These Croatian bomber wings would come under the control of German 3rd Air Wing of the 52nd Luftwaffe Fighter Group (III/JG 52), of the 4th Air Fleet. (*Getty Images*)

Croatian members of a bomber wing. Notice the Junkers Ju 88 bombers in the background. (*Museum of Modern History*)

The Croatian Air Badge. (*Author's collection*)

BOMBARDERI IZT. BOJISTE

Cuff band worn on the lower left sleeve of the uniform. The inscription reads '*Bombarderi IZT. Bojist*' ('Eastern Front bomber'). (*Author's collection*)

A photograph taken sometime in 1944, during an anti-partisan operation. Here we see German, Cossack and Croatian soldiers atop an Italian Carro Armato M13/40. After Italy surrendered in September 1943, the Germans, Croatians, Serbian Chetniks and Tito Partisans all rushed to disarm Italian units and take their weaponry. The most successful were the Partisans and the Germans. (*Museum of Modern History*)

A decorated member of the *Poglavnik* Bodyguard Division in 1944. (*Museum of Modern History*)

Croatian police recruits and their German trainer. The Germans raised numerous police battalions made up of Croatian men and employed them under the German Higher SS Command in the Balkans. Throughout the war the Germans would try to employ Croatian manpower, and thus reduced the number of men available to serve in the Croatian Armed Forces. (*Author's collection*)

Two members of the Croatian NDH, sometime in 1943. (*Author's collection*)

An extremely rare photograph of two members of the Zagreb Cavalry Regiment. (*Author's collection*)

Four Croatian soldiers, two members of the police and two members of the army. (*Croatian History Museum*)

Poor-quality image of high-ranking Croatian officials. The man in the centre appears to be Stijepo Perić, who became Foreign Minister on 5 November 1943. (*Photo courtesy Michael Duff collection*)

Zagreb, 10 April 1941. A parade of the newly-created army of the Independent State of Croatia. (*Photo courtesy of the Museum of Modern History*)

General Slavko Kvaternik, who was the Croatian Defence Minister from 10 April 1941 to 4 January 1943. (*Photo courtesy of the Museum of Modern History*)

Croatian members of the *369. Infanterie Division*, sometime in 1944. (*Croatian History Museum*)

The next is a series of five photographs taken in 1944. These are members of a German-sponsored Croatian police battalion coming upon a building covered with communist graffiti. (*Museum of Modern History*)

Members of a German-sponsored Croatian police battalion inspect communist graffiti on the wall of a home. (*Museum of Modern History*)

The Croatian policemen seem to be looking inside the building, as if deciding what to do next. (*Museum of Modern History*)

Inside they find an old woman whom they appear to be expelling from the home. (*Museum of Modern History*)

A slightly damaged photograph showing a Croatian member of the German sponsored police battalions marching through the village. In the background a small structure is burning. (*Museum of Modern History*)

Croatian police recruits practice with a small trench mortar, some time in the winter of 1942/43. (*Museum of Modern History*)

Members of a Chetnik band. The flag reads: 'С вером у Бога, за краља и отаџбину' ('For King and Fatherland, with Faith in God'). (*Museum of Modern History*)

An *Ustaše* tank unit employing the FIAT Ansaldo Carro Veloce 33 on parade in Zagreb, sometime in 1941. It was a turretless tankette that carried twin 6.5mm machine guns. The vehicle was little more than a small armoured car. Each vehicle is painted with a large 'U' for '*Ustaše*' with the Croatian chequerboard symbol inside the letter. (*Croatian History Museum*)

A Croatian tank commander riding a Panzer III tank. The belt buckle and other insignia identify him as a member of the *Ustaše*. He is wearing the Croatian armoured badge above his right breast pocket. (*Museum of Modern History*)

A 1942 photo taken in Bosnia, of Jure Francetić and Rafael Boban. (*Museum of Modern History*)

A parade of NDH soldiers in Zagreb, circa 1942. (*Museum of Modern History*)

Members of the *Poglavnik* Bodyguard Division parade in Zagreb, sometime in 1944. (*Museum of Modern History*)

Croatian artillery. (*Museum of Modern History*)

Croatian troops, equipped by the Italians, enter Zagreb on 10 April 1941. When the invasion of Yugoslavia began on 6 April 1941, the Italians employed Croatian volunteer forces - many of which had been created from men wanted by the Yugoslav state for political reasons.

A propaganda photograph showing the Croatian leader, Ante Pavelić, visiting NDH recruits as they trained, circa 1943.

planned for the second half of 1943 included *Kugelblitz, Schneesturm,* and *Herbstgewitter*. These operations all took place, but they couldn't prevent the Italian capitulation which occurred on 8 September 1943. The collapse of the Italian forces was like a shot in the arm for Tito's Partisan army and to a lesser extent, the Chetnik forces of Draza Mihailovich. The Italian collapse represented a double-edged sword. On the one hand, the Chetniks were able to acquire more military hardware from the Italians, but on the other hand, the Italian Army had always shielded and protected the Chetniks from the Croatians and from Tito's Partisans. Now that protection was gone.

Some Italians chose to either join the Chetniks or the Partisans against their former allies. In some cases, the Partisans convinced many Italians by threatening violence, but others joined willingly. In this way, about 4,000 men of the Italian *Isonzo, Bergamo,* and *Zara* Divisions joined Tito's guerrillas. The summer months of June through August 1943, were spent expanding and reorganizing the Croatian Army. Some minor operations were also launched by the NDH forces. The 11. and 12. *Ustaše* Regiments, raised in the spring of 1943, were quickly followed by the 13., 14., and 15. *Ustaše* Regiments which were organized in the summer of 1943. The German-raised *Polizei Gendarmerie Bataillon* was expanded to regimental status, and its title was changed to *Polizei Regiment Kroatien*. The Italians had also been busy raising a Croatian Legion in May 1943, about four months before their collapse. This Italian-sponsored Croatian Legion was sent to Lake Garth in northern Italy, where it was formed into a 1,800-man combat regiment of two infantry battalions, one artillery battalion of only two batteries, an engineer company, and a replacement battalion. This unit was later sent to the Gorizia-Tarviso area near the Italian-Slovene border, and used for guard duty by the Germans when the Italians surrendered. Later still, they were sent to Stockerau Training Camp, where the regiment was disbanded. Its men were used to reinforce the *373. Kroatische-Deutsch Legion Infanterie Division* and *392. (deutsch-kroatische) Infanterie Division*. While Croatia continued to expand the size of her armed forces, desertions to the partisans continued.

On 11 July 1943 for example, the Croatian 7. *Jäger* Regiment of the 4. *Jäger* Brigade was assisting part of the *7. SS Freiwilligen Gebirgs Division Prinz Eugen* in retaking the towns of Krivaja and Clovo, some 20km southwest of Kladanj. While the battle was in progress, large numbers of men from the 7. *Jäger* Regiment deserted. In fact, total losses in numbers of deserters from the Croatian 4. *Jäger* Brigade between June and October 1943 was over 1,000 men. In the end, both towns were taken by the Germans. Axis losses stood at four dead (three of them Croatian), thirteen wounded (eleven of which were Croatians), and 100 Croatian soldiers who deserted. Partisan losses amounted to about 200 dead. Two days later the *II. Bataillon* of the 1. Regiment/ *7. SS Freiwilligen Gebirgs Division Prinz Eugen,* and the 7. Croatian *Jäger* Regiment finally broke the Partisan resistance in the area of Kladanj. The region southeast of Olovo, some 30km north of Sarajevo, was also cleared. During this operation close supervision of the 7. *Jäger* Regiment by its officers and the German *SS* unit prevented further desertions. Efforts by the *369., 373.,* and *392.* (*deutsch-kroatische*) *Infanterie Division* to help train the Croatian army, were also interrupted as much as possible by the guerrillas.

For example, on 27 July 1943 in the area of operations of the *373.* (*deutsch-kroatische*) *Infanterie Division,* a Croatian *Domobran* company that was undergoing training under the leadership of German NCOs from the *373. Infanterie Division,* were surprised by the Tito Partisans and ambushed just south of Klujc. Four German NCOs were killed, along with forty-one Croatian recruits. In addition, thirteen Croatian recruits were listed as missing.[2] Weapons losses included five light machine guns, two heavy machine guns, and seventy rifles. Apparently more than half of the Croatian company had lost their weapons, and over one-third had either been killed or was missing.

Chapter 11

THE CONSEQUENCES OF ITALY'S SURRENDER

The summer and autumn of 1943 was a turning point in the partisan war in Yugoslavia. Soviet military assistance to the Partisans had increased beginning in the summer, helping Tito's forces to better deal with Axis attacks. It was also then that the Western Allies, in particular the British, decided to arm Tito's army, and stop supporting Draza Mihajlovic's Chetniks. The communists had done a wonderful job of gathering together overwhelming evidence about how the Chetniks had established a *modus vivendi* with both the Italians and Germans. While it was true that some Chetnik bands had agreed to leave German and Italian forces alone, so they could concentrate on destroying the communist threat, and that Italy was actually arming many of these Chetnik bands, not all Chetnik forces had made this agreement. Nevertheless, the Partisans were finally able to convince London that they should stop supporting Mihailovic's Chetniks.

Arms from the West now began to flow to the Tito communists. Italy's surrender to the Allies in that same year was the straw that broke the camel's back, as it were, of the German and Croatian attempt to defeat the guerrillas. The collapse of Fascist Italy in September 1943 was also a double-edged sword to the Croatian state. While it got rid of the meddling and land-hungry Italians, their very absence required that the already dispersed German and Croatian forces now had to cover a much larger area, with the same number of troops. The Germans would eventually need to bring into Yugoslavia additional forces. In addition to no longer having the dubious support of the Italian Army, the fears which the Germans held, about Italian weapons being handed over to the Chetniks or Tito communists, predictably came true.

Chetnik units and in particular Tito's forces rushed to disarm Italian Army units in Yugoslavia, in order to claim as much war booty as possible. For the communist Partisans, this was a gift from the Gods. With this large influx of additional weapons and munitions, Tito could expand his army. Entirely new brigades and divisions sprang up, aided by the massive amount of Italian war materiel which was captured. In addition, some Italian formations decided to join the guerrillas. The Germans were disgusted with their erstwhile Italian allies for having surrendered. It was also bad enough that in addition to surrendering, large numbers of Italian weapons would help arm more Partisan divisions. Divisions that would help destroy German and Croatian forces. But to join the fight against their former Axis allies was seen by the Germans and Croatians as a treacherous and reprehensible act. Henceforth, from the autumn of 1943 to the end of the war, whenever German forces would capture Italians serving with the guerrillas, they would be shown no mercy. The Croatians, who had always been starved of sufficient military hardware, also tried to cash in on the Italian debacle, sending their 2. and 3. Mountain Brigades to Karlovac in order to disarm the Italian *Lombardia* Division, which was stationed there at the time of the surrender.

This particular Italian division did not resist the Croatians, and dissolved quietly on 9 September 1943. The Germans likewise rushed to disarm their former Italian allies, not so much to acquire their equipment, but rather to prevent those arms from falling into guerrilla hands. The Germans also feared an Allied landing along the Dalmatian coast, so rushed there to cover the coastline. The *7. SS Freiwilligen Gebirgs Division Prinz Eugen,* supported by elements of *369. (deutsch-kroatische) Infanterie Division,* the so-called 'Devil' division, managed to obtain the surrender of Italian forces in Mostar, and then turned towards Split, on the Dalmatian coast, where they took on and defeated the *Bergamo* Division. When it was over, about 18,000 Italians were in German and Croatian hands at Split alone. The Partisans had great successes in exploiting the military situation. Shortly after the Italian surrender, the guerrillas took over control of Tuzla, north of Sarajevo. This area had been swept clean of guerrillas by the *369. (deutsch-kroatische) Infanterie Division 'Teufel'* in June and July 1943. Now the region was once again infested with roving bands of partisan fighters. Fortunately for Tito's army, and unfortunately for the Germans and Croatians, a total of eleven out of fifteen major Italian brigades and divisions surrendered to the partisans. Thus, the lion's share of weapons and equipment fell to Tito's communist forces. Shortly thereafter, German intelligence began to intercept radio communication from Partisan brigades and divisions that they had never heard of before. It was deduced from these intercepted messages that Tito's Partisan army had grown exponentially – all thanks to a treasure-trove of captured Italian weaponry.

As previously stated, with the arms cache taken from the Italians, Tito's guerrilla army was able to raise numerous new brigades and divisions. The Italian controlled islands in Croatian territory fell to the communists, while major centres like Jajce were also lost to the Partisans. The guerrillas wasted no time in employing their newly acquired arms and units, overrunning numerous Croatian Army garrisons. Some NDH commands gave up without a fight while others, mainly those made up of *Ustaše* forces, fought until they were overwhelmed. Between 17 October and 10 November 1943, the communist Partisans threw two and a half divisions against the city of Gospic. Gospic was being garrisoned at the time by the 4. *Ustaše* Brigade, plus the forming 3. Battalion of the 3. Croatian Garrison Brigade. Other smaller units inside Gospic included a company of *Domobrans* and the Home Guard Volunteer Battalion Gospic, which was made up of older-age militiamen. These Croatian forces stood their ground throughout the siege, and handed the partisans a rare tactical defeat, since the city could not be taken. Banja Luka was similarly besieged and attacked, and here too the guerrillas were unsuccessful.

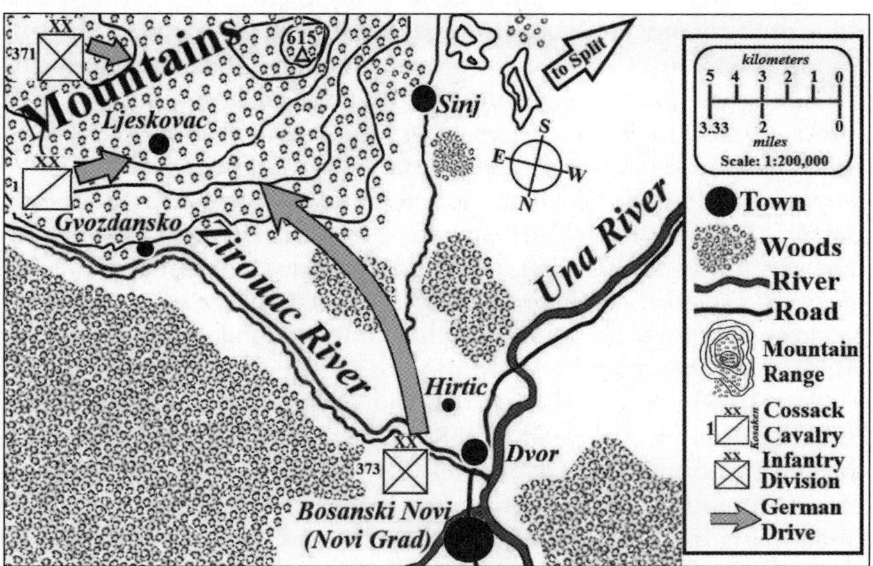

Figure 26. *Unternehmen Panther* (Operation Panther), 10–27 December 1943.

The city of Travnik was also attacked from 10–15 November 1943, but the main Croatian Army units in the town, which included two cavalry battalions fighting on foot, were likewise able to hold off the Partisans until German reinforcements arrived to repel the guerrilla assault. Between 10–27 December 1943 the *373. (deutsch-kroatische) Infanterie Division* launched Operation Panther, just east of the city of Bosanski Novi,[1] between Bihac and Banja Luka. The *373. (deutsch-kroatische) Infanterie Division* moved from Bosanski Novi in a southeasterly direction, towards Ljeskovac. From the east, elements of *1. Kosaken Kavallerie Division* and *371. Infanterie Division* moved west towards the same objective. On 1 December 1943 the *369. (deutsch-kroatische) Infanterie Division* was fighting Partisan units in the region of Travnik. A day later the Germans launched *Unternehmen Kugelblitz* (Operation Lightning Ball) in the region southeast of Sarajevo. On 3 December the Germans were reporting stiff guerrilla opposition in the region of Tuzla. The units involved in this region included the *7. SS Freiwilligen Gebirgs Division Prinz Eugen,* the Bulgarian 24. Infantry Division, *1. Gebirgs Division,* the Croatian 2. Mountain Brigade, and a battlegroup of the *187. Infanterie Division.*[2]

The *369. Kroatische Legion Infanterie Division* soon joined the above-named Axis forces in *Unternehmen Kugelblitz* in the region northeast of Visoko, about 12km northwest of Sarajevo. Before *Kugelblitz* was over, the 24. Bulgarian Infantry Division had to be withdrawn because it refused to follow German orders. Many men from this Bulgarian division deserted and soon formed a guerrilla detachment fighting under Tito's command. The Partisans lost a total of 9,000 men during the course of *Unternehmen Kugelblitz,* which had been aimed at their forces in eastern Bosnia. Soon after, another operation was begun, *Unternehmen Schneesturm* (Operation Snow Storm), which netted another 2,000 guerrillas killed. Still, the bulk of Tito's army in eastern Bosnia had been able to outmanoeuvre the German and Croatian anti-partisan drives and escape into the high mountain ranges. The *369. (deutsch-kroatische) Infanterie Division* also participated in *Unternehmen Schneesturm,* and in an operation which followed in January 1944 titled *Waldrausch* (Operation Forest Run).

German reinforcements to Croatia now even took on an improvised form, for example, the German *367. Infanterie Division,* which had been formed in Germany in October 1943, was sent to the Zagreb area in November of that year. There it remained a part of the garrison, while undergoing training until April 1944, when it was sent to the Russian front. The Independent State of Croatia had tried to enlarge its army during the summer and autumn of 1943, in order to accommodate the large areas which were evacuated by the Italian army after their surrender. With this in mind, three Croatian regional commands were established in these now-vacant regions, which up until then had encompassed the Italian 1st and 2nd Occupation Zones. Several new Croatian army units were raised, and conscription of the Muslim and Croatian population in those areas which the Croatian state had been previously prohibited from recruiting by the Italians now began. A Croatian Coastal Brigade of perhaps four to six battalions was established in Split.

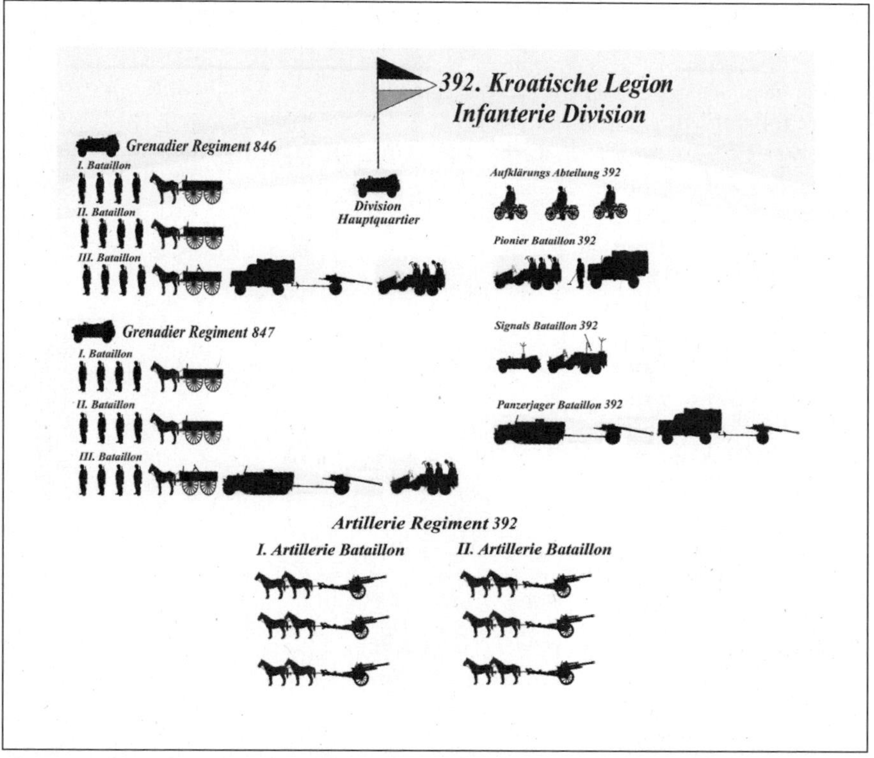

Figure 27. Schematic diagram of the *392. (deutsch-kroatische) Infanterie Division*. The organization was different than for its sister divisions. The major change was the addition of a third reconnaissance company (bicycle-mounted) and the elimination of a third (heavy) artillery battalion. (*Author's line drawing*)

In the town of Zenica, a brigade of infantry was formed, while in Susak a Home Guard Volunteer Regiment was raised for employment in the Istrian peninsula. The third and last of the German-Croatian Legion divisions, *392. (deutsch-kroatische) Infanterie Division,* now made its appearance in Croatia in January 1944. It was immediately posted to the area around Senj. Its 12,000 men would spend the rest of the war not far from the Dalmatian coast. While the *369. (deutsch-kroatische) Infanterie Division* had been nicknamed the 'Devil' division, the other two Croatian Legion divisions had also been given honorary titles. The *373. (deutsch-kroatische) Infanterie Division* for example, was named the 'Tiger' division, while the *392. (deutsch-kroatische) Infanterie Division* was called the Croatian 'Blue' division, just like the *250. (spanisch) Infanterie Division* which incidentally, was withdrawn in October 1943 from the Eastern Front, just as *392. (deutsch-kroatische) Infanterie Division* was being activated. The major combat units of *392. (deutsch-kroatische) Infanterie Division* included:

846. (deutsch-kroatische) Grenadier Regiment –
- *I. Bataillon*
  - *1. Kompanie*
  - *2. Kompanie*
  - *3. Kompanie*
  - *4. Kompanie*
- *II. Bataillon*
  - *5. Kompanie*
  - *6. Kompanie*
  - *7. Kompanie*
  - *8. Kompanie*
- *III. Bataillon*
  - *9. Kompanie*
  - *10. Kompanie*
  - *11. Kompanie*
  - *12. Kompanie*
  - *13. Kompanie*
  - *14. Kompanie*

847. (deutsch-kroatische) Grenadier Regiment –
- *I. Bataillon*
  - *1. Kompanie*
  - *2. Kompanie*
  - *3. Kompanie*
  - *4. Kompanie*
- *II. Bataillon*
  - *5. Kompanie*
  - *6. Kompanie*
  - *7. Kompanie*
  - *8. Kompanie*
- *III. Bataillon*
  - *9. Kompanie*
  - *10. Kompanie*

11. Kompanie
12. Kompanie
13. Kompanie
14. Kompanie

392. (*deutsch-kroatische*) *Artillerie Regiment* –
I. Bataillon (105mm guns)
II. Bataillon (105mm guns)

392. (*deutsch-kroatische*) *Aufklärungs Abteilung* –
1. Radfahr Kompanie
2. Radfahr Kompanie
3. Radfahr Kompanie

392. (*deutsch-kroatische*) *Panzerjäger Abteilung*
1. Panzerjäger Kompanie – 75mm Pak 40 *geschleppte* (towed)
2. Panzerjäger Kompanie – 75mm Pak 40 *geschleppte* (towed)

392. (*deutsch-kroatische*) *Pionier Bataillon* –
1. Pionier Kompanie
2. Pionier Kompanie

392. (*deutsch-kroatische*) *Nachrichten Abteilung*
1. Nachrichten Kompanie
2. Nachrichten Kompanie

392.(*deutsch-kroatische*) *Feldersatz Bataillon* –
1. Feldersatz Kompanie
2. Feldersatz Kompanie
3. Feldersatz Kompanie
4. Feldersatz Kompanie (added in 1945)

There were other, smaller units which the Croatians formed at this time, and included the Home Guard Volunteer Battalion Gospic, Dubrovnik, Trebinja, Knin, and the Home Guard Volunteer Regiment Zadar. In March 1944 the so-called 'garrison brigades' were established to act as static guard units and local security services for the corps commands. These garrison units were based in major towns and cities. They were formed by using the existing garrison units and combining them with the Home Guard volunteer battalions and regiments. The standing Croatian Army also organized three replacement brigades that were to supply recruits to the regular NDH forces. This reorganization was completed during the first six months of 1944, although another major reorganization of the Croatian Armed Forces was ordered later still, in November 1944. That reorganization was begun a month later, in December 1944. The Croatian Army as it stood in January 1944 looked like this on paper:

1. Corps Region – Zagreb with:
1. Mountain Brigade – Kutina,

1. Mountain Regiment – Kutina
5. Mountain Regiment – Vim

3. Mountain Brigade – Banja Luka, with about 3,200 men split up into the following regiments:

3. Mountain Regiment – Ramekin
11. Mountain Regiment – Bosanko Gradisca

4. Mountain Brigade – Lipik, with:

4. Mountain Regiment – Daruvar
8. Mountain Regiment – Pakrac

2. *Jäger* Brigade – Donji Lapac,

1. *Jäger* Regiment – Vrtoce
10. *Jäger* Regiment – Lapac

1. Garrison Brigade – Krizevci, with:

1. Battalion – Varazdin
2. Battalion – Hercegovac
3. Battalion – Koprivnica
4. Battalion – Bjelovar
I. Battery – Krizevci-Bjelovar
Engineer Company – Krizevci

2. Garrison Brigade – Karlovac, with:

1. Battalion – Karlovac
2. Battalion – Karlovac
3. Battalion – Dugaresa
4. Battalion – Jastrebarsko/Domagovici
5. Battalion – Ogulin/Crikvenica
I. Battery – Karlovac
II. Battery – Karlovac

3. Garrison Brigade – Gospic, with 5,300 men split up into the following units:

1. Battalion – Bilaj/Ribnik (450 men)
2. Battalion – Knin (1,100 men)
3. Battalion – Gospic (1,100 men)
Gospic Home Guard Battalion – Gospic (1,000 men)
Perusic Home Guard Battalion – Perusic (600 men)
Kosinj Home Guard Battalion – Kosinj (300 men)
6. Replacement Battalion – Lesce/Jance
I. Battery – Gospic
Engineer Company – Knin

4. Garrison Brigade – Sisak, with:

1. Battalion – Sisak (474 men)
2. Battalion – Petrinja (380 men)
3. Battalion – Turopolje (400 men)
I. Battery – Petrinja

Zagreb Garrison Brigade – Zagreb, with:

1. Battalion – Zagreb-Leskovac (800 men)
2. Battalion – Zagreb (550 men)
3. Battalion – Turopolje (600 men)

1. Replacement Brigade – Zagreb, with:
   1. Battalion – Zagreb
   2. Battalion – Zagreb
   3. Battalion – Odra
   4. Battalion – Lomnica
   Susak Home Guard Defence Regiment – Susak[3]

Zenica Brigade – Zenica (just east of Travnik), with:
   1. Battalion – Zenica (375 men)
   2. Battalion – Vranduc (300 men)
   3. Battalion – Zenica (450 men)
   4. Battalion – Lasva (330 men)

2. Corps Region – Brod

1. *Jäger* Brigade – Doboj with about 6,000 men split into the following two regiments:
   4. *Jäger* Regiment – Derventa (2,543 men)
   6. *Jäger* Regiment – Vinkovci (2,355 men)

3. *Jäger* Brigade – Brod, with:
   5. *Jäger* Regiment – Vrpolje
   8. *Jäger* Regiment – Gorjani

4. *Jäger* Brigade – Dvor, with about 4,500 men split into the following two regiments:
   7. *Jäger* Regiment – Dvor (2,425 men)
   13. *Jäger* Regiment – Bosanski Novi (1,300 men)

5. Garrison Brigade – Nova Gradisca, with:
   1. Battalion – Nova Gradisca
   2. Battalion – Novska
   3. Battalion – Osijek
   4. Battalion – Doboj/Zelah
   I. Battery – Rudice/Cazin
   I. Motorized Artillery Platoon – Osijek
   II. Motorized Artillery Platoon – Banja Luka
   Engineer Company – Nova Gradisca

6. Garrison Brigade[4] – Doboj, with:
   1. Battalion – Derventa
   3. Battalion – Teslic
   4. Battalion – Tuzla/Doboj/Kotorska
   5. Battalion – Kladanj

7. Garrison Brigade – Mitrovica, with:
   1. Battalion – Ruma (587 men)
   2. Battalion – Vinkovci (371 men)
   3. Battalion – Mitrovika (519 men)
   4. Battalion – Zemun/Petrovardin/Kamenica

10. Garrison Brigade[5] – Tuzla, with:
   1. Battalion – Medjasi
   2. Battalion – Zivinice
   3. Battalion – Miricina
   5. Battalion – Srebrenica

6. Battalion – Teocak
7. Battalion – Zvornik
8. Battalion – Celic/Brcko
9. Battalion – Gracanica
10. Battalion – Samac

2. Replacement Brigade – Vinkovci, with:
1. Battalion – Vinkovci
2. Battalion – Mostar
3. Battalion – Mostar
4. Battalion – Vinkovci

3. Corps Region – Sarajevo

2. Mountain Brigade – Konjic, with:
2. Mountain Regiment – Jablanica
6. Mountain Regiment – Gradina (2,128 men)

8. Garrison Brigade – Sarajevo, with 6,500 men split up into the following units:
1. Battalion – Sarajevo/Travnik/Bugojno
2. Battalion – Zvornik/Ranjevici/Jabuka
3. Battalion – Bjelemici/Ustikolina
4. Battalion – Kotorac/Vijake/Mednik
5. Battalion – Gorazde
I. Battery – Travnik
II. Battery – Sarajevo
III. Motorized Artillery Platoon – Sarajevo

9. Garrison Brigade – Dubrovnik, with:
1. Battalion – Hum/Poljice/Jasenica
2. Battalion – Mostar/Domanovici/Stravljena
3. Battalion – Gacko
4. Battalion – Milniste
5. Battalion – Mimi/Mrcinc/Gruda
6. Battalion – Sinj I Split
I. Battery – Sinj

3. Replacement Brigade – Sarajevo, with:
1. Battalion – Sarajevo
2. Battalion – Visoko
3. Battalion – Mokro
4. Battalion – Pale

In addition to the above forces there existed three armoured car battalions which were numbered sequentially: 1–3. The 1. Armoured Car Battalion was attached to the 1. Corps, the 2. Armoured Car Battalion was attached to the 2. Corps, and the 3. Armoured Car Battalion was attached to the 3. Corps. There were other units which were independent of the Croatian Army commands. They included the railway security battalions, which we have discussed already, and the Mobile Brigade containing three battalions which were at this time located in the following areas:

1. Battalion (motorized) – in Döllersheim Training Camp, Austria.
2. Battalion (motorized) – in Bred and Gromacnik.
3. Battalion (motorized) – in Travnik and Lasva.

As stated earlier, there were three armoured trains which were now stationed as follows: the 1. Armoured Train in Brod, the 2. Armoured Train in Zagreb, and the 3. Armoured Train in Kakanj. The commander of motorized replacements had three battalions of motorized troops which supplied replacements of men and machines to all Croatian mechanized units. These were stationed as follows:

The 1. Motorized Replacement Battalion was at Zagreb.
The 2. Motorized Replacement Battalion was stationed in Brod.
The 3. Motorized Replacement Battalion was located in Sarajevo.

To those forces already mentioned we must add three Croatian labour regiments, numbered 1–3. The 1. Labour Regiment and the 3. Labour Regiment both contained four construction battalions, while the 2. Labour Regiment contained a total of five construction battalions. In addition, the Croatian army was also supported by one Croatian police and one *Gendarmerie* unit, whose numbers would continue to grow, primarily due to the recruiting efforts of the German Police & *SS* command. The seven Croatian police battalions raised under German auspices, then grew to ten by the end of 1943. By the spring of 1944 the Germans were raising the 14. and 15. Croatian Police Battalions. In fact, there were so many battalions formed that regimental headquarters were organized to control these new units. Several independent units were also created, such as the 1. and 2. Croatian Police Assault Gun Batteries, which were raised in February 1944. The police regiments formed were as follows:

Polizei Freiwilligen Regiment 1 Kroatien – this regiment had the original first three Croatian police battalions (i.e. – I., II., and III.).

Polizei Freiwilligen Regiment 2 Kroatien – created in April 1944 and initially only had one battalion, the first (I.). In May 1944 another battalion was formed for this regiment (the II.), while a *'III. Bataillon'* came into existence in August 1944. These three battalions were completely different from the *I.-III. Bataillone* of the *Polizei Freiwilligen Regiment 1* named above.

Polizei Freiwilligen Regiment 3 Kroatien – formed in May 1944 from the 11., 12., and 13. Croatian Police Battalion, which were mere re-designations of the 11., 12., and 13. Croatian Railway Security Battalions that had been transferred over to the German *Ordnungspolizei* (Order Police) command in Croatia in December 1943. This regiment was stationed in the town of Ruma on 17 August 1944.

Polizei Freiwilligen Regiment 4 Kroatien – created in July 1944 by using the 7. & 10. Croatian Police Battalions, plus the newly raised 15. Croatian Police Battalion.

Polizei Freiwilligen Regiment 5 Kroatien – this regimental headquarters was created in August 1944 but it was not ready until September, or one month later. It was in September that one newly created Croatian police battalion, designated the *'I.'* could be assigned to it. The regiment remained the only one battalion regiment until January 1945 when a *'II. Bataillon'* was finally added. A month later in February a *'III.'* and final battalion was added.

Polizei Freiwilligen Bataillon 1 Kroatien – created in May 1944 when the original 1. Croatian Police Battalion was absorbed into the *Polizei Freiwilligen Regiment 1 Kroatien*. This battalion was directly attached to the headquarters of the *Befehlshäber der Ordnungspolizei Kroatien* (Supreme Commander of the Order Police in Croatia). As such, it was at the disposal of that higher police headquarters. The battalion was stationed in Zagreb.

Polizei Freiwilligen Bataillon 2 Kroatien – like the '1.' above, this was a completely new unit formed in May 1944 and assigned to the *Kommandeur der Ordnungspolizei* in Zagreb.[6]

Polizei Freiwilligen Bataillon 3 Kroatien – like the 1. and 2. Police Battalions above, it was also raised in May 1944 and assigned to one of the *KdO* commands, specifically to the one located in Osijek.

Polizei Freiwilligen Bataillon 4 Kroatien – this was the old 4. Croatian Police Battalion which had been created in 1943 and now remained an independent battalion-sized unit. It was re-designated as the '4.' and assigned to the *KdO* command in Sarajevo.

Polizei Freiwilligen Bataillon 5 Kroatien – as above, this was the 'old' 5. Battalion and remained an independent unit. It was assigned to the *KdO* command in Banja Luka.

Polizei Freiwilligen Bataillon 6 Kroatien – as above, this was the old 6. Battalion, and was stationed in Split.

Polizei Freiwilligen Bataillon 8 Kroatien – as above, this was the old 8. Battalion which was now assigned to the *KdO* command in Zagreb, alongside the 2. Battalion.

Polizei Freiwilligen Bataillon 9 Kroatien – As above, this was the 'old' 9. Battalion, and was attached to the *KdO* in Osijek, like the 3. Battalion.

In addition to these Croatian police forces, the Germans also created two Croatian police artillery batteries (numbered 1. and 2.) in January and February 1944. The 1. Police Artillery Battery (*Polizei Geschütz Batterie 1*) was posted to Osijek, while *Polizei Geschütz Batterie 2* was located in Zagreb. A Police NCO School (*Polizei Unterführer Schule*) also operated in the city of Brod between April and December 1944. A Croatian Police Cavalry Squadron (*Polizei Reiter Schwadron*) is known to have existed and was formed in the first quarter of 1944, but not much else is known about its movements and whereabouts. Most likely, it would have been stationed either in Brod or Zagreb. In September 1944 the Police Replacement Battalion located in Osijek was redesignated as *Polizei Freiwilligen Ausbildungs Bataillon Kroatien* (Police Volunteer Training Battalion Croatia). Finally in April 1944 a *Polizei Wach Bataillon Kroatien* (Police Guard Battalion Croatia) was raised, but it was destroyed in August of that year. Shortly afterwards a new Guard Battalion was created using new recruits and the remnants from the original guard unit and stationed in Zavidovice. In December 1944 the *ORPO* raised a *Polizei Panzerjäger Kompanie Kroatien* (Police Anti-Tank Company Croatia), which immediately became a part of the *BdO* command in Zagreb.

Chapter 12

1943–1944: THE WRITING ON THE WALL

The *Ustaše* ground forces at the beginning of 1944 were organized into numerous brigade-sized units and were far superior in both size and effectiveness to the regular Croatian Army forces. The only other Croatian units of comparable or better fighting quality to the *Ustaše* ground forces were the German-raised Croatian Legion divisions, though they too were not immune from bouts of morale loss and desertions, especially as the war dragged on and it became clear to all but the most fanatical or ignorant that the Germans were going to lose the war. On paper, the *Ustaše* organization looked like this in January 1944:

Poglavnik Bodyguard Brigade – Stationed in Zagreb with:
Ustaše Bodyguard Regiment –
  1. *Ustaše* Battalion
  2. *Ustaše* Battalion
2. *Ustaše* Bodyguard Regiment –
  1. *Ustaše* Battalion
  2. *Ustaše* Battalion
  Poglavnik Ustaše Cavalry Battalion
    1. *Ustaše* Cavalry Squadron
    2. *Ustaše* Cavalry Squadron
    3. *Ustaše* Cavalry Squadron
  Poglavnik Ustaše Armoured Battalion[1]
  Poglavnik Ustaše Life Guard Battalion[2]
  Poglavnik Ustaše Artillery Battalion
    I. *Ustaše* Artillery Battery
    II. *Ustaše* Artillery Battery
    III. *Ustaše* Artillery Battery

Poglavnik Ustaše Engineer Battalion –
1. *Ustaše* Engineer Company
2. *Ustaše* Engineer Company
3. *Ustaše* Engineer Company

Zagreb Ustaše Garrison Brigade – Stationed in Zagreb with:
Ustaše Garrison Battalion
2. *Ustaše* Garrison Battalion
3. *Ustaše* Garrison Battalion
4. *Ustaše* Garrison Battalion

1. *Ustaše* Brigade – Stationed in Sarajevo with:
2. *Ustaše* Infantry Battalion
24. *Ustaše* Infantry Battalion
29. *Ustaše* Infantry Battalion

2. *Ustaše* Brigade – Stationed in Vinkovci with:
6. *Ustaše* Infantry Battalion
15. *Ustaše* Infantry Battalion
16. *Ustaše* Infantry Battalion
18. *Ustaše* Infantry Battalion
1. *Ustaše* Replacement Battalion

3. *Ustaše* Brigade – Stationed in Karlovac with:
5. *Ustaše* Infantry Battalion
10. *Ustaše* Infantry Battalion
13. *Ustaše* Infantry Battalion
30. *Ustaše* Infantry Battalion
2. *Ustaše* Replacement Battalion

4. *Ustaše* Brigade – Stationed in Otocac with:
9. *Ustaše* Infantry Battalion
19. *Ustaše* Infantry Battalion
20. *Ustaše* Infantry Battalion
31. *Ustaše* Infantry Battalion
34. *Ustaše* Infantry Battalion
Otocac Ustaše Defence Battalion[3]

5. *Ustaše* Brigade[4] – Stationed in the towns of Varazdin, Bjelovar, and Kopavnica with:
Ustaše Infantry Battalion
7. *Ustaše* Infantry Battalion
20. *Ustaše* Infantry Battalion
35. *Ustaše* Infantry Battalion

6. *Ustaše* Brigade – Stationed in Mostar with:
1. *Ustaše* Infantry Battalion[5]
2. *Ustaše* Infantry Battalion
3. *Ustaše* Infantry Battalion
4. *Ustaše* Infantry Battalion
26. *Ustaše* Infantry Battalion

7. *Ustaše* Brigade – Stationed in Bihac with:
1. *Ustaše* Infantry Battalion
2. *Ustaše* Infantry Battalion

3. *Ustaše* Infantry Battalion
4. *Ustaše* Infantry Battalion
5. *Ustaše* Infantry Battalion
6. *Ustaše* Infantry Battalion

8. *Ustaše* Brigade – Stationed in Zadar with:
1. *Ustaše* Infantry Battalion
2. *Ustaše* Infantry Battalion
3. *Ustaše* Infantry Battalion
4. *Ustaše* Infantry Battalion
6. *Ustaše* Infantry Battalion
8. *Ustaše* Infantry Battalion
11. *Ustaše* Infantry Battalion

9. *Ustaše* Brigade – Stationed in Mostar and Jablanica with:
Ustaše Infantry Battalion
2. *Ustaše* Infantry Battalion
3. *Ustaše* Infantry Battalion
4. *Ustaše* Infantry Battalion
5. *Ustaše* Infantry Battalion

10. *Ustaše* Brigade – Stationed in Banja Luka with:
Ustaše Infantry Battalion
2. *Ustaše* Infantry Battalion
3. *Ustaše* Infantry Battalion
4. *Ustaše* Infantry Battalion
5. *Ustaše* Infantry Battalion
6. *Ustaše* Infantry Battalion

11. *Ustaše* Brigade – Stationed in Sarajevo and Zvornik with:
1. *Ustaše* Infantry Battalion
3. *Ustaše* Infantry Battalion
4. *Ustaše* Infantry Battalion
6. *Ustaše* Infantry Battalion

12. *Ustaše* Brigade – Stationed in Zvornik, Lukavac, and Bosanski Brod with:
14. *Ustaše* Infantry Battalion
23. *Ustaše* Infantry Battalion
25. *Ustaše* Infantry Battalion
26. *Ustaše* Infantry Battalion
29. *Ustaše* Infantry Battalion

13. *Ustaše* Brigade – Stationed in Vinkovci with:
6. *Ustaše* Infantry Battalion[6]
16. *Ustaše* Infantry Battalion
Djakovo Ustaše Defence Battalion
Zupanja Ustaše Defence Battalion

14. *Ustaše* Brigade – Stationed in Nova Gradisca with:
Ustaše Railway Security Battalion
3. *Ustaše* Railway Security Battalion
4. *Ustaše* Railway Security Battalion

15. *Ustaše* Brigade – Stationed in the surrounding Zagreb area with:
    Ustaše Infantry Battalion
    6. *Ustaše* Infantry Battalion
    7. *Ustaše* Infantry Battalion
16. *Ustaše* Brigade – Stationed in Bred and Derventa with:
    Bred Ustaše Defence Battalion
    Derventa Ustaše Defence Battalion
    2. *Ustaše* Railway Security Battalion
17. *Ustaše* Brigade – Stationed in Ogulin with:
    Ogulin Ustaše Defence Battalion
    Vrbovska Ustaše Defence Battalion
    Susak Ustaše Defence Battalion
    Rijecica Ustaše Defence Battalion
    Ozalj Ustaše Defence Battalion
    Karlovac Ustaše Defence Battalion
18. *Ustaše* Brigade – Stationed in Gospic with:
    Otocac Ustaše Defence Battalion
    Brinje Ustaše Defence Battalion
    Senj Ustaše Defence Battalion
    Lovinac Ustaše Defence Battalion

Ustaše Camp Brigade[7] – Stationed in the following labour camps: Jasenovac, Laborgrad, and Pag Island, north of Zara with:
    Ustaše Guard Battalion
    2. *Ustaše* Guard Battalion
    3. *Ustaše* Guard Battalion
    4. *Ustaše* Guard Battalion
    Ustaše Mobile Battalion
    Ustaše Artillery Battalion (two weak batteries)

In the early months of 1944, the Partisans had been concentrating on disrupting the Zagreb-Zemun railway line, which was one of the chief communication and supply arteries in the Balkans for the Germans and their Axis allies. This rail line travelled from Croatia and on through Serbia, where it then veered south through Yugoslav Macedonia and into Greece. The city of Jajce had been Tito's primary headquarters in the beginning of 1944, but after the Germans and Croatians forced him out of this region, he moved his staff and command headquarters to Drvar. There in a mountainside cave, he set up shop. He would be left undisturbed until the beginning of the summer of 1944, when the Germans would launch their most ambitious anti-partisan operation of the war: Operation *Rösselsprung* (Knight's Move). This anti-partisan drive would begin on 25 May 1944 and not only included a multi-pronged land offensive, but had been timed to coincide with a daring SS paratrooper assault on Tito's mountain hideout. The aim of this parachute drop was to capture or kill Tito himself. For this operation, the Germans employed the following principal combat units:

1. Gebirgs Division
7. SS Freiwilligen Gebirgs Division Prinz Eugen
92. Infanterie Regiment (*motoriziert*)
II. Bataillon/Jäger Regiment 1 Brandenburg (*motoriziert*)
III. Bataillon/Jäger Regiment 1 Brandenburg (*motoriziert*)
500. SS Fallschirmjäger Bataillon

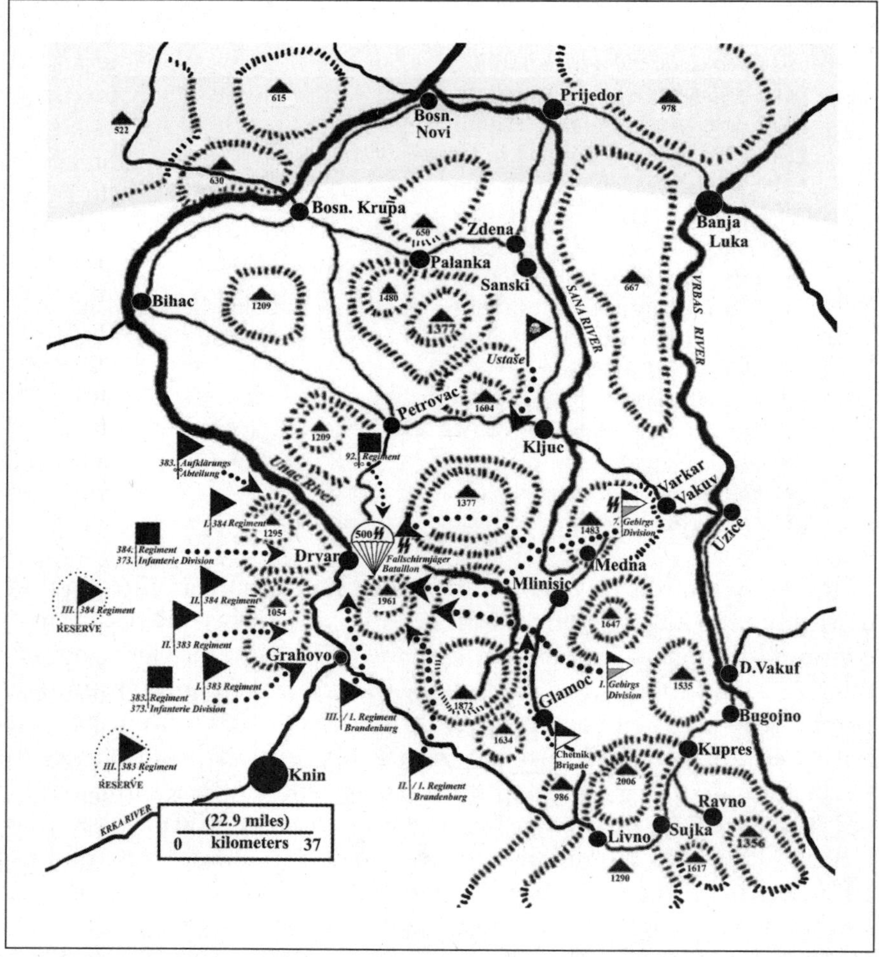

Figure 28. Operation *Rösselsprung* (Knight's Move), May 1944. (*Author's line drawing*)

Croatian forces included the *373. (deutsch-kroatische) Infanterie Division,* plus a token force of one *Ustaše* infantry battalion from the *3. Ustaše* Brigade at Karlovac. The Germans also used a brigade of Serbian Chetniks in their assault. This was a complete about-face in German policy towards the Chetniks, who in the beginning of 1943 were being disarmed and imprisoned by the Germans. But it seemed that the collapse of Fascist Italy in 1943 had forced the Nazis to reconsider employing these anti-communist Serbian forces.

Nothing works better to create military pragmatism and expediency, than continued military reversals. However, using the Chetniks on the German side brought its own kind of trouble. For example, this Serbian Chetnik brigade had to be employed away from the *Ustaše* unit, lest they fall into temptation to attack one another.[8] Placing these two groups together was like striking a match to gasoline. As stated earlier, the aim of this operation was not merely the destruction of the bulk of the estimated 80,000–100,000 Partisans in Croatian territory, but the capture or elimination of Marshal Josip Broz Tito himself. The plan was to land *500. SS Fallschirmjäger Bataillon* in the town of Drvar and on top of Tito's mountain hideout. Initial success, gained at a very bloody cost in German lives, was lost when Tito was able to escape through another opening in the cave, where he had been cornered, fleeing the German trap on a nearby train which had been standing by for just such an occasion. A Soviet-piloted but American-manufactured DC-9 plane later took him to Italy, from where he once again returned to Yugoslav territory, this time wisely making his headquarters on the Dalmatian island of Vis. A whole brigade of Partisans and an entire British commando battalion would defend him there. It was not until the autumn of 1944 that Tito once again felt safe enough to move his headquarters and himself to the Yugoslav mainland. The last major anti-partisan operation of any significance in Yugoslavia was Operation *Rubezahl,* which was to be launched on 12 August 1944. Originally planned as an offensive against the partisan concentrations in Montenegro, it had to be altered to a defensive operation to prevent an estimated thirteen Partisan divisions from crossing into Macedonia and Serbia in an attempt to block the German withdrawal from Greece, which was just getting started. The major units involved in this attempt included the following formations:

1. Gebirgs Division
7. SS Freiwilligen Gebirgs Division Prinz Eugen
13. Waffen Gebirgs Division der SS Handschar
21. Waffen Gebirgs Division der SS Skanderbeg[9]

The operation was a success and most of Tito's thirteen divisions were prevented from entering Macedonia and Serbia. The summer and autumn of 1944 saw an increase in the number of desertions from the Croatian army. The *Ustaše* formations did not suffer as badly as the regular NDH forces, but were not exempt from this either, or from low morale. As the saying goes, the handwriting was on the wall and it wasn't much of a surprise when in September 1944, large-scale Croatian military units began to defect *en masse* to the Tito Partisans. This was magnified by an offer of amnesty, which Tito had made to all men and units of the NDH who would desert or lay down their arms by September and October 1944. An exception was made for those individuals who had committed war crimes. In September 1944 alone the Croatian 1. Anti-Aircraft Artillery Battalion, 1. Mountain Brigade, and 1. *Jäger* Brigade went over to the partisans almost to a man. In the second half of September the Tito guerrillas, by now organized like conventional fighting units, launched a serious assault on the Croatian stronghold of Banja Luka.

Major Croatian units stationed there included the 3,000 strong 3. Mountain Brigade and 10. *Ustaše* Brigade. In spite of this strong Croatian army and *Ustaše* presence, the Partisans pressed on with their attack. It was only by the intervention of the 1. Cossack Cavalry Division and the 3. *Ustaše* Brigade that disaster was averted. The Croatian troops that had been besieged in Banja Luka were surprised but nevertheless very happy to see Cossack cavalrymen coming to their rescue. In fact, the Cossacks operating under the German army command in NDH territory were so good and performed so well against the communist partisans, that they were soon nicknamed by the Croatian troops as the 'North Croatian Fire Brigade'. The Cossacks went on to fight major battles on Croatian territory – at Metilka, Glina, Kostajnica, Banja Luka, Varazdin, Dakovo and many others. In spite of successful defences like the one at Banja Luka, Croatian military ineffectiveness continued to increase. Surprisingly, a rift in the Tito camp appeared in the spring and summer of 1944, when Tito offered amnesty to all Croatian forces that would desert and join his army – regardless of whether or not they had fought the communist movement in the past. This led to the large-scale defection of numerous Croatian Army and even a few small *Ustaše* units and outposts into the guerrilla camp. As this occurred the Serbians, who had up until then been in the majority in the communist guerrilla army, began to get alarmed at the increasing numbers of ex-Croatian Army personnel who were now filtering through into Tito's army. Especially disturbing was the fact that many of these new 'converts' had fought the Partisans and royalist Serbian Chetniks from the very beginning. Tito himself was a Croat, which did not soothe Serbian sentiments. This Serbian paranoia came to a boiling point and created an incident in late April 1944 when several Serbian-run and dominated partisan detachments from the Kordun region deserted and went over to the Germans:

> On 26 April 1944 the partisan commander of the Kordun region, Joco Eremic, deserted to the Germans, taking with him several hundred soldiers. On 15 May his associate, Stevo Kosanovic Jabucar, Assistant Commissar of a group of partisan detachments, led about ninety partisans over to the Germans. The Regional Committee reacted swiftly and offered them amnesty if they returned, which most of them did.[10]

What is amazing about this event is that it occurred so late in the war and at a time when all but the most naïve or most fanatical knew that Tito's forces were on the winning side. Though this was certainly a small and isolated incident within the basically tight-knit Partisan movement, it nevertheless illustrates the hatred and suspicions that both Serbs and Croats felt for one another – so much so that even in the 'proletarian movement' of Josip Tito's communist army, the inner fears of these two peoples allowed it to be shown. It is certain that although no other Serbian-run Partisan detachment deserted, probably quite a large number of them contemplated just such a move due to their fears about a Croatian domination of the post-war Yugoslav government. Hundreds of years have passed but the hatred felt by these two people has never quite been able to be resolved. Add to this explosive mixture the addition of the Muslim 'question' and you have what happened, and what continued to occur in the 1990s with the formal breakup of Yugoslavia. Today, even though relations between Serbia and Croatia appear to be formal and correct, below the surface, hatred and bitterness form the core of the actual relationship between Serbians and Croatians.

The atrocities of the Second World War and those committed during the breakup of Yugoslavia in the 1990s were seared into the collective memory of Serbians, Croatians, and Muslims. If a future war is ever to be fought between both nations, the war, I am sure, will be fought with equal ferocity and loathing. On the Croatian side, Pavelić also had to deal with those within his own officer corps who now began to waver in their support for a Croatian Fascist solution for an independent Croatian state. It was in this way that in the summer of 1944 the *Ustaše* Minister of Police, Colonel Mladen Lorkovic, and the *Ustaše* Defence Minister, Krilnik Ante Vokic, began secret negotiations with the Croatian Peasant

Party in order to try and establish contact with the Western Allies. Their attempt was to seek a separate peace with the Western powers in order to avoid being conquered by Tito's communist Partisans. Their hope was to try and keep Croatia's independence alive in a post-war Europe. The negotiations however got nowhere, basically because the Allies wanted nothing to do with the Croatians. The decision to allow Tito full control of the former Yugoslavia had already occurred. It had also been agreed that the Soviet Union would have Yugoslavia in its sphere of influence, and this ran contrary to retaining an independent rump Croatia, which would be free of communist influence. Tito was to be the de-facto ruler and that was not up to debate. Soon Pavelić found out about the treachery in his own ranks, and had both formerly close *Ustaše* officers arrested.

It was an embarrassing scandal within the Croatian Fascist camp, especially since both chief conspirators were high-ranking government leaders, and one out of the two (Ante Vokic) had the title of *Ustaše Krilnik*, an honorary *Ustaše* title that only one other person held: Ante Pavelić himself. It was thus that after Vokic and Mladen's demise, Ante Pavelić took direct and complete control of the Croatian Armed Forces and eventually appointed himself 'Supreme Commander' in November 1944. The *Ustaše* Chief of Staff, Colonel Tomislav Sertic, was then replaced by Pavelić's personal appointment of *Ustaše* Colonel Ivica Herencic, whom he considered to be extremely loyal. Heavy fighting continued in NDH territory in the autumn of 1944 with no end in sight. In October 1944 the city of Travnik was surrounded by strong Partisan forces and besieged from all sides. Inside the city was a Croatian garrison of some 1,800 to 2,000 men. They included the following:

400 men of the *Polizei Freiwilligen Bataillon 5 Kroatien*[11]
300 men of the I. Battalion/8. Garrison Brigade
400 men of the local *Ustaše* Guard Battalion
500–700 men of the 3. Mobile Battalion
80v100 men of the I. Artillery Battery/8. Garrison Brigade

The Partisan assault continued incessantly until 22 October 1944 when the Croatian defences were finally pierced and the city fell to the Partisans. Last ditch efforts by the *Ustaše* in the city barracks ended after their ammunition ran out. The surviving Croatian troops were then ordered to fix bayonets by the garrison commander, Colonel Bona Bonic.[12] Those who had survived up until then knew very well that they were about to die. Yet, not a single one of them threw down their weapons and surrendered. The final battle inside the city barracks were filled with the maddening screams of the dying and the yells and battle cries of those about to die. During those last few minutes of the battle, Colonel Bonic fell bravely while leading his men in a suicidal bayonet charge. One account says that he was mowed down by a partisan with a Beretta Model 38 submachinegun. In any event, his courage showed great heroism.[13] For his actions, he was posthumously promoted to general and awarded the Golden Ante Pavelić Medal for Bravery. He was also lauded by his nation when the radio announcement was made declaring his death. The defence and final fall of Travnik in late October 1944 has been compared to the defence of Vukovar by the Croatian Defence Forces in 1992.[14] The city of Dubrovnik also fell that month in much the same way, with its defenders fighting until the very end. Sadly, the bravery of the Croatian troops in the defence of these towns has never been acknowledged.

On 6 December 1944 Knin came under direct Partisan artillery fire from the guerrilla forces that were chasing the NDH units that had shortly before, evacuated the cities of Split and Sibenik. The German *264. Infanterie Division (bodenstandig)*, which had made its appearance on Croatian soil in October 1943, was also withdrawing towards Knin. When it had arrived, it had been posted to the areas surrounding those two cities on the Dalmatian coast (i.e. – Split and Sibenik). The *264. Infanterie Division* (*bodenstandig*) was never an elite infantry unit, owing to the fact that it was basically a static formation that had been raised from elderly reservists and even moderately wounded men who could no longer face the rigors of the Russian front or battles in France. There were also sick men who could not serve in regular front-line units because they suffered from one ailment or another. This German unit together with several other minor Croatian forces was now surrounded in and around the city of Knin and was eventually destroyed. What remnants survived of the division fought their way to Bihac, alongside Croatian Army survivors of the siege. After the battle for Knin, control of the whole Dalmatian coast was in dispute and the German and Croatian forces were put on the defensive. The Croatian Navy, as it was, was wholly inadequate for controlling the Dalmatian Coast. In the summer of 1944, the Croatian Navy (*Hrvatska Mornarica*) had consisted of about 1,000 men, eight motor boats, one torpedo boat, and two escort ships – all under *Kriegsmarine* (German Navy) command. These reverses on land once again sapped the fighting morale of the NDH forces, even those of the Air Force and Navy as witnessed by a passage from the German Army High Command War Diary in late December 1944:

> On 24 December the Croatian coastal flotilla tried to put out to sea at Fiume [Rijeka – the author] to join the enemy. One boat with the flotilla commander escaped, while the other craft returned and were disarmed. After the head of the Croatian state had ordered strong measures to be taken, War Minister Steinfl convened a Croatian war council. The Foreign Office also took part in the proceedings. On 5 January [1945] the Commander in Chief of the Navy informed the Wehrmacht Operations Staff that he was forced to take severe measures to suppress the mutineers who were hauling down the flags, occupying all ships, and disarming the crews. He proposed incorporating all vessels into the German Navy and manning them with German crews, then activating a Croatian Naval Legion for employment in the North Sea and the Baltic Sea to serve as a nucleus for a future Croatian Navy. Croatian naval forces on the land should be organized into security battalions within German units; training of Croatian officer applicants and enlisted men should continue.[15]

This was just one of numerous examples of how the Croatian Armed Forces had lost much of its effectiveness due to large and numerous defections coupled with military reversals. It's no small wonder then, that towards the end of 1944 the number of *Ustaše* troops available (114,000–130,000 men) far outnumbered the regular Croatian Army NDH units. At this time the NDH was estimated at no more than 38,000–90,000 men, depending on which source you believe. In November 1944 an announcement was made that the Croatian Armed Forces would once again undergo yet one more reorganization. This time the *Ustaše* brigades were to be merged with what was left of the Croatian Army *Jäger*, Mountain, and Garrison brigades to form mixed divisions. It was hoped that by mixing the mostly effective and loyal *Ustaše* units with the mostly ineffective and demoralized regular Croatian Army formations, that those regular NDH forces could become effective. At the very least, it would make it more difficult for them to desert. In December 1944 the reorganization of those forces began to take shape. The new force, now dubbed the *Hrvatske Oruzane Snage* (Croatian Armed Forces) looked like this on paper:

1. Infantry Corps: Zagreb area with:
    Poglavnik Bodyguard Division: Zagreb & northwest of Virovitica.
        1. *Ustaše* Bodyguard Regiment: Northwest of Virovitica (Podravina and Bilogora).
        2. *Ustaše* Bodyguard Regiment: Northwest of Virovitica.
        Poglavnik Ustaše Cavalry Battalion: Northwest of Virovitica.
        Poglavnik Ustaše Armoured Battalion: Zagreb.
        Poglavnik Ustaše Artillery Battalion: Northwest of Virovitica.

Poglavnik Ustaše Life Guard Battalion: Zagreb (Pavelić's own personal escort).
Poglavnik Ustaše Engineer Battalion: Virovitica.
Poglavnik Ustaše Replacement Battalion: Zagreb.

1. Croatian Storm Division;[16] at Virovitica & Zagreb.
20. Infantry Regiment: Virovitica (Bilogora & Podravina).
21. Infantry Regiment: Virovitica (Vrbovec, Popovaca, Voloder).
22. Infantry Regiment: Zagreb (still forming – not combat ready yet).
20. Artillery Battalion: Virovitica (Vrbovec, Popovaca, Podravina).
21. Artillery Battalion: Virovitica
Storm Division Mobile Battalion (motorized): Virovitica.

2. Croatian Infantry Division:[17] Zagreb, Leskovac, Sambor, Bistra, Krapina, Sesvete.[18]
20. *Ustaše* Brigade (formerly the *Ustaše* Zagreb Garrison Brigade).
15. *Ustaše* Brigade
20. Infantry Brigade
3. Engineer Training Battalion[19]

4. Croatian Infantry Division: Dos. Novi, Sisak, Petrinja, Kostajnica.
7. *Jäger* Brigade (formerly the 4. *Jäger* Brigade).
8. *Ustaše* Brigade
19. *Ustaše* Brigade

5. Croatian Infantry Division: Bjelovar.
5. *Ustaše* Brigade[20]
11. *Jäger* Brigade
1. Artillery Battery
2. Artillery Battery

Croatian Infantry Division: Bihac.
10. *Jäger* Brigade (formerly the 2. *Jäger* Brigade)
7. *Ustaše* Brigade
VIII. Artillery Battalion

13. Croatian Infantry Division:[21] Karlovac.[22]
3. *Ustaše* Brigade
17. *Ustaše* Brigade
12. *Jäger* Brigade
I. Artillery Group
1. Artillery Battery
2. Artillery Battery

16. Training & Replacement Division: Zagreb.
21. Replacement Brigade (formerly the 1. Replacement Brigade)
23. Replacement Brigade (formerly the 2. Replacement Brigade)
21. *Ustaše* replacement Brigade
3. *Ustaše* Brigade – Karlovac[23]

2. Infantry Corps: Brod region with:
2. Croatian Infantry Division: Vinkovci.
1. *Jäger* Brigade (formerly the 3. *Jäger* Brigade).
2. *Ustaše* Brigade

13. *Ustaše* Brigade
VII. Artillery Battalion
1. Artillery Battery
2. Artillery Battery
6. Croatian Infantry Division: Banja Luka.[24]
10. *Ustaše* Brigade
15. *Jäger* Brigade (formerly the 5. Garrison Brigade)
III. Battalion/8. *Jäger* Regiment[25]
1. Artillery Battery
2. Artillery Battery
7. Croatian Mountain Division: Northwest of Brod (N. Kapela, Batrina).
1. Mountain Brigade (reformed).
4. Mountain Brigade
I. Artillery Battalion
1. Artillery Battery
2. Artillery Battery
VI. Artillery Battalion
1. Artillery Battery
2. Artillery Battery
12. Croatian Infantry Division: Brcko.[26]
Mountain Brigade (formerly the 10. Garrison Brigade)
12. *Ustaše* Brigade
2. Engineer Replacement Battalion.
XII. Division Artillery Battalion.
1. Artillery Battery
2. Artillery Battery
3. Artillery Battery
14. Croatian Infantry Division: St. Brod (later still: Ivanić-Grad, just SE of Zagreb).[27]
14. *Ustaše* Brigade: Nova Gradisca,
19. *Jäger* Brigade: Osijek-Brod-Zagreb rail line.[28]
15. Croatian Infantry Division: Doboj.
16. *Jäger* Brigade (formerly the 6. Garrison Brigade).
16. *Ustaše* Brigade
3. Infantry Corps: Sarajevo with:
8. Croatian Infantry Division: Sarajevo.[29]
1. *Ustaše* Brigade
11. *Ustaše* Brigade
18. *Jäger* Brigade (formerly the 8. Garrison Brigade).
1. Artillery Battery
Independent Units:
Mobile Brigade (motorized): Dugoselo
1. Mobile Battalion: Bozjakovina
2. Mobile Battalion: Dugoselo
1. Independent Artillery Battery (motorized): Bozjakovina

One engineer company (motorized).
One repair & maintenance company (motorized) – Dugoselo.
Ustaše People's Brigade – Vinkovci.
Ustaše People's Regiment *'Baranja'*
Ustaše People's Regiment *'Vuka'*
Ustaše People's Regiment *'Posavlje'*
Ustaše Camp Brigade: Jasenovac
1. *Ustaše* Guard Battalion
2. *Ustaše* Guard Battalion
3. *Ustaše* Guard Battalion
4. *Ustaše* Guard Battalion
Ustaše Mobile Battalion (motorized)
Ustaše Artillery Battalion
1. Artillery Battery
2. Artillery Battery

Notes on the Croatian divisions

1. Croatian Storm Division – this Division not only had the most fanatical *Ustaše* units, but the best Croatian Army units. Its morale was high. The next-best formation after this division was 8. Croatian Infantry Division. This division was thrown into battle in December 1944 before it was fully formed, since its 22. Infantry Regiment was still undergoing training. One source states that the division was 6,000 men strong, while another quotes a figure of 9,000 men. Perhaps this apparent discrepancy can be attributed to the missing 22. Infantry Regiment. The Mobile Battalion had one reconnaissance company made up of armoured cars and two tank companies made up of Czech and Italian light tanks and tankettes. At full strength, it had a total of nine infantry and two artillery battalions. During the winter of 1944/45 the Croatians received a large batch of Finnish light-blue uniforms which they put to use in the 1. Croatian Storm Division and other units. The division was committed on 25 December 1944, holding an attacking Russian force at bay on the banks of the Drava River for six weeks until supplies and ammunition ran out. In early February 1945 the Division was ordered to withdraw lest it be enveloped and destroyed.
2. Infantry Division – had a total of 5,000+ men in eleven battalions. It acted as the Zagreb garrison and its surrounding areas. It was positioned in the line Zagreb-Leskovac-Sambor-Horvati-Bistra-Krapinska-Toplice-Krapina-Zabok-Sesvete-Marija-Bistrica-Vel. Gorica. Its morale was average. Like the 1. Croatian Storm Division, the 2. Division was under the operational control of the German *LXIX. Armeekorps.*
3. Infantry Division – this division had around 7,500 men in eight *Ustaše* infantry, six Army (NDH) *Jäger,* and one artillery battalion. Its morale was very good. The operational area was in the region of Zupan-

ja-Vinkovci-Osijek. Like all of the other Croatian units, this division was assigned to a Croatian corps command, but was under the operational control of the nearest German corps' command. In this case, the 3. Croatian Infantry Division was under the operational control of the German *XXXIV. Armeekorps.*

4. Infantry Division (General Antun Nardelli) – this unit had about 7,000 men in seven *Ustaše,* four NDH *Jäger,* and four Home Guard battalions, plus three artillery batteries. It operated in the area of Sisak-Petrinja-Kostajnica-Divusa-Bos. Novi. It was under the operational control of the German *LXIX. Armeekorps.* Strangely, while Croatian sources listed this division as an infantry formation, German situation maps listed this unit as a mountain formation.
5. Infantry Division – this unit had 6,000 men in six *Ustaše,* and four NDH *Jäger* battalions, plus two artillery batteries. It operated in the areas of Varazdin-Koprivnica-Krizevoi-Bjelovar-Djurdjevac-Virje. Its morale was average. It was under the operational control of the German *LXIX. Armeekorps.*
6. Infantry Division – this unit had about 4,000–4,500 men in six *Ustaše* and four NDH *Jäger* battalions, plus two artillery batteries. It operated in the regions of Pakrac-Garesnica-Sunja-Dubica-Prijedor -Kotor-Varos-Hrvacani-Medari. It was under the operational control of the German *LXIX. Armeekorps.*
7. Infantry Division – This unit was also weak like the 6. Infantry Division – having perhaps 4,000–4,500 men in four mountain, four *Jäger* and two weak artillery battalions. The two artillery 'battalions' only had two batteries each. Although it's operational area was Brod-Kutjevo-Velika-Pakrac-Medari-Sava River. It was dispersed along the rail line following the localities of Kriz-Novska-Nova Kapela-Batrina-Pozega. Strangely enough, the German situation maps do not list a Croatian division as mountain unit, but rather as a regular infantry division. It was under the operational control of the German *LXIX. Armeekorps.*
8. Infantry Division (led by General Roman Domanik) – this unit had perhaps about 7,000 men in seven *Ustaše,* and seven NDH *Jäger* battalions, plus one artillery battery. Its morale was very good. Its area of operations was Sarajevo- Zvomik-Visoko-Ilidza-Stambolcic-Praca. The Division was under the operational control of the German *V. SS Freiwilligen Gebirgs Armeekorps.*
9. Infantry Division (led by General Ivan Tomašević) – this unit was a much under-strength formation and contained perhaps around 3,500–4,000 men in four weak *Jäger,* and three weak *Ustaše* battalions, plus one artillery battalion of two batteries. The headquarters of the 7. *Ustaše* Brigade, a sub-unit of the 10. Infantry Division, was at Bihac, with its 1st Battalion in Lapac, II. Battalion at Kiotoc, and III. Battalion in Otokoc. The headquarters of the 10. *Jäger* Brigade (another sub

unit) was at Skocaj. The German *XV. Gebirgs Armeekorps* had operational control of the Croatian 10. Infantry Division.

10. Infantry Division (led by Colonel Slavko Cesarić) – this division had about 6,000 men in six *Ustaše*, and ten weak NDH *Jäger* battalions, plus one engineer battalion (two companies), and three artillery batteries. One of the 12. Division's sub-units, the 3. Mountain Brigade headquarters, was located in the Zupanja area, while the 12. *Ustaše* Brigade, another sub-unit was at Zvornik-Lukavac-Gracanica-Bos. Samac-Bosanski Brod. It was under the German *LXVIII. Armeekorps* command until January 1945 when it came under the operational control of the German *XXXIV. Armeekorps.*
11. Infantry Division (led by Colonel Jaroslav Šotola) – this unit contained the 14. *Ustaše* Brigade with the 1., 3., and 4. *Ustaše* Railway Security Battalions. It also had the 19. *Jäger* Brigade, with the 4.–10. Railway Security Battalions – in total, about 4,000 men under the command staff of the German *Eisenbahnsicherungsstab Kroatien* (Railway Security Staff Croatia).
12. Infantry Division (led by General Zorko Čudina) – this unit had the 16. *Ustaše* Brigade with three battalions: *Ustaše* Defence Battalions *Brod, Derventa,* and the 2. *Ustaše* Railway Security Battalion. The 16. *Jäger* Brigade was also a sub-unit of this division. It had the 16. and 17. Railway Security Battalions, and the 1., 3., & 4. *Jäger* Battalions. In all, about 3,000–3,500 men in eight battalions. It was under the operational control of the German *XXXIV. Armeekorps,* and later the *XXI. Gebirgs Armeekorps.* Its 16. *Ustaše* Brigade operated between Derventa-Brod, while the 16. *Jäger* Brigade operated between Derventa-Teslic-Doboj- Zenica.
13. Training & Replacement Division (led by General Milivoj Durbešić) – this unit contained about 9,000 recruits and training personnel in twelve replacement battalions and four artillery replacement batteries. One source says that it had sixteen battalions, but this seems to include the artillery batteries, referring to them as 'battalions'. It is known that in April 1945 a '22. *Ustaše* Replacement Brigade' was added to this division. It could well be that at this time the 3. Replacement Brigade, having four battalions and known to be in the Sarajevo area, was finally merged with the Division, becoming this new '22. *Ustaše* Replacement Brigade'. This additional replacement brigade would have added an additional 3,000 men to the 16. Training & Replacement Division by April 1945. The division was not fully armed and equipped so was not a combat unit and could not be deployed for battle.

In February 1945 an additional three Croatian infantry divisions were formed: the 9. Mountain Division (led by General Božidar Zorn), the

11. Infantry Division (led by Colonel Juraj Rukavina), and the 13. Infantry Division (led by General Tomislav Rolf). The 9. Mountain Division was now attached to the 3. Infantry Corps in Sarajevo, though for operational purposes, it was under the German *XXI. Gebirgs Armeekorps*. Its area of operations included its home base of Mostar, plus the areas of Jablanica-Ostrozac-Konjic-Tarcin and Sarajevo. It had about 6,000 men split into two brigades: the 2. Mountain Brigade and 9. *Ustaše* Brigade. The total number of battalions included five mountain and three *Ustaše* battalions, plus three artillery batteries. The 11. Infantry Division was formed from the 4. and 18. *Ustaše* Brigades, and the 13. Infantry Brigade. It had a total of some 7,000 men in eight *Ustaše*, and seven *Jäger* battalions, plus only one artillery battery. The 4. *Ustaše* Brigade in particular, had suffered heavy casualties and had a complement of four battalions instead of the original eight that it had contained in December 1944. The division was posted to Gospic, with its area of operations being Gospic-Licki-Osijek-Perusic-Licki-Novi-Brusane-Rizvanusa-Karlobag-Senj-Brinje Kosinj-Vrhovine. It was attached to the German *XV. Gebirgs Armeekorps*, but in March 1945 the Croatians would form an additional two corps headquarters staffs – the 4. and 5. Army Corps, and would assign the 11. Infantry Division to the newly created '5. Corps'. The 13. Infantry Division, which had been forming since December 1944, was created using the 3. and 17. *Ustaše* Brigades, plus the 12. *Jäger* Brigade. In addition, the 1. Artillery Battalion was added to the division.

This battalion had two artillery batteries. As stated previously, this division was stationed in Karlovac, and in March 1945 was attached to the newly-created Croatian 5. Army Corps, although it would serve under the operational control of the German *LXIX. Armeekorps*. It contained about 6,500– 7,000 men in fourteen battalions and two artillery batteries. Its area of operations encompassed Karlovac–Draganici–Dugaresa–Mahicno–Recica–Jaska/Ozalj–Ogulin–Susak and Svarca. It should be stated that in the autumn of 1944, the Germans had made the conscience decision to employ a small German liaison staff, in each Croatian division. It was through this small German staff, which formed part of the Croatian divisional headquarters, that the unit received its orders when under the direction of a German corps' command. What is immediately obvious, when one looks at the Croatian Order of Battle for December 1944, is that an effort was being made by the Croatian government to improve the fighting strength of its divisions. This was achieved, by mixing *Ustaše* units with regular NDH army units in each division. The logic was that the more reliable *Ustaše* troops would help to prevent the regular NDH units from either surrendering or melting away in battle. The second thing that stands out, is that even though the war was winding down, the Croatian Army was still trying to expand its ranks. This is attested to by the creation of two more corps commands and the reorganization of the army, which continued into March and April 1945.

The Croatian Army command, at the directions of Ante Pavelić, began a propaganda campaign geared to remind the NDH forces that the Partisan amnesty period, where NDH soldiers could surrender and not face trial or prison, was now over. The flyers handed to the troops stipulated clearly how no mercy would be shown to anyone serving in the Croatian Army. The best that an NDH soldier could hope for was to be captured by a partisan unit composed of Croatians, which might allow the soldier to be taken prisoner. There was no such mercy shown to NDH soldiers who surrendered to Serbian Partisans, especially if it contained former Chetniks, who had switched sides and were now under Tito's communist army. In that instance, the NDH soldier who surrendered was shown no mercy. All *Ustaše* soldiers who surrendered could only expect to be shot. For them, the end of the war would bring a terrible retribution. As 1944 came to an end, it was clear to all that the writing was on the wall. Defeat loomed ahead, and there seemed to be no way to prevent it from happening.

Chapter 13

1944: VICIOUS FIGHTING

Rückzug

As 1944 was coming to an end, the military situation facing the Axis all across Europe looked bleak. In April 1944 the *Wehrmacht* still had 7,849,000 men under arms. The disastrous spring, summer and autumn campaigns in France, Italy and the Russian front had reduced that number greatly. In November 1944, the strength of the *Wehrmacht* was around six million men, although this figure had been achieved by the call-up of older and younger males, and a thorough combing-out of the various German industries for additional recruits. By 1944, there were so-called 'stomach battalions' – made up of men who had stomach ulcers and other alimentary-canal ailments that, under normal circumstances, would have made them 4F (not fit to serve). These men gathered together in units and were placed on coastal defence or as fortress troops. Other, similar 'medical battalions' were created and placed in limited-duty missions, like garrison and guard duty. Around 1,000,000 German soldiers had surrendered to Allied forces from 6 June to 31 December 1944, and that did not include the German soldiers killed on the western front. Between those dates around 30,000 Germans had been killed in France, with a further 80,000 wounded and about 210,000 missing and presumed captured.

On 1 May 1944, the *Ostheer* (German Army in the East) could still boast of having some 2,460,000 troops,[1] with an additional 300,000 Finns, and 550,000 Hungarians and Romanians. However, the Soviet 1944 summer offensive reduced that number by 450,000 men. Thus, by the end of July 1944, the *Ostheer* could count only on about 2,000,000 men. Out of those two million soldiers, approximately 400,000 (20 per cent) were actually *Osttruppen*. Facing these tired and worn out *Landsers* were approximately 6,000,000 Russian troops. In the Balkans, the Germans could count on around 300,000 men, while the Croatian Army contained somewhere in the neighbourhood of 140,000 soldiers by November 1944. However, Germany's enemies had far more troops. By the autumn of 1944 the Russians alone had around 6,450,000 soldiers, with another 100,000 soon to join the Red Army. By November 1944 Tito's Partisan army had a strength of about 650,000 men. The Bulgarians, who had switched sides and were now allied to the Soviet Union, had fielded some 455,000 troops divided into three armies, which had entered Serbia in September 1944 against the Germans. The situation therefore, of the German and Croatian forces in November 1944 was grim, as the German Armed Forces High Command War Diary recorded:

> On 30 December the Commander in Chief Southeast reported that as many forces as possible were being moved forward to support the Second Panzer Army on the northern bank of the Drava. This was done at great risk, since it had been necessary to abandon the Drina front and to leave the Drava front unoccupied. After the transfer of 1. Gebirgs Division and the 118. Jäger Division to the Second Panzer Army, the following organization was in effect: Mostar Area: The 369. (deutsch-kroatische) Infanterie Division was assigned several fortress battalions to replace the regiment of the 118. Jäger Division which had been withdrawn. The Commander in Chief Southeast hoped to manage with this one division, although it served only as a screen and both flanks were still open. Eastern Sector: The 181. Infanterie Division held both sides of Visegrad. The 22. (Luftlande) Infanterie Division had taken up positions along the Drina front. It was questionable whether the 181. Infanterie Division would be sufficient, since the enemy in that sector was expected to exert strong pressure. Units were needed to occupy the uncovered Drina front, where Partisans were now able to move freely. Syrmian Front: Tito Partisan divisions and seven Bulgarian divisions oppose the German forces in this area. The 41. Festungs Division was to be employed in order to allow the withdrawal of units from the 1. Gebirgs Division, the 118. *Jäger* Division, and 13. Waffen Gebirgs Division der SS 'Handschar'. The following forces employed in this sector represented a minimum: the 7. SS Freiwilligen Gebirgs Division; the 41. Festungs Division; and the 117. Jäger Division. On the Drava Front: until now only the 11. Luftwaffe Feld Division was employed. Wide, unoccupied areas were held by the partisans. The 297. Infanterie Division was to be employed in mopping up resistance and to act as a security force. It was urgent that those areas be occupied because of threats from across the river. One brigade of the 1. Kosaken Kavallerie Division was approaching from the northwest. Bihac Area: Apart from the Drina front, this area was the most susceptible to enemy pressure.

> In weakened condition, the XV. Gebirgs Armeekorps could not be expected to stop the enemy. It was intended to employ the 1. Gebirgs Division, elements of which were already in the area. Now, however, the 104. Jäger Division would have to be brought forward as fast as possible to avoid a setback in this strategic sector. Southern boundary of Croatia (between Nevesinje and Visegrad): No forces were available. The interior: Weak security forces, consisting of Croatian units of doubtful reliability, were not sufficient for the protection of roads and railways. There were no forces for fighting constantly increasing Partisan activity or for protecting valuable industrial plants. There are no reserve forces available. The forces listed above represents the minimum strength to hold Croatia. They would be further weakened by the withdrawal of air, naval, and police forces, and by the growing unreliability of the Croatian units. The Commander in Chief Southeast asked for a decision as to whether the order withdrawing large units would remain in effect. Unless the order was changed, he does not think it would be possible to defend Croatia.[2]

The German Armed Forces High Command War Diary chronicled the situation with exacting accuracy. Even though the Croatians continued to reorganize and expand their meagre forces, it would amount to very little in terms of improving the effectiveness of the Croatian Army. For example, the Germans organized twelve of the German-raised Croatian police battalions into a Croatian *Gendarmerie* Division, but this new headquarters could not gather the battalions together from their diverse positions, localities, and duties. Thus, a new 'paper division' was formed; one that could not employ all of its battalions together and for all intents and purposes was useless. Another example of the futility of the Croatian reorganization efforts was the Croatian 14. Infantry Division, whose headquarters was raised to control the three *Ustaše,* and seven NDH army railway battalions along the long stretch of rail line between Zagreb-Brod-Osijek. Since the battalions could not be concentrated for employment as a whole unit (they were dispersed along the entire rail line), it was ludicrous to form a divisional staff for these battalions and a waste of scarce staff and cadre personnel battalions. I must admit however, that on Ante Pavelić's situation map, the addition of another white-and-red checkered divisional flag must have looked impressive and reassuring. Aside from these 'aesthetics' however, the addition of these useless staffs added no real fighting value to the capacity of the Croatian Army to resist Tito's partisan army. As 1945 arrived, the Croatian military was still not ready to properly defend its national borders. On 21 January 1945, the Croatian government – still bent on expanding and reorganizing their forces – submitted a proposal through the Commander in Chief Southeast to activate a Croatian Guard Corps. This unit would be titled the '*Poglavnik* Bodyguard Corps,' and was to comprise the cream of the Croatian Armed Forces:

> *Poglavnik* Bodyguard Division
> 1. Croatian Storm Division (led by General Ante Moškov)
> 5. Croatian Infantry Division (led by General Rafael Boban)[3]
> Mobile Brigade (mechanized)

The German Commander in Chief Southeast quickly rejected the idea, as witnessed in the OKW (German Armed Forces High Command) War Diary:

> On 29 January the Wehrmacht Operations Staff and the Commander in Chief Southeast expressed the opinion that the request should be denied, since it would create a new command headquarters which might prove difficult to control and might seek to escape German influence. As the head of the Croatian State [Pavelić] had personally made this proposal, the Foreign Office agreed that it should not be flatly refused. The Commander in Chief Southeast was accordingly informed that the request had been denied because it would dissipate forces which could be better employed in already existing units.[4]

This passage is very indicative of the mistrust that by 1945 the Germans had of the Croatian Armed Forces and of Ante Pavelić as well. This began in earnest in the autumn of 1944 when even some high-ranking members of the fanatical and reliable *Ustaše* in the Croatian government, had attempted to contact the Western Allies in order to seek a separate peace. Another German OKW War Diary entry, dated '19 January', or just two days before Pavelić's proposal to form an elite corps, emphasized the German fear that elements in the Croatian State were still involved in an attempt to join the Western Allies:

> Reports from army group intelligence described preparations of the *Ustaše* to transfer units to the Lika (northwest Croatia) area and to contact the British in case of a German withdrawal. It was therefore considered advisable to watch the Slovenian units and the Chetniks in Istria. Special attention was to be given pro-British sentiment.[5]

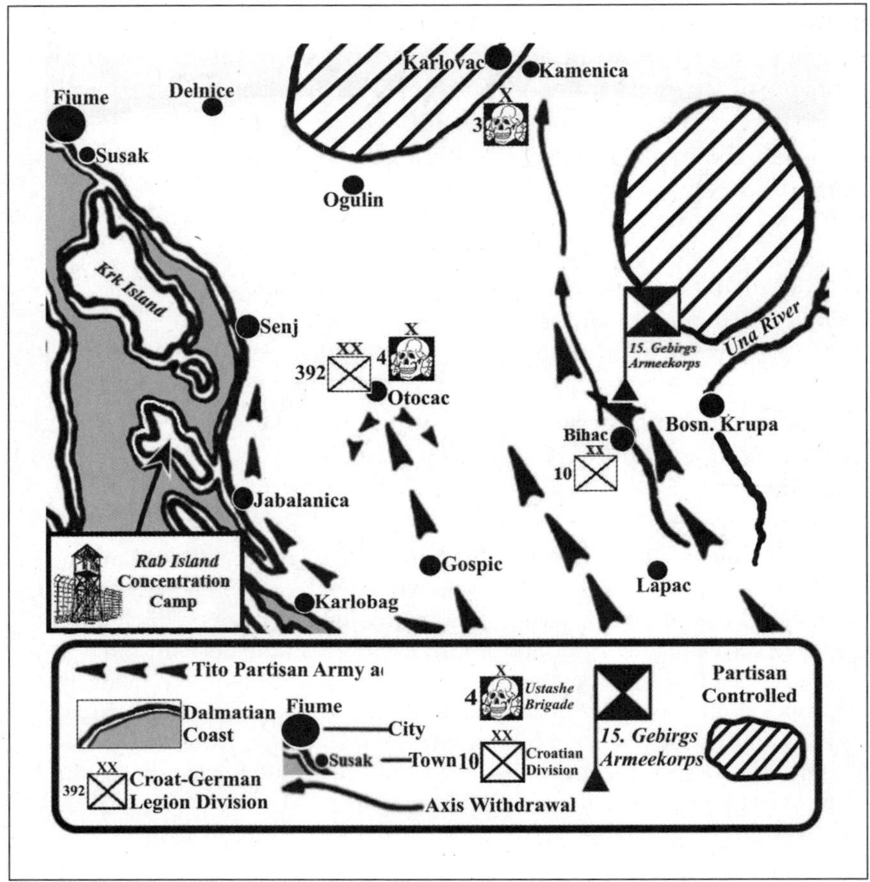

Figure 29. Partisan army advance along the Dalmatian Coast, January 1945.

Meanwhile, the military situation in the Balkans continued to develop in favour of the Partisans and against the Croatians and Germans. On 2 January 1945 the remnants of the *373. (deutsch-kroatische) Infanterie Division* and the small cadre of the *264. (bodenstandig) Infanterie Division* which had survived the debacle at Knin were fighting their way back to the German lines, after having failed in their counter-attack near Knin. In the process of this withdrawal the town of Gracac was also lost. The OKW War Diary for 2 January 1945 listed the following report:

> The situation at Bihac has become more acute because of enemy pressure from the north and south. The remnants of the 264. (bodenstandig) Infanterie Division and 237. Infanterie Division were to fight their way back to German lines, since their attack had failed. North of this area the German position is especially weak. Two companies of the

> 373. (deutsch-kroatische) Infanterie Division had literally run away. Cannoneer battalions in cooperation with units of the 392. (deutsch-kroatische) Infanterie Division were constructing a security line. The enemy employed pincer tactics to destroy the defending forces in this area. Two fortress battalions were to be sent as reinforcements.[6]

That only two meagre fortress battalions were all the reinforcements that could be spared for the defence of Bihac and Gospic is indicative of the critically weak state in which the Axis forces found themselves in at the beginning of 1945. One of those two fortress battalions earmarked for the *392. (deutsch-kroatische) Infanterie Division* was the *VIII. Bataillon* of the German *999. Strafebrigade* which had recently seen action on Pag Island off the Dalmatian coast.

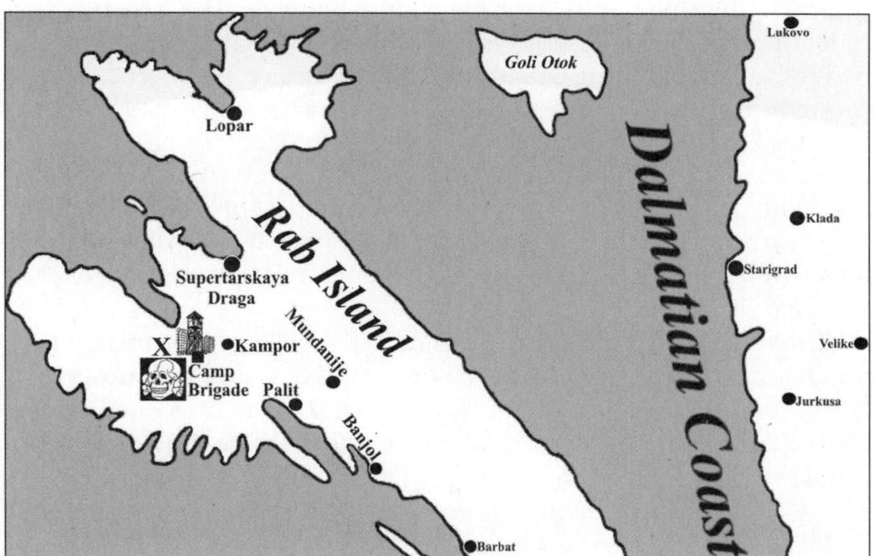

Figure 30. Close-up view of the location of the Rab Island concentration camp.

It had begun its defence of Pag Island with 856 men, but had lost 130 men. Thirty had also been wounded, and an additional 100 had been captured by the Partisans. It was these types of reinforcements that was what the Germans had left. It's no small wonder then, that towards the end of January 1945 both Otocac and Bihac were on the verge of falling. If they fell the Partisans would be within striking distance of Senj, Susak, and even Rijeka (Fiume). In effect, the whole Dalmatian coast up to the Istrian peninsula was in danger.

Kämpf bis zum Schluss

Towards the end of January 1945 both Otocac and Bihac were on the verge of falling to Tito's Partisan Army. Once they fell the communists would be within striking distance of Senj, Susak, and even Rijeka (Fiume). In effect the entire upper Dalmatian coast area up to the Istrian peninsula was in danger. On 3 January 1945 the Partisans attacked Mostar and Travnik once again, specifically in the area between the Sarajevo-Brod Road. A counter-attack was planned against these forces in the region of Travnik by the German *104. Jäger Division* on the left flank of the *392. (deutsch-kroatische) Infanterie Division*, but the 10. Croatian Infantry Division on the left flank of *392. Infanterie Division* soon gave way to Partisan attacks and towards the second week of January it was dislodged from its positions and withdrew in disarray. This unexpected turn of events postponed the German attack indefinitely. Of course, this was exactly what the Partisan command had hoped when the 10. Croatian Infantry Division had been attacked. An attempt was made to restore the combat readiness of the 10. Croatian Infantry Division in February when the Divisional Headquarters was relocated to Kamenica, just east of Karlovac. The Croatian forces had a few minor successes; most notably the re-conquest of Srijem in January and February 1945 and the retaking of Ljubbuski and Metkovic, but these were tactical victories which would not change the overall strategic situation.

The worst calamity to befall the Axis in the Balkans in February 1945 was the breakthrough at Mostar by the Partisans and the subsequent destruction of Croatian forces there. As the German Armed Forces High Command War Diary had forewarned, the withdrawal of the elements of the German *118. Jäger Division* for its supporting role in the upcoming German counter-attack in Hungary, *Unternehmen Frühlingserwachen* (Operation Spring Awakening), had left the flanks of the *369. (deutsch-kroatische) Infanterie Division*, which was defending Mostar, dangerously exposed. An attempt to stiffen the Axis defences there had been made when several fortress battalions from the *964. Festung Brigade* had been ordered there. Those battalions ordered to this threatened sector included the *12. Festung Infanterie Bataillon*, *16. Festung Infanterie Bataillon*, and *3. Festung Artillerie Bataillon*. Unfortunately for the defenders of Mostar, events there began to unfold very quickly in the beginning of February 1945, so much so that the fortress brigade arrived in time to take part only in the defence of Sarajevo.[7] The only other supporting unit in the area that could possibly lend the *369. (deutsch-kroatische) Infanterie Division* any help was the 6,000 men of the newly forming Croatian 9. Mountain Division. The German Armed

Forces High Command War Diary once again describes quite vividly, what transpired and the effects it had on the Axis military situation:

> On 10 February the Commander in Chief Southeast submitted a report on the situation at Mostar, which in the meantime had become worse. The enemy intended to cut off Mostar by envelopment from both sides and had concentrated ten brigades, including one armoured brigade, for this purpose. At the same time, Nevesinji was threatened by three brigades. The situation was similar to that which had occurred previously at Knin. The Croatian units were of no value and even the troops of the Croatian Legion [the *369. (deutsch-kroatische) Infanterie Division*] were no match for the enemy. Intending to hold Mostar, if possible, the Commander in Chief Southeast moved up all available elements of the 10. Mountain Corps, in spite of the fact that in doing so he weakened the Gorazde sector and deprived the 22. (Luftlande) Infanterie Division of their rear communications. To run a greater risk was not justified. The Commander in Chief Southeast requested permission to employ mobile tactics on both sides of Mostar and to withdraw from Nevesinji if necessary. Otherwise, the German cadre personnel would be endangered, the units of the Croatian Legion would break up, and the front could no longer be held together. To hold Nevesinji might mean the loss of all heavy equipment there. An early decision was requested. The Wehrmacht Operations Staff gave the approval. Permission to employ mobile tactics and to abandon Nevesinji was granted by telephone on the same day and was confirmed in writing on 12 February [1945]. However, the consent of the Führer was required for the withdrawal from Mostar.[8]

In the next four days, however, Partisan attacks proved too strong and too rapid for the German and Croatian forces to deflect. Mostar was enveloped and the fate of the capital city of the province of Herzegovina was sealed. The following report from the same war diary, dated 13:45 hours, 14 February 1945 describes the events:

> After the collapse of the front west of Mostar, during which the Croatian units had been routed, the enemy advanced to the commanding heights west and north of Mostar. Only weak German cadre units still offered resistance. After some initial success, the reconnaissance battalion of the 117. Jäger Division had been annihilated. All available forces were thrown into a counterattack against the enemy advancing eastward towards the exposed northern flank. Already the advance guard had reached Zandra, ten kilometres northeast of Mostar. The counterattack was intended to crush the enemy and to prevent the road to Sarajevo from being cut. Success was uncertain, and the situation was not expected to be restored even after the abandonment of Nevesinji, ordered for the night of 13

> February, and the employment of forces that had been committed there. Therefore, permission to evacuate Mostar was requested for the following reasons – a) Enemy forces north of Mostar had been strengthened. b) All available German forces had already been committed. c) Forces from the evacuated Visegrad bridgehead had arrived too late and in inadequate strength. d) The situation south of Sarajevo had become acute and required additional support. e) There was danger that the forces at Mostar would be encircled, thereby preventing the 21. Gebirgs Armeekorps from being in a position to intercept an enemy thrust further to the rear.[9]

By 16 February 1945 Mostar was in Partisan hands and the newly forming 9. Croatian Mountain Division had been smashed. Worse still, the *369. (deutsch-kroatische) Infanterie Division* had been routed and had lost all of its heavy weapons. Additionally, the unit had suffered an extremely heavy loss of German cadre officers:

> On 16 February the Commander in Chief Southeast reported on the loss of Mostar and the general plan of action which would follow. On the same day, the chief of staff of the army group reported by telephone that events at Mostar had taken the same turn as at Knin. The German cadre personnel had fought well but had lost two regimental and five battalion commanders. After troops of the 369. (deutsch-kroatische) Infanterie Division had run away, it had been impossible to hold the line alone. The Commander in Chief Southeast would report on the consequences of this action.[10]

The only successful operation of any significance that could be attributed to the Croatian Army in February 1945 was the combined Croatian-Cossack-German operation launched in the first week of February against Partisan forces in the region of Virovitica, near the Drava River. This was the operational area of the German *LIX. Armeekorps*. Code-named *Werwolf* (Werewolf), it was aimed at the estimated six partisan divisions which were identified operating in that area of Slavonia a month earlier. By the beginning of the second week in February the ancient town of Virovitica, complete with its very own castle, was recaptured by the Axis forces:

> 11 February 1945: Operation Werewolf: Virovitica was taken by storm on the afternoon of 9 February. The 7. SS Freiwilligen *Gebirgs* Division Prinz Eugen was able to affect a juncture with the 2. Kosaken Kavallerie Division. The attack continued to the north. A damaged bridge at Barcs was repaired. The enemy fell back. The 7. Croatian Division was to mop

up the area to the north. Southeast of Zagreb the situation was improved by the arrival of police forces.[11]

The units involved in this operation had included elements of *7. SS Freiwilligen Gebirgs Division Prinz Eugen , 297. Infanterie Division, 104. Jäger Division,* 1. Croatian Storm Division, *Poglavnik* Bodyguard Division, 7. Croatian Mountain Division, *1. Kosaken Kavallerie Division,* and *2. Kosaken Kavallerie Division*. The major Croatian unit which was employed was the 7. Mountain Division (led by General Stjepan Perčić).[12] By the end of the second week in February, Operation Werewolf was winding down:

> 13 February 1945 – Operation Werewolf: mopping up continued north of the Drava River. The 7. Croatian Division advanced slowly. South of Zagreb the situation was unchanged: It had not been possible to relieve a group encircled there. German forces still continued to resist at Bihac.[13]

Virovitica was not soon recaptured by the Partisans. In fact, it was the town in which the *15. Kosaken Kavallerie Korps* assembled in order to choose a new *Ataman* (leader of all Cossacks) in early March 1945.[14] The representatives of this all-Cossack Congress, from all of the regiments within the *15. Kosaken Kavallerie Korps,* assembled at the great hall in the old castle overlooking the town. They chose for the very first and last time a non-Cossack commander to lead them: German General von Pannwitz.[15] German forces were still continuing to resist at Bihac. It was there that the remnants of the German and Croatian forces, which perhaps numbered about 1,000 men, had been bypassed and surrounded in the following localities:[16]

1. Five hundred and sixty German troops with two French tanks and eight heavy machine guns at: Izacic, Papari, Muslic and Selo. These villages and hamlets were approximately 9km, 6km, and 5km northwest of Bihac, respectively.
2. A small German garrison in Turija, about 6km north-northwest of Bihac, with about twenty-five light machine guns, belonged to the *373. (deutsche-kroatische) Infanterie Division.*
3. The *1.* and *2. Kompanie* of the *II. Bataillon/646 Infanterie Regiment* in Pokoj, about 4km north of Bihac.[17]
4. The Veterinary Company of the 6. Croatian Infantry Division, located in Brekovica, about 7km north of Bihac.
5. Twenty-five Germans and seventy-five *Ustaše* troops surrounded in a bunker at Ostrozac, about 10km northeast of Bihac.

The German and Croatian withdrawal proved to be only partially successful, as the *369. (deutsch-kroatische) Infanterie Division* was reported in the OKW War Diary as having been wiped out alongside the 9. Croatian Mountain Division. A heavy loss of officers in the *369. (deutsch-kroatische) Infanterie Division* had weakened its command structure, which ultimately led to the Division's demise. Now the Partisan Army began to approach Sarajevo and Visegrad much closer, threatening the German and Croatian forces stationed there. On 21 February, the Partisans were reportedly making headway in their attacks against Travnik. The Germans blamed the Croatian forces there for the current guerrilla advances. On 24 February *Unternehmen Wehrwolf* was finally concluded, and a body count netted a grand total of 1,988 enemy guerrillas killed. The month of March 1945 saw an increase in Partisan advances and attacks all across Croatia. Croatian forces were particularly well engaged in fighting guerrilla units in the Papuk Mountains. Desertions from the Croatian Army still continued to plague the Croats, as the following German report stated:

> 18 March 1945: Additional Red Cross ships departed from Rhodes. Fighting continued in Sarajevo. After 120 men of a Croatian division deserted, the balance of the division was disarmed. Enemy reinforcements arrived at Doboy. Partisans were active again at Bihac.[18]

Four days later, on 22 March 1945 the Germans were once again blaming the Croatian Army units in the Bihac area of withdrawing and threatening German units there with encirclement as a result of their retreat.

Chapter 14

BIS ZUM BITTEREN ENDE

The situation in the Bihac area was so tenuous that the German *104. Jäger Division* was called upon to be shifted to that area as support. By 3 April the evacuation of Sarajevo had begun, and did not end until 7 April 1945. Bijeljina was likewise evacuated on 4 April, while Zenica was abandoned on 12 April 1945. An *Ustaše* battle group, nicknamed 'Battlegroup Nardelli' after its commander, made initial headway from Bijeljina, but was soon blocked from escaping and returned to the town for lack of ammunition. Their fate most likely was a grim one as the Partisans were not prone to taking *Ustaše* prisoner, especially at this late stage in the war. The logic being that only the most loyal and fanatical *Ustaše* would remain fighting by this time. A list of the still-employable Croatian Army units was listed by the Germans in their OKW War Diary entry for 5 April 1945:

1. Infantry Corps: Zagreb.[1]
    - *Poglavnik* Bodyguard Division, stationed in Zagreb and surrounding area.
    - 2. Croatian Infantry Division, stationed in Zagreb and surrounding area.
    - 16. Croatian Training & Replacement Division, stationed in Zagreb and surrounding area.
    - 1. Croatian Storm Division, stationed in Zagreb and surrounding area.
    - Croatian Mobile Brigade, stationed in Dugo Selo (east of Zagreb).[2]
    - Croatian Infantry Division – Bjelovar.
2. Infantry Corps: Brod.
    - 6. Croatian Infantry Division, stationed in Dubica
    - 7. Croatian Infantry Division, stationed in Bred area.
    - 14. Croatian Infantry Division, stationed in Bred area.
    - 15. Croatian Infantry Division, stationed in Doboj.

Under the German *XXXIV. Armeekorps:*[3]

3. Croatian Infantry Division stationed Vinkovci.

12. Croatian Infantry Division stationed in Brcko, then Doboj.[4]

3. Infantry Corps: Sarajevo.

8. Croatian Infantry Division was located in Sarajevo.

The battlegroup of the 9. Croatian Mountain Division was located west-southwest of Sarajevo, then it moved and was located around Gevesnica and Bjelovar.

Under the German *XXI. Gebirgs Armeekorps*:

Kampfgruppe of the *369. (deutsch-kroatische) Infanterie Division*, located at Senj, just northwest of Bihac. The division withdrew from the town when Senj was captured by Tito's partisans on 8 April 1945.

Under the German *XV. Gebirgs Armeekorps*:

The remnants of *392. (deutsch-kroatische) Infanterie Division* who, at this time, like the *369. (deutsch-kroatische) Infanterie Division*, was located in and around Senj. Like its sister division, it withdrew from Senj when it was taken by partisan forces on 8 April 1945. The 10. Croatian Infantry Division was at Bihac after its recapture in March 1945, then it was moved to Sisak.[5] At this time, the *373. (deutsch-kroatische) Infanterie Division* was marching towards Bihac. A battlegroup of the 11. Croatian Infantry Division – Moved from Diroselo, then to Gospic, Perusic, and Otocac. At Otocac, the remnants of the 11. Croatian Infantry Division put up a brave defence, but the town was lost on 17 April 1945.

Under the German *LXIX. Armeekorps*:

13. Croatian Infantry Division – Karlovac.

Croatian Infantry Division – Bjelovar (see 1. Croat Infantry Corps).

The 13. Croatian Infantry Division was reformed in April 1945 to include the following units:

28. Infantry Regiment
29. Infantry Regiment
Corps Reconnaissance Battalion
Ustaše Replacement Battalion
Ustaše Engineer Battalion.[6]
Artillery Group
1. Artillery Battery
2. Artillery Battery

The 13. Croatian Infantry Division now had a complement of six infantry battalions and two artillery batteries, with a total strength of around 6,000 men. The 5. Croatian Infantry Division began reorganizing itself as an 'assault' division in April 1945. It did not become fully operational again until early May. Its new units included the 23. Infantry Assault Regiment, located in Koprivnica and Pogacnik, the 24. Infantry Assault Regiment (in Bjelovar), and the 25. Infantry Assault Regiment in Ciglena, Trojstvo, and the Zlijeb Forest area. Total strength was around 6,000 troops. It was assigned to the *Poglavnik* Bodyguard Corps in mid-April 1945. A newly-forming unit which came into existence in April 1945 was the 18. Croatian Assault Division. It had been formed from the following units:

a) Remnants of the *Ustaše* Camp Brigade, most of which was smashed by the partisans in March 1945.
b) 19. *Ustaše* Brigade
c) 11. *Ustaše* Brigade
d) 4. Garrison Brigade.[7]

The 18. Croatian Assault Infantry Division looked on paper as follows:

30. Infantry Assault Regiment
31. Infantry Assault Regiment
32. Infantry Assault Regiment
No support units whatsoever.

The Croatian command, as can be seen, completely ignored the German refusal to allow the formation of an elite Croatian corps. They picked their best divisions and assigned them to the 1. Infantry Corps, which was soon re-designated as the '*Poglavnik* Bodyguard Corps.' In addition, two new corps commands were established in mid-April: the 4. & 5. *Ustaše* Corps. The 2. and 3. Corps were also renamed *Ustaše*. By the beginning of May 1945, the Croatian corps commands were located as follows:

North of the Sava River: *Poglavnik* Bodyguard Corps (4½ divisions), 4. *Ustaše* Corps (three divisions).
South of the Sava River: 2. *Ustaše* Corps (three divisions), 3. *Ustaše* Corps, 5. *Ustaše* Corps.

Total NDH strength, counting the regular Army and *Ustaše* units, was around 150,000 men although one source puts the number at around 200,000.[8] Still a third source states that the figure was exactly 220,000 men.[9] A more logical figure as to the actual number of Croatian troops that were still in the field, would be somewhere in the neighbourhood of 130,000–150,000.[10] The difference in these varying figures may or may not take into account the Croatian Legion divisions (i.e. the *369., 373.,* and *392.* (*deutsch-kroatische*)

Infanterie Division), but in the penultimate case, the figure of 220,000 is for Croatian troops that surrendered at Blieburg, and the Croatian-German Legion divisions were supposedly not among them. By April 1945, these three Legion divisions were almost completely depleted. In fact, towards the end of the war, the *392. (deutsch-kroatische) Infanterie Division* had to resort to blending their weakened battalions with the local *Ustaše* unit in the area of Otocac, men from the 4. *Ustaše* Brigade.[11]

This may have been a very practical move on the part of the *Ustaše* brigade, since closer ties between both units probably prevented either of them from being completely destroyed, and the presence of the German officers in the *392. (deutsch-kroatische) Infanterie Division* probably helped to keep the majority of the *Ustaše* troops from losing heart. The slow destruction of the Croat-German Legion divisions would continue however. For example, on 28 April 1945 the *369. (deutsch-kroatische) Infanterie Division* could only boast of having an effective combat strength of only 515 men in its entire *370. Infanterie Regiment*. The other regiments in the division were in a similar state. By 9 May 1945, the total number of men still in the division was 3,036 (160 officers and 2,876 NCOs and enlisted men). On 17 April 1945 *369. (deutsch-kroatische) Infanterie Division* arrived north of Brod, while in Syrmia the entire Axis line of defence was being pulled back. Sarajevo had already been evacuated on 6 April, and the German *XXI. Gebirgs Armeekorps* was now located in the Zagreb area. Already the *XCI. Armeekorps* had assumed responsibility for northwestern Croatia, while its former sector was given to the German *XXXIV. Armeekorps*.

Towards the end of April, the *373. (deutsch-kroatische) Infanterie Division* was fighting the partisans in the area of Kostajnica, but by 3 May 1945 the division was withdrawing towards Sisak. From there it next moved towards Zagreb. The *392. (deutsch-kroatische) Infanterie Division* was located north of Rijeka (Fiume) in late April. On 24 April it released all of its Croatian personnel from further service. Its German cadre then withdrew towards the Austrian border. On 11 May 1945 the *369. (deutsch-kroatische) Infanterie Division* surrendered and was disarmed between Goricica and Prosenisko. Close to 3,000 men of this division managed to reach Blieburg, just inside the Austrian border. There they surrendered to advancing British armoured forces.

The first week of April 1945 saw the last anti-Partisan drive launched just west of the Papuk Mountain range, between the towns of Daruvar and Pakrac. A total of four Partisan brigades were estimated to be in this region, and the units of the German *XXXIV. Armeekorps*, which had recently taken over this sector, were used to launch this last operation against the guerrilla enclave. Elements of the German *117. Jäger Division, 41. Festung Division,* and the ethnic-German *7. SS Freiwilligen Gebirgs Division Prinz Eugen,* were all employed against the Partisans. In addition, the Croatian 7. Infantry Division was used as a blocking force during this last sweep.

A minor Croatian success had occurred from 10–13 April, when the Croatian 3. Infantry Division (led by General Stjepan Mifek) had been able to delay a partisan drive against Vinkovci. This town fell on 13 April however, as did the towns of Vukovar and Osijek. Valpovo fell on 14 April and Donji Miholjac on 15 April. Gospic and Otocac were evacuated after 29 April 1945, as the newly reformed 11. Croatian Infantry Division fought its way from Gospic to Zagreb. The communist forces that had been assembled for the final push to capture the Croatian capital and included the following formations:

> In the area of the upper Drava River his [Tito's] 3. Army was stationed; Seven divisions with 95,000 men. In Syrmia was the 1. Army: ten divisions with 130,000 men. In northern Bosnian Croatia was the 2. Army with twelve divisions and 100,000 men and in Central Dalmatian Croatia the 4. Army with fourteen divisions and 95,000 men. Tito organized seven divisions as army reserve. In addition to these troops at his disposal, were the Soviet armoured corps and Bulgarian units. Everything was ready for a frontal attack against the rest of Croatia.[12]

In the region of the Drava and Sava Rivers the Partisan 3. Army was operating. It was in this area that one regiment of the newly organized 18. Croatian Assault Division launched a limited, though successful counter-attack which temporarily reconquered Bubanj – an important high plateau and arrived at Virovitica. Another minor feat was the successful Axis defence of the region between Hecegovac and Garesnica, along the Ilova River. Here the *7. SS Freiwilligen Gebirgs Division Prinz Eugen* and remnants of the *369. (deutsch-kroatische) Infanterie Division* took part. Croatian units involved in this operation included the 8. Croatian Infantry Division, and 9. Croatian Mountain Division of the 3. Croatian Corps. By 1 May however, the order to withdraw was given, and the Germans and their Croatian partners left the Ilova River and headed north. The newly created 18. Croatian Assault Division was later cut-off, due in part to the right of the German *11. Feld Division* (L) on its flank, after a brave stand at

Djakovo. On account of this encirclement, the 18. Assault Division was almost wiped out.

On 5 May the German *41. Festung Division* and the Croatian 7., 8. and 9. Division withdrew northwest of Ivanicgrad. A day later they retreated even further, to Dugoselo and Vrbovac, just east of Zagreb. The Croatian Storm Division was holding positions around Bjelovar in the beginning of May, but was soon ordered to withdraw along with the rest of the Croatian Army. On 6 May the Croatian government left the capital city of Zagreb and headed for Carinthia, along the Austrian-Slovene border region. Ante Pavelić had already fled the city and eventually managed to escape to Argentina by being smuggled through Italy under the protection of sympathetic Croatian Catholic clergy with connections to the Vatican. The Croatian Army and its command were thus left to fend for themselves in the first week of May 1945. What remained of the top Croatian Army officer corps was formed into an ad-hoc headquarters which not only included senior NDH generals and colonels, but high-ranking civilian officials as well.

Some of those loyal Croatian generals and colonels who remained by their troops at this, their most desperate time, included General Herencic, Metikos, Servatzy, and Generals Boban and Pericic. General Moskov also refused to abandon his post, preferring to remain as commanding officer of the '*Poglavnik* Bodyguard Corps'. As stated earlier, perhaps between 130,000–220,000 Croatian troops, and about 100,000 civilians now began to withdraw north through Slovenia in an attempt to reach Austria in order to avoid having to surrender to the communist partisans and the fate that awaited them under Tito. Again, I emphasize how inaccurate the figure of 220,000 Croatian soldiers is, given this period of the war. At best, no more than 130,000–150,000 troops were left in the Croatian Army. I believe that the figure of 220,000 troops is a mistake, and probably occurred by adding the number of civilians (100,000) who accompanied the withdrawing Croatian army. Tito's guerrilla army entered Zagreb on 10 May 1945. Between 9–10 May 1945 the main Croatian column moved through Slovenj Gradec (Windischgrätz in German) in Slovenia. On 11 May Davograd (Unterdrauberg in German) was reached and then the column was halted just south of the town.

Beyond Davograd lay the Austrian border and what was hoped would be political asylum for all Croatians who were fleeing the partisan advance. Blocking any further advance of the Croatian Army was the Slovenian 51. Partisan Division, which had taken up positions in and around Davograd. It was a very brave move on the part of this lone Slovene Partisan division, especially in light of the fact that no further Slovene Partisan support could be expected any time soon. This 'division' only had a few thousand men in its ranks. This was an especially risky act, given that the bulk of the elite Croatian divisions were spearheading the NDH column. Wishing merely to retire into Austria, and not wanting any further bloodshed, the Croatian command made several attempts to peacefully pass through the town, but were denied passage by the Slovene communists, who responded by launching a mortar attack on the leading Croatian Army positions, beginning at 14:00 hours on Sunday, 13 May 1945. The Croatians were given no choice but to fight. The large Croatian column was now deployed in the following manner:

a) On the left flank was General Boban's 5. Croatian Infantry Division, with Colonels Slaher and Servatzy.
b) In the centre was the 2. Croatian Infantry Division, reinforced by a company of *Ustaše* tanks of mixed Italian, German and French origin, and a reinforced complement of Croatian policemen of *Polizei Bataillon Kroatien III* that had made the withdrawal all the way from Banja Luka.
c) On the right flank were the remnants of the Montenegro Volunteer Corps which had been recently seized by Serbian separatist, Dr Sekula Drljevic, and renamed the Montenegrin National Army.

The bulk of the *Poglavnik* Bodyguard Corps was not committed initially in order to keep some elite units in reserve. The 'Montenegrin National Army,' headed by General Milan Pencic, was a pro-Croatian former Yugoslav Army officer who was an adherent of Dr Sekula Drljevic. These Montenegrin *Chetniks* were loath to squander their men in any fight, so could not be called on to make a determined attack against the blockading Slovenian Partisan force, unless absolutely pressed. Croatian artillery batteries soon began responding to the communist mortar attack, supporting the NDH forces at the head of the column, which were now deploying to attack. The Montenegrins, plus the Croatian 2. and 5. Infantry Division were ordered to make a frontal assault against Davograd and seize the town by storm. In spite of a furious defence put up by the companies of the 51. Partisan Division, the leading Croatian Army assault units entered the northern Slovenian town by the following morning.

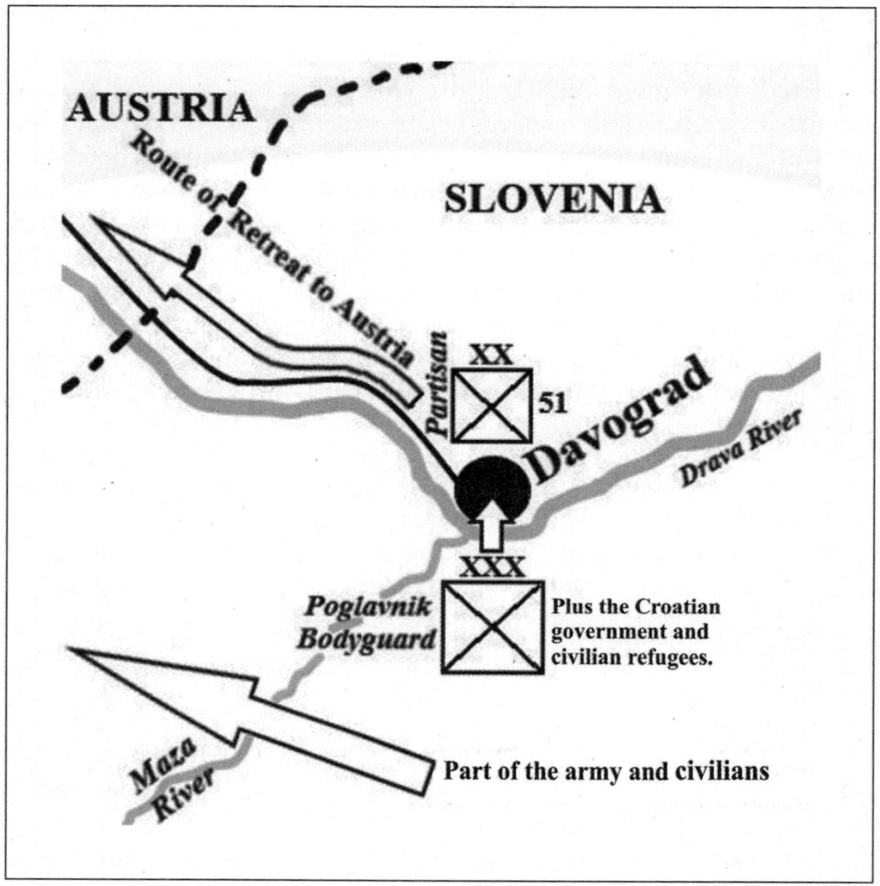

Figure 31. The fight for Davograd, 13 May 1945. (*Author's line drawing*)

The battle was fierce and according to the accounts, no quarter was given and no quarter was asked. The Slovenian partisans showed great bravery knowing that they faced the entire Croatian Army. The Croatians for their part, showed unrelenting rage against men who were intending to prevent their flight, and by virtue, condemn both Croatian soldiers and civilians to the 'mercy' of the Tito communists. After breaking through the Slovenian partisan division, parts of the Croatian Army column wasted no time in continuing the march, but the delay had cost them one very valuable and precious day. The bulk of the Croat forces and civilians however, had veered left, crossing the lesser Meza River just north of Crna and on towards the Austrian border. The NDH forces were now moving west-northwest in the direction of the frontier crossing by Blieburg. This move had been necessitated by the fact that strong Partisan forces had arrived north of Davograd and were blocking any northern withdrawal towards the Austrian border town of Lavamund. On Monday, 14 May the leading Croatian column again came under intense fire and the *Ustaše* tank company was once again called forward. This *Ustaše* mechanized unit was led by a very daring First Lieutenant, named Kovacevic.

He would be one of tens of thousands killed brutally after the Croatian prisoners were handed back to Tito's communists by the British Army. Once again, the road was being blocked by a unit of the Slovenian partisans. The delay in having to fight their way through the town of Davograd, had allowed time in which additional Slovene partisan forces could be brought in. In fact, earlier in the day the same Slovenian guerrillas had ambushed a German column trying to escape into Austria. The burning and charred metal carcasses of that earlier column were still lying in and around the roadside when the Croatian column came upon them and was attacked themselves. Between 08:00 and 17:00 hours the Croatians attacked what turned out to be elements of the Slovenian 14. Partisan Division. This unit had been thought wiped out in February 1944, but the formation had performed so well, that the Partisan Command had revived the division in the summer of 1944, replenishing her ranks with almost 90 per cent new personnel. Once again, the now desperate Croatians broke through the ambush and by that same afternoon of 14 May the leading elements of the entire Croatian Armed Forces were immediately south of the Austrian border town of Blieburg.[13] It was there that they first encountered a British armoured column that halted their advance. Croatian attempts to move further into Austria were met by the following response from the English commander: 'All Croatian forces are to surrender and return to Yugoslavia. If Croatian troops resist and fight their way through, British tanks and aircraft will open fire.'[14]

By far the largest Croatian column was the one which headed for Blieburg, but smaller NDH columns also fought their way through Slovenia to try and reach Austria and Italy. Approximately 35,000 reached Klagenfurt and 5,000 headed towards St. Paul-Wolfsberg-Judenberg, while about 210,000 soldiers and civilians were stopped at Bleiburg.[15] Not wanting to fight the Western Allies whom Croatia had no quarrel with, and in order to prevent further civilian casualties, the Croatian command council decided that resistance would be futile, irresponsible, and counterproductive. They thus agreed to lay down their arms and surrender to the British, although they agreed to vigorously resist their forced repatriation into almost certain death, regardless of any guilt. The British agreed to these conditions, mainly because they wished to disarm the Croatian Army in order to avoid taking further casualties – especially after the war was over. The promise of refuge from repatriation was conveniently left up to decide at a later date. The Croatian capitulation party included General Ivo Herecic and Vjekoslav Servatzy, along with the *Ustaše* Colonel Danijel Crlen.[16] As early as 17 May 1945 about 7,000 Croatian officers were gathered up in Krumpendorf near Klagenfurt, and told that they would be transported to Italy, where they were to be given asylum. Captain Josip Hecimovic, a Croatian *Domobran* officer, vividly described what transpired next, and shows what awaited the rest of the Croatian Army and civilian authorities:

> A British delegation arrived at Krumpendorf and a high-ranking officer gave a speech. General Rupcic translated it. We were to go to Italy. In Italy the Croatian Armed Forces would be given asylum. Croatian officers and soldiers obeyed the command and loaded the men on trucks. We were taken to a railway station near the border. We left by train before evening. We arrived at Jasenica, Slovenia instead of Italy. Of course, we discovered now that we had been deceived, but nothing could be done about it. The train stopped at Jasenica, where over a thousand Communist soldiers besieged us. Some of them ran into the train shooting at us officers. There were only officers in this transport. They drove us out of the train and filed us in ranks along the track. Shouts from the enemy soldiers ensued – 'Did you think that you could escape? One yelled 'At any rate you came into our hands and now we'll judge you!' They began to question each individual about his rank in the army and his home town in Croatia. Immediately they separated some and shot them in the necks with revolvers. Frightful things occurred before our eyes. We had no protection from anyone. We were disarmed and so could not defend ourselves. This was just the beginning of the tragedy and of the many pains which Croatian soldiers and citizens suffered in Tito's death marches. We were not treated in the way prisoners of war should be treated. All over the world, the armies that had capitulated were afforded prisoner's rights and later were permitted to live as free citizens. This was not granted to the Croatian Army nor to the Croatians. Instead of being sent back to our homes, for the war had ended on all European battlefields, we, the Croatian soldiers and citizens, had to undergo sufferings and losses which exceeded by far the war pains and casualties. After the war ceased, our way of the Cross began! There followed mass executions, slaughters, tortures, poisonings, and atrocities that are almost inconceivable to the human mind.[17]

The rest of the Croatian Armed Forces and the accompanying civilian refugees were treated in much the same manner, regardless of whether they were responsible for any war crimes or not. The manner in which they were killed is a testament to the characteristic Balkan cruelty when it comes to taking revenge. The numbers of people killed is quite staggering:

Near Maribor (Marburg) – 40,000.
Near Kocevje – 30,000.
Near Tesko Celo (St. Vid) – 25,000.[18]

In addition, perhaps around 30,000 more were murdered in the following localities:

Huda Luknja – 9,600
Bezigrad – 450
Hrastnik – 700
Lasko – 700
Reichenberg – 400
Kostanjevica – 700
Crna – 300
Kamnik – 450
Near Zagreb – 11,000
Gracani – 600
Sosice – 500
Vrgin Most – 1,300
Dubocac – 350
Podravski Kiostar – 250
Virovitica – 300
Butmir-Kasindol – 350
Kravarsko – 500
Sisak – 1,550

The Croatian author and former death march survivor Josip Hecimovic has stated that the deaths which occurred in the above localities (not including those at St. Vid, Kocevje, and Maribor) totalled an astounding 163,000 killed.[19] This number, even when taking into account civilian losses, seems a bit high. German estimates vary as to how many Croatians were killed after they were handed back to the Tito communists. One states that around 100,000 were killed,[20] while other figures claim that between 100,000 and 150,000 were murdered.[21] One other source, published in Zagreb in 1990, states that only 60,000 'Quislings' lost their lives in the death marches during the summer of 1945.

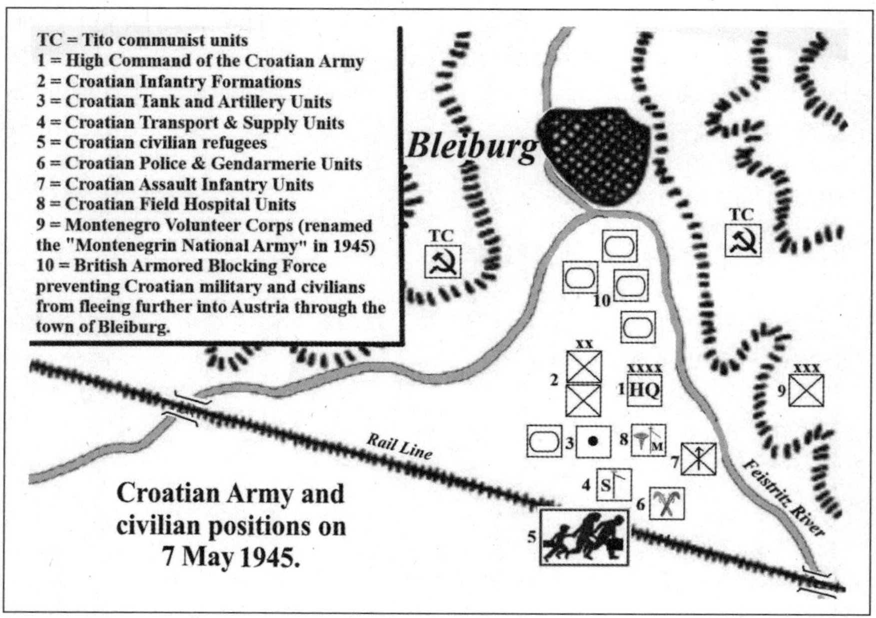

Figure 32. Final positions of the Croatian Army, 7 May 1945.

And of that number, around 10,000 were German soldiers.[22] While one is keen on believing that around 10,000 Germans were caught up in this Croatian *Gotterdämerung*, enough contradictory evidence exists to suggest that more than 60,000 Croatian soldiers were killed. This source, although published in Croatia, may be suspect to bias. The same can be said however, about the figures quoted by Captain Hecimovic. The truth certainly lies somewhere in between. What caused such cruelties to be inflicted on the Croatian nation? We must return again to the Balkan mentality of an eye for an eye, and then some! The *Ustaše* atrocities had the most detrimental effect on the Croatian state, for they were like recruiting posters for the Chetnik and communist guerrilla movements. But what of the 'Jewish question' in Croatia? Of the estimated 70,000 Jews living in Yugoslavia at the beginning of the war 21,000 lived in the newly created Independent State of Croatia in April 1941.

Of that number exactly 12,315 were living in Zagreb alone, while 8,000 were living in the countryside.[23] In the autumn of 1941 3,600 Jews were interned in the Croatian camps of Jasenovac, Laborgrad, Stara Gradisca, and Gredjarn while 2,400 were in the camp at Pag Island, which also housed around 4,500 Serbians. Upon hearing that the Italian Army was going to occupy the island, the *Ustaše* killed 4,500 of the estimated 6,900 Serbs and Jews in the camp.[24] By 1942 the Jewish community in Zagreb had been reduced to about 4,000 since around 7,000 had fled to the Italian zone where they were safe from persecution. Of these 7,000 people about 4,500 sought refuge in Dubrovnik. Once Italy surrendered 2,662 of the 7,000 Jews in Italian territory were caught in German sweeps and were eventually sent to Auschwitz. From Croatia an additional 4,927 Jews were also sent to Auschwitz in 1942.[25]

There was no love lost between the *Ustaše* and the Jewish population in Croatia. Like all extreme nationalistic political movements, the society that the *Ustaše* fanatics wanted to create was exclusive, not inclusive. Hundreds of years of religious intolerance in the Balkan Peninsula did not help the situation. No precise figures can be obtained as to how many of the Jews in the mainland camps were killed, but a rough total figure of just how many Croatian Jews were killed in Croatia, or deported to concentration camps seem to be 12,589. When we compare this last figure in relation to the total number of Jews estimated to be living within the Yugoslav borders in 1941 (about 60,000), we come up with a figure of 21 per cent of the Jews killed or deported. While Serbian groups have always pointed an accusing finger at the Croatian people, we must realize that it was a miniscule few who perpetrated these acts, and the Croatian nation should not be held accountable for the acts of the *Ustaše* fanatics.

Serbian circles have repeatedly pointed out how they and the Jewish community suffered terrible abuses at the hands of the 'Croatian Fascists.' Yet a published work conclusively shows that Serbians participated in *pogroms* against the Jewish community of Yugoslavia, and their wartime propaganda showed it.[26] Serbian losses at the hands of the *Ustaše* massacres have been estimated to have been as high as 750,000 by post-war Yugoslav communist government figures. A figure of 200,000 killed seems to be a more precise picture. One other source, which also quotes another official history estimates that the number of Serbians, Romani, and Jews killed in the entire Yugoslavia during the war was around 350,000.[27] This larger number of 350,000 probably also includes those Serbian communist military combatants lost through the war effort, plus those civilians who were killed by the tens of thousands who were unfortunate enough to be living in the war zone and who suffered through indirect fire, bombings, reprisal shootings by the Germans, etc. Another 240,000 Serbians were forcibly converted to Catholicism, and thereby saving themselves from persecution, before this practice was stopped. General Lothar Rendulic, a German officer who led troops in the Balkans, and was very intimately aware of the inner workings of the Croatian state, had this to say regarding the *Ustaše* actions and their repercussions:

> While German troops were still in several places in Croatia, the Croatians began a beastly persecution of the Orthodox. At this time at least a half million people were killed. An unbelievable governing mentality was responsible, as I heard in August 1943 when I received the answer to a question of mine from a government functionary in the circle of the Chief of State. When I said that I could not at all understand how it was possible, in spite of all hatred, to kill half a million people, he answered: Half a million is libelous. No more than 200,000 were killed! Against that type of thinking, one can do nothing with arguments. During the period of my command, signs appeared of a new persecution of the Orthodox. That persecution caused me no end of trouble and I finally had to put a stop to it with energetic measures and threats of force.[28]

Recently, an impartial investigation into just how many people perished in the Croatian camp of Jasenovac revealed that about 165,000 human beings died there. Although this is a far cry from the 1,500,000 espoused by the post-war Yugoslav government, it is nevertheless a frightening figure.[29] The Serbians also are guilty of crimes, since they too had begun to practice genocide on the Muslim and Croatian Catholic population from almost the very beginning of the war. Whether this was in response to the *Ustaše* persecution or vice-a-versa is irrelevant in so far as the cruelties that were perpetrated by all parties involved meant that they all equally had a share of the guilt. Serbian Chetnik attacks against the Croatian population in the villages of Ilici, Cim, and other small hamlets in Herzegovina were performed as early as 13–16 April 1941. This campaign of terror continued into June especially in the localities of Avtovac, Ljubinje, and Nevesinje.

The districts of Vlasenica, Srebrenica, Bogatica, Visegrad, Gorazde, Cajnice, and Foca were all hit by the Chetniks, who tried to kill off as much of the Croatian population as possible. In Foca itself, an estimated 1,000 Croatian men, women, and children were slaughtered while in the surrounding countryside another 5,000–6,000 Croatians lost their lives.[30] The Muslim population was not spared the wrath of the Chetnik murder spree, nor later, the communist retribution that was meted out. In December 1941 and January 1942 Chetnik attacks caused the lives of some 2,000 Muslims in the region of Foca, in southeastern Bosnia. The *Ustaše* even joined in these attacks, killing an additional 500 Muslims in the same region. It is interesting to note that in a reversal of their earlier policies, these same *Ustaše* units began recruiting the Muslim population into the Croatian Armed Forces in 1942. In late August 1942 additional killings of the Muslim population occurred. This time the Chetniks were at it once again. The worst atrocities happened in the pre-dominantly Muslim region of the Sandzak (Sandjak), and are vividly described by the following quote:

> The worst of the Chetnik terror against the Muslims occurred in Sandjak and southeastern Bosnia in January and February 1943. According to a statement originating with the Chetnik Supreme Command dated 24 February 1943, these were punitive counter measures prompted by the 'aggressive actions of the Muslims who attacked Serbian villages and killed some Serbian people'. Chetnik units which had been mobilized in December 1942 in Montenegro and readied for the planned but delayed 'March on Bosnia' were ordered early in January and again early in February to undertake what were known as 'cleansing actions' against the Muslims, first in the county of Bijelo Polje in Sandjak and in February in the county of Cajnice and part of the county of Foca in southeastern Bosnia, and in part of the county of Pijevlja in Sandjak. Chetnik losses were minimal; Muslim losses were estimated at about 10,000 persons. More details are revealed in the reports that Major Djurisic, the officer in charge of these operations, submitted to the Chief of Staff of the Supreme Command (Mihailovic). According to Djurisic's report of January 10th, thirty-three Muslim villages had been burned down, and 400 Muslim fighters (members of the Muslim self-protection militia supported by the Italians) and about 1,000 women and children had been killed, as against 14 Chetnik dead and 26 wounded. The cleansing action carried out in early February took an even more staggering toll: according to Djurisic's report of February 13th, in this action the Chetniks killed about 1,200 Muslim fighters and about 8,000 old people, women, and children. Chetnik losses in the action were 22 killed and 32 wounded.[31]

What all of these reports and numbers show is that the war in Yugoslavia was fought uncompromisingly by all sides involved. Given the very nature of the war, we can argue that aside from the *Ustaše* fanatics, the Croatian Army behaved incredibly chivalrous towards that part of the population that did not wish to see itself in an independent Croatian state. The regular Croatian draftee was fighting not for the extermination of any race, as they were fighting for a free Croatia.

It is thus unfortunate that initially, the Italians did not allow the Germans to install a more moderate Croatian government, as they had wanted. This fact alone makes the tragedy of Bleiburg, where both the guilty and the innocent were made to pay equally all the more tragic. But in all wars, it is the victor, who gets to judge the vanquished, and in the case of the Croatian Army, they would not be the exception to this rule, rather they would be the perfect example of this old maxim.

The final order of battle for the Croatian Army in mid-May 1945 was as follows:

Poglavnik Bodyguard Corps (General Ante Moskov)
Poglavnik Bodyguard Division
1. Croatian Storm Division
2. Croatian Infantry Division
5. Croatian Infantry Division
16. Croatian *Ustaše* Training & Replacement Division.
Croatian Mobile Brigade (two mobile battalions & 1 battery)
2. *Ustaše* Corps (General Vjekoslav Maks Luburic)[32]
12. Croatian Infantry Division
14. Croatian Infantry Division
18. Croatian Infantry Division
3. *Ustaše* Corps (General Metzger)
3. Croatian Infantry Division
7. Croatian Infantry Division
8. Croatian Infantry Division
9. Croatian Infantry Division
4. *Ustaše* Corps (Unknown)
4. Croatian Infantry Division
6. Croatian Infantry Division
15. Croatian Infantry Division
5. *Ustaše* Corps (General Herencic)
10. Croatian Infantry Division
11. Croatian Infantry Division
13. Croatian Infantry Division

It appeared from anyone looking at the situation, that the Croatian Army was in an impossible position. This was the story of that impossible military situation, and how the NDH forces were able to overcome these challenges. In the end, in spite of deficiencies in all types of armaments and weapons; of having to fight two separate guerrilla movements (the communists an Serbian Chetniks) from the very start of the war; and in spite of being hamstrung by a meddling Italy and Germany, the Croatian nation was able to field and maintain an army that served her cause to the bitter end. What better praise can any army ever receive than this?

Figure 33. Silhouette of the Hotchkiss H 39 tank. The Croatian Army employed several of these tanks, as well as Italian-made CV-33 tankettes, Czech 35(t) and German Panzer III tanks.

Figure 34. Silhouette of the German Panzer III/N tank. The Croatian Army employed twenty-five of these vehicles.

Figure 35. The FIAT Ansaldo Carro Veloce 33. It was a turretless tankette that carried twin 6.5mm machine guns. The vehicle was little more than a small armoured car. It was outmatched even against light tanks. Because of this, the Italian tank crews sarcastically nicknamed them the 'mobile coffin', because its crew were sure to get killed in them.

Figure 36. The Czech-built 35-T tank. It was built between 1936–40 by Škoda, ČKD. A total of 434 vehicles were produced. It carried a 37mm KwK 34(t) anti-tank gun.

We know for sure that the Croatian Armed Forces received the following armoured vehicles between 1941 and 1945: ten Italian CV 33/35 tankettes, four Polish TKS tankettes, twenty-five Panzer III/N tanks, ten Panzer IV/F1 tanks, five Panzer IV/G tanks and fifteen SdKfz. 251 halftracks. In addition, the Croatian Army initially employed a few old French Renault FT tanks from the First World War.

Appendix I

THE CROATIAN AIR FORCE, 1941–1945

Figure 37. The Croatian Air Force emblem.

The air wing of the Croatian Armed Forces was composed of the 4th Croatian Air Force Regiment (*4. zrakoplovna pukovnija*). This unit contained the 4th Fighter Wing, and the 4th and 5th Bomber Wings. The Armed Forces of the Kingdom of Yugoslavia surrendered on 17 April 1941 to a combined invasion of German, Italian and Hungarian forces. Croatia, which had in December 1918 helped to form Yugoslavia, known as the Kingdom of the Serbs, Croats, and Slovenes until 1928, took the opportunity and declared its independence on 10 April 1941. The Croatian Air Force Legion (*Hrvatska zrakoplovna legia*) was established in Zagreb in July 1941 with 360 officers, NCOs and men. All of these men were volunteers. It was organized to support *Luftwaffe* operations during the invasion of the Soviet Union.

Command of the Croatian Air Force Legion was given to Colonel Ivan Mrak. The Legion was composed of the 4th Air Force Regiment. This unit contained the 4th and 5th Bomber Wings. These two bomber wings were commanded by Major Franjo Dzal. Major Dzal led fifteen officers, ninety-three NCOs and ninety-five men in two units, the 10th and 11th Fighter Squadrons.

The 5th Bomber Wing was under the control of Major Vjekoslav Vicevic. This Wing contained the 12th and 13th Bomber Squadrons with a grand total of thirty-seven officers, 110 NCOs and five airmen. Later on, Major Vladimir Graovac would take control of this bomber Wing. On 15 July 1941 the Croatian Air Force Legion left for Germany for training. The 4th Wing was moved to an airfield near Fürth, while the 5th Wing was sent to two air bases near Greifswald. By September 1941 the fighter squadrons were ready. On 6 October the 10th Squadron was sent to the Eastern Front. The 11th Squadron followed in December 1941. The Wing formed part of the German 3rd Air Wing of the 52nd *Luftwaffe* Fighter Group (III/JG 52), of the 4th Air Fleet. This German air fleet was attached to Army Group South, which was then advancing through Ukraine. A chronic shortage of fighter aircraft forced the Wing to reorganize in January 1942 as the Reinforced 10th Fighter Squadron (*Ojacano 10. lovacko jato*). In April, the designation: 'Dzal's Fighter Wing' (*'Lovacka skupina Dzal'*) was officially established. Its German designation however, was 15th Fighter Squadron/52nd Fighter Group. The unit flew its Messerschmitt Bf 109s very successfully against the Red Air Force, scoring 263 combat kills. Fourteen pilots gained ace status, each destroying at least ten enemy aircraft. The top ace was Lieutenant Mato Dukovac, with forty victories to his credit. The Bomber Wing served on the Eastern Front for eight months, from October 1941 till February 1942 as 10th Squadron/3rd Bomber Wing (10/KG3). The Croatian airmen employed the Dornier Do 17 bomber. They used this German plane from June to October 1942 as the 15th Croatian Squadron of the 53rd Bomber Group (15 Kroatische Schwadron/53-KG), operating the Junkers Ju 88 bomber under 1st Air Fleet, which was attached to Army Group Centre in Belorussia (White Russia). The Wing carried out a grand total of 1,332 combat missions before returning to Croatia in October 1942. On 21 July 1944 the Croatian Air Force Legion was disbanded. It was regrouped as the Croatian Air Force Training Wing (*Hrvatska zrakoplovna izobrazbena skupina*). The Wing was led by Colonel Dzal. It possessed two squadrons, 15/JG52, which was still operating in Ukraine,[1] and the newly formed 1st Croatian Dive-Bomber Squadron (*1. Kroatische Stukastaffel*). This squadron contained six Junkers Ju 87R2s under 9th Ground Attack Group (SG9). Initially, the Wing saw action in East Prussia, but was later sent to Posen, West Prussia, and later to Frankfurt in February 1945. Most of the airmen managed to return to Croatia by March 1945.

Principal Planes Employed

Figure 38. The Messerschmidt Bf 109 fighter.

Figure 39. The Junkers Ju 87 R2 dive-bomber

Figure 40. The Dornier Do 17 light bomber.

Figure 41. The Junkers Ju 88 multi-purpose bomber.

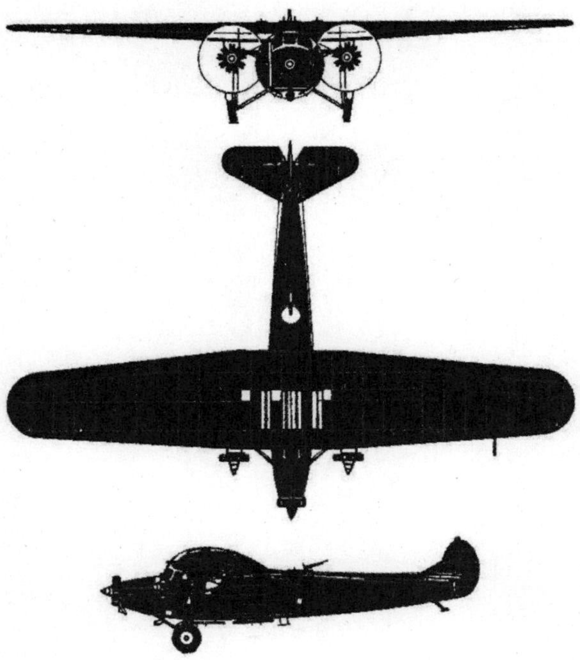

Figure 42. The Fokker F.VIIB employed as a bomber.

Figure 43. The Junkers Ju 52 transport plane. The German airmen and soldiers affectionately referred to the plane as '*Tante Ju*' ('Auntie Ju').

Appendix II

THE CROATIAN NAVY, 1941–1944

Figure 44. The torpedo boat *TA 48*. This small torpedo boat was originally used by the Austrian Hungarian navy as *T78*. She was then employed by the Yugoslav navy up until 1941, listed as *T3*. The Italians captured the vessel in April 1941 and put her into service. She was seized by the Germans after the Italian surrender in September 1943. The Germans then transferred the boat to the Croatian navy. Under the Croatian navy she still carried the old Yugoslav designation of *T3*. The *Kriegsmarine* reclaimed the torpedo boat on 14 December 1944 after the Croatian navy was disbanded. It was then that she received her final designation: *TA 48*. She was sunk by Allied bombers in Split harbour on 20 February 1945.

The Croatian navy, as it existed under the Independent State of Croatia, was divided into three naval commands: the Northern Command (located initially at Crkvenica, then at Susak), the Central Command (stationed in Makarska, but later moved to Split), and Southern Command (located in the city of Dubrovnik). There was also a Riverine Flotilla that was established in the autumn of 1941. Its home base at in the town of Zemun. This riverine flotilla had been created to patrol the Sava and Danube Rivers, which were the major rivers that ran NDH territory. The Italians, who jealously guarded their dominance over the Adriatic Sea, forbade the Croatians from having ships larger than fifty tons. Like their meddling on land, Italian rules limited the size and growth of Croatian naval forces. A Naval Infantry Battalion was created in Zagreb in the spring of 1942, and eventually stationed in Zemun. This naval battalion never served along the Adriatic Sea, and was employed as a ready reaction force for the Croatian riverine flotilla. When Italy suddenly surrendered and switched sides in September 1943, the Croatians were no longer encumbered by Italian restrictions. The Croatians were now free to create vessels larger than 50 tons and also to occupy the better harbours that had been used by the Italian navy along the Croatian coast of the Adriatic Sea. The German Kriegsmarine assumed overall support for the Croatian naval force. The largest vessel that it ever had was the German-built torpedo boat *TA 48*. At its height in October 1943, it contained 1,262 personnel. The navy was officially disbanded on 14 December 1944.

NOTES

Author's Note

1 The Dayton Accords were signed by all parties on 14 December 1995.

2 Schmidt assumed this role on 1 August 2021.

Foreword

1 Leo Valiane, Editorial Section – Italian daily, *Corriere delia Sera,* dated 24 May 1980.

Chapter 1: Background to the Balkans

1 Speech given by Abraham Lincoln at the Illinois Republican State Convention, Springfield, Illinois, 16 June 1858.

Chapter 2: The Balkan Troubles

1 Zbor: The Yugoslav National Movement. It was a Serbian Fascist movement founded in 1935. This movement has been replaced by numerous Serbian ultranationalist and right-wing parties. These include the Serbian Dveri Movement. Then there is also the ultra-nationalist Serbian Radical Party, whose members were deeply involved in the atrocities committed during the breakup of the former Yugoslavia in the 1990s. Other far right parties in Serbia today include Obraz, the clerical-Fascist 'Serbian Action' Party; the Serbian Party Oath Keepers (similar in ideology as the US Oath Keepers), the Serbian Right Party, the Party of Serbian Unity, the ultranationalist youth movement called the '1389 Movement', and the neo-Nazi *Nacionalni stroj Stranka* (National Alignment Party), which no longer exists. Nevertheless, there are currently a total of eleven right-wing parties being represented in the Serbian National Assembly. The dream of a 'Greater Serbia' therefore, is still very much alive.

2 When the nation of Czechoslovakia was finally occupied in March 1939, Slovakia became an independent Fascist state under Father Tiso (a defrocked Catholic priest). The Czech territories became the German 'protectorates' of Böhmen (Bohemia) and Mähren (Moravia).

3 David G. Williamson, *The Age of the Dictators*. New York: Routledge Publishing, 2007, p. 435.

4 The German war machine was dependent on oil coming from the oil wells at Ploesti, in Romania, and the oil wells near Lake Balaton in Hungary.

Chapter 3: The Independent State of Croatia

1 Mark Mazower, *Hitler's Empire. How the Nazis Ruled Europe*. Penguin Books: New York, 2008, p. 345.

2 Jozo Tomasevic, *War and Revolution in Yugoslavia, 1941-1945: Occupation and Collaboration*. Stanford: Stanford University Press, 2002, and: Tomasevic, op. cit., p. 138.

3 The 1931 Yugoslav census was employed in obtaining these estimates. Other sources used to obtain the figures included: Tomasevic, op. cit., p. 592, as well as: Jere Jareb, *Pola stoljeća hrvatske politike 1895-1945*. 1960; reprint Zagreb; Institut za suvremenu povijest, 1995, pp. 87–8, and Fikreta Jelić-Butić, *Ustaše i NDH*. Zagreb: Liber Zagreb-Skolska Knjga, 1978, p. 106.

4 The history of the Roma is a colourful one. Their ancestors originally lived on the Indian subcontinent. Specifically, they were an Indian tribe whose homeland was located in the northwest corner of the Gupta Empire. Around the year 500 AD, the Gupta rulers ordered the tribe to leave their ancestral home and head west, in what was supposedly a 'diplomatic mission'. There are two versions for the reason why they were forced to leave. One reason was possibly to escape the Hunnic invasion of the Indian subcontinent, which began around the same time. The other possible motive is more unsavoury and pejorative. According to the story, this particular Indian tribe had earned a reputation for ceaseless squabbling with their neighbours and for banditry. When they came to the attention of the Guptas, the decision was made to get rid of them, by sending them away. The tribe travelled west, passing through Afghanistan and Persia until they reached the Middle East. It was in the early Middle Ages that they entered the Balkans. In order to be more readily accepted by the people living there, they claimed to be Christian Egyptian pilgrims. It was from this claim, that Europeans began to call them 'Gypsies' (from the word 'Egyptian'). Once they entered the Balkans, they began to mix with the local people, becoming the mixed-race Romani of today. Like the Jews, the Romani have been the subject of persecution throughout history. In fact, some German municipalities had ordinances in their books, as late as the mid-1970s, that were geared to minimize the '*Ziegeuner*' (Gypsies). The term 'Gipsy' is no longer proper, as it is considered offensive. Interestingly, the Jews have a similar history to the Romani. Originally, the Israelites were a Semitic people living in what is today southern Iraq and the nation of Kuwait. Back then the region was known as Mesopotamia. Sometime around

2000 BC the Israelites left southern Mesopotamia and began to wander west. No one knows for sure why the Israelites left during that time, but we know it was connected to the political strife occurring in the Sumer city-state of Ur. The political conflict that followed the downfall of the Third Dynasty of Ur around 2004 BC, is most likely what prompted the exodus, as various Semitic tribes in the city and surrounding countryside vied with one another to position themselves for control of this southern Sumerian city-state. This occurred after the collapse of the Third Dynasty ruler, Ibbi Sin (ruled 2028–2004 BC). If that is the case, then the Israelites proved to be on the losing end of this power struggle, apparently having to flee the region. Another more unsavoury explanation has them forcibly evicted by other Sumerian tribes who found them too quarrelsome and haughty to deal with. In any event, they left Mesopotamia and wandered westward until reaching the land of Canaan.

5 J. Lee Ready, *The Forgotten Axis. Germany's Partners and Foreign Volunteers in World War II.* McFarland & Company: Jefferson, 1987, p. 172.

6 Hugh Gibson and Sumner Welles (eds), *Ciano Diaries 1939-1943, Complete, Unabridged Diaries of Count Galeazzo. Italian Minister for Foreign Affairs 1936-1943.* New York: Doubleday & Co., 1946, p. 247.

7 Estimates as to the number of people killed during the Great Purge range from a low figure of 700,000 to a high figure of 1,200,000.

Chapter 4: Reinforcements

1 Edmund Glaise von Horstenau, *Ein General im Zweilicht: Die Erinnerungen Edmund Glaises von Horstenau* (*Veröffentlichungen der Kommission für Neuere Geschichte Österreichs*). Wien: Böhlau Verlag, 1980, 3 vols, Vol. 2, p. 55.

2 How Jure Francetić died was both accidental and unexpected. Colonel Francetić was a wanted man, both by the Tito communists and by the Serbian Chetniks. By then the Black Legion had earned a terrible reputation. During the war, it was impossible for an *Ustaše* soldier to surrender to the Chetniks. He would simply be tortured before being killed. As for Tito's Partisan forces, the best thing for an *Ustaše* soldier to do was to surrender only during a period of grace which was offered a few times throughout the war. Of course, initially, as in the 1943 amnesty offer, this pardon only applied to the Croatian Home Guard and not to the fanatical *Ustaše* forces. Only in the 1944 amnesty offer did the clemency include *Ustaše* troops. Even then, the Partisans would not accept anyone who had taken part in any atrocities. If you had taken part in any massacres, it was not advisable to surrender. Colonel Francetić was headed from Zagreb on 22 December 1942 to assume command of forces in Lika. His aircraft developed engine trouble along the way and crash-landed near Slunj, in the Kordun region. Mija Abicic, who was the pilot who was flying the *Ustaše* commander to Lika, had

been responsible for inspecting the plane before take-off. His plane log was never recovered but we can assume that he did the routine inspection before a plane takes off. When the engine stalled, the plane coasted for a minute or two before coming down. Upon crash-landing, Francetić ordered Abicic to disable to the plane so that the Partisans could not use it. That delay cost them their lives. A firefight soon ensued when Partisan troops arrived. Both men were wounded in the abdomen and were quickly captured by the Tito Partisans. The communists on the scene reportedly tortured Francetić when they realized who he was. According to the official Yugoslav government report, both men were taken to a local hospital where Francetić died on 27 December 1942 of his wounds. The fate of Mija Abicic is not known, but he likely was killed as well.

Chapter 5: The Guerrilla War Begins

1 Ernst Percy Schramm, *Kriegstagebuch Des Oberkommandos Der Wehrmacht*. Munich: Bernard & Gräfe Verlag, 1982, 8 vols, Vol. 3, p. 223.

2 On 31 March 1943 the division was reclassified as the *118. Jäger Division*.

3 Schramm, op. cit., Vol. 3, pp. 238–9.

4 Schramm, op. cit., Vol. 3, p. 241.

Chapter 6: Recruitment and Further Operations

1 Lüters was promoted to *General der Infanterie* on 1 February 1943.

2 On 25 August 1943 *Generalmajor* Lüters became the first commander of the newly-created *XV. Gebirgs Armeekorps*.

Chapter 7: Croat-German Reinforcements and Operations

1 Franz Schraml, *Kriegsschauplatz Kroatien: Die deutsch-kroatischen Legions-Divisionen 369., 373., 392. Inf.-Div (kroat.)*. Neckargemünd: Kurt Vowinckel Verlag, 1962, pp. 36–7.

Chapter 8: Expansion of NDH and German Forces

1 This regiment came from the 6. Croatian Infantry Division in Mostar, which was not involved in the new reorganization. To replace the missing 13. Infantry Regiment, the 6. Croatian Infantry Division was assigned the newly formed 1. Volunteer Infantry Regiment. The 6. Croatian Infantry Division was now composed of 1. Volunteer Regiment and the 14. Infantry Regiment. For some reason, the 1. Volunteer Infantry Regiment was later incorporated into the 6. *Ustaše* Brigade.

2 Schraml, op. cit., pp. 155–7.

3 Police Training Battalions I and II.

4 SE represents *Heeresgruppe Südost* (Army Group Southeast).

5 *BddTK stands for: Befehlshaber der deutschen Truppen in Kroatien* (Commander of German Troops in Croatia).

6 *F/2. Pz. A., stands for: Heeresgruppe F/2. Panzerarmee* (Army Group F/2nd Tank Army).

7 *XV. Geb. Korps* stands for *XV. Gebirgs Armeekorps*, or '15th Mountain Corps'.

8 'F/E' stands for *Heeresgruppe F/Heeresgruppe E* (Army Group F/Army Group E), where Army Group F was subordinate to Army Group E.

9 Where 'E' stands for *Heeresgruppe E* (Army Group E).

Chapter 9: German Influence Increases in NDH Territory

1 Police Training & Replacement Battalion I and II.

2 The rank of *SS Oberführer* was one that was peculiar to the *SS*. It was a rank somewhere between colonel and brigadier-general.

Chapter 10: Major German-Croatian Anti-Partisan Drives

1 The *369. (deutsch-kroatische) Infanterie* Division was nick-named the 'Devil' Division.

2 The thirteen that went missing with their weapons and equipment were most likely deserters to the Partisans. The German joke that the Croatian Army was the weapons and troop replacement unit for Tito's Partisan army appears to have been based partly on reality.

Chapter 11: The Consequences of Italy's Surrender

1 Bosanski Novi is now known as Novi Grad.

2 This division was redesignated as the *42. Jäger Division* on 22 December 1943.

3 This unit was selected for employment on the Istrian peninsula.

4 There was no 2. Battalion in this brigade.

5 There was no 4. Battalion in this brigade.

6 Five such command headquarters existed in Croatia in the summer of 1944, and were immediately subordinated to the *BdO* command. The *KdO* commands were located in (1) Zagreb, (2) Osijek, (3) Sarajevo, (4) Banja Luka, and (5) Knin.

Chapter 12: 1943–1944: The Writing on the Wall

1 Two tank companies containing outdated Czech and Italian-made tanks.

2 This battalion contained four companies drawn from Pavelic's fanatical personal bodyguard.

3 From 1942 onwards, all former garrison battalion (sixteen in all) were forcibly conscripted into the *Ustaše* organization.

4 This was the former '1. *Ustaše* Assault Regiment', also known as the Black Legion, for the completely black uniforms which its men wore. The regiment had contained initially two, then three battalions and had been led by *Ustaše* Major Jure Francetic. The Germans later asked the Croatian government that this unit be disbanded because of the excesses that it caused against both the Serbian and Muslim population. Ante Pavelić did remove Francetic in order to appease the Germans, but instead of punishing him Francetic was promoted. This only shows that Pavelic was not concerned about the Serbs or Muslims.

5 Sequential numbering of the *Ustaše* infantry battalions was often duplicated in the brigades.

6 This battalion was initially in the 2. *Ustaše* Brigade.

7 This *Ustaše* brigade was made up of camp guards and other prison personnel. When it was grouped together into a combat unit in March 1945, it was almost immediately decimated by the Tito Partisans. The I. Battalion was destroyed at Sunja, while the II. Battalion was wiped out at Bosanski Novi. The III. Battalion, which was at Lepoglava when it was attacked, was likewise eliminated, while the IV. Battalion met its end in Jasenovac itself. A month after being wiped out (April 1945); the remnants of the *Ustaše* Camp Brigade were regrouped and formed into the 30. Assault Infantry Regiment of the newly-raised 18. Croatian Assault Division.

8 This proved similar to the problem the Germans encountered when employing both Hungarian and Romanian forces on the Russian Front. The Germans often had to place German or Italian units between the Hungarians and Romanians, or else what would happen is that invariably the Romanians and Hungarians would begin to shoot at each other. This enmity between the Hungarians and Romanians stemmed from Hungary's loss of the region of Transylvania, which at the end of the First World War was given to Romania by the Entente powers, on account of their aid against the Central Powers.

9 On 11 September 1944 the Skanderbeg Division had a strength of 4,944 men, of which 3,504 were Albanians. On that same day the partisans attacked the division's headquarters, and killed eighteen members of the staff. On 17 September 1944, the *50. Waffen Grenadier Regiment der SS* was disbanded after 1,176 of its members deserted that day. After the *Oberbefehlshaber Südost* (Commander-in-Chief Southeast) ordered on 3 October 1944 that the division be disbanded. After releasing most of the Albanians except for about 100 diehard volunteers, the 800-strong German cadre staff from the now-disbanded division set off towards Croatia. They were met along the way by 1,800 German naval personnel who were now ordered to join the small battlegroup and act as infantrymen.

10 Jill A. Irvine, *The Croat Question: Partisan Politics in the Formation of the Yugoslav Socialist State.* Boulder: Westview Press, 1993, p. 172.

11 These German-raised Croatian police units contained a cadre of German police officers and NCOs.

12 One source states that Bonic died on 2 October 1944, although this is doubtful.

13 Gaj Trifkovic, *Sea of Blood: A Military History of the Partisan Movement in Yugoslavia 1941-45.* Amherst: Helion and Company, 2002.

14 In 1992, Vukovar was defended by lightly-armed Croatian Defence Forces which had few or no heavy weapons. After months of merciless Serbian artillery and tank pounding, the city was taken in hand-to-hand fighting. The battle was so tough and so costly that after it was all over, the Bosnian Serb command vowed never again to commit its forces to such street fighting unless absolutely necessary. The Bosnian Serbs were the ones who coined the phrase that Vukovar was the 'Stalingrad' of the Croatians. After the Serbian forces captured the town, they committed numerous massacres – the most infamous was the execution of wounded Croatian soldiers in the town hospital, as well as civilians, including women and children. Most of the Croatian and Muslim women in the town were first raped before being murdered. The terrorist and Serbian mafia leader, Željko Ražnatović, took part in the siege. Known as 'Arkan's Fighters', this Serbian gangster and his unit (Belgrade mafia members, but mostly former Red Star Belgrade hooligans), had a particularly heinous habit of slicing off the breasts of women that they had just raped, before killing them.

15 Schramm, op cit., Vol. 8, pp. 1424–5.

16 1. Croatian Storm Division began forming on 9 October 1944. The artillery sections were formed from Boban's Bobanova Bojna's *Ustaše* unit- the second most notoriously infamous *Ustaše* formation after the well-known 'Black Legion'.

17 This division had around 4,500–5,000 men at any one time. It was equipped primarily with Italian and Czechoslovakian weapons, with a sprinkling of small weapons from a stock of captured British arms.

18 Schramm, op. cit., vol. 4, p. 1312.

19 Added after December 1944.

20 This was the former *Crne Legije,* i.e. the Croatian Black Legion.

21 NARA RG-331, Roll 447, Frames 75-135.

22 This division contained around 10,000 men in December 1944. It was considered a good formation. It took heavy losses during the winter of 1944/45, given that by February 1945 it only had around 6,500 men. It defended Karlovac until May 1945. Tito's forces finally overran the town between 7–12 May 1945.

23 Note: this *Ustaše* brigade would help to form the 13. Croatian Infantry Division in February 1945.

24 NARA T-311, Roll 196, Frames 189, 447, 777, 873; and NARA RG 226 (OSS doc. num. 109636, 110433, 126034).

25 This battalion was acting as the reconnaissance unit of the division.

26 This division had poor morale and consisted of around 6,000 men.

27 This division contained around 4,500–5,000 men. Apparently, the only role this division was tasked with, was to protect the Zagreb to Slavonska Brod rail line. As such, it was not under Croatian control, but under the German *Eisenbahn-sicherungsstab Kroatien* headquarters.

28 Schramm, op. cit., Vol. 4, p. 1312.

29 NARA RG-242, T-311, R. 184, F. 0437, 0513; Roll 189, F. 0785. The division was listed as one of the best in the Croatian Army. Its strength in December 1944 was an astounding 16,858. Most of the personnel were Bosnian Muslims. The only problem with this division is that it lacked armament, especially in heavy weapons. The morale of the division was excellent. In February 1945 its strength was listed as only 7,000 men. It is improbable that the division would have suffered close to 10,000 casualties in several months. More than likely, many men were transferred to other NDH divisions as entire units or as replacements. This theory merits weight, given that a month later, on 1 March 1945, the 11. *Ustaše* Brigade of the division was handed over to the new 17. Infantry Division, which was in the stages of being formed in the region of Zenica.

Chapter 13: 1944: Vicious Fighting

1 Of the 2,460,000 troops in the *Ostheer*, approximately 492,000 were Eastern volunteers wearing the German field grey uniform.

2 Schramm, op. cit., Vol. 8, pp. 1401–02.

3 The 5. Infantry Division was considered the third best combat division in the Croatian army, after the *Poglavnik* Bodyguard Division and 1. Storm Division.

4 Schramm, op. cit., Vol. 8, p. 1425.

5 Ibid., p. 1415.

6 Ibid., p. 1401.

7 Hans Peter Klausch, *Die 999er. Von der Brigade 'Z' zur Afrika-Division 999: Die Bewärungsbataillone und ihr Anteil am antifaschistischen Widerstand.* Frankfurt am Main: Roederberg Verlag, 1986, p. 356.

8 Schramm, op. cit., Vol. 8, p. 1414.

9 Ibid., p. 1415.

10 Ibid.

11 Ibid., p. 1423.

12 German reports refer to this Croatian division as an 'infantry' formation, and not as a 'mountain' division as the Croatians labelled it.

13 Schramm, op. cit., Vol. 8, p. 1424.

14 Fifty thousand Cossacks fighting on the German side under German general Helmuth von Pannwitz. This corps was soon taken over by the *Waffen SS* and renamed the 15. SS Cavalry Corps. This transfer was merely a 'paper' one since the *Heer* uniforms remained and no *Waffen SS* officers were assigned to the unit.

15 Samuel J. Newland, *Cossacks in the German Army, 1941-1945.* London: Frank Cass, 1991, p. 164.

16 NARA microfilm series T-501, Roll No. 266, Frame 000536.

17 This was a regional defence regiment made up of older reservists.

18 Schramm, op. cit., Vol. 8, p. 1181.

Chapter 14: *Bis zum bitteren Ende*

1 This corps was redesignated as the *Poglavnik* Bodyguard Corps in mid-April 1945.

2 The Mobile Brigade joined the 1. Corps in mid-April 1945, when the 1. Corps was redesignated as the Poglavnik Bodyguard Corps. The 5. Croatian Infantry Division was reorganized in April and its units renamed as the 23., 24., and 25. Infantry Regiments. It had been assigned to the German *LXIX. Armeekorps* in early April, but by mid-April the 5. Division was reassigned to the Croatian command.

3 This German corps was located along the Syrmian front lines in April 1945. Tito's First Partisan Army launched a full-scale attack against *XXXIV. Armeekorps,* beginning 12 April 1945. Tito's divisions eventually broke through the lines of the corps. This led to the capture of Zupanja, Vukovar, and Vinkovci. Zagreb was the ultimate goal, but in late April and the beginning of May 1945, the Croatian capital was defended by the 1. Croatian Infantry Division, as well as the German *41. Festungs Division* and *181. Infanterie Division.* This Croatian and German force held off Tito's partisans until the end of the war. The Croatian government did not leave Zagreb until 6 May 1945. A day later, Germany surrendered unconditionally.

4 The 12. Croatian Infantry Division was effectively wiped out by the Partisans. It had been reduced to a mere 900 men by the end of April 1945. The division did not fall apart, but had been destroyed in heavy fighting!

5 The 11. Croatian Infantry Division had an operational strength of only 2,000 men. The 10. Croatian Infantry Division lost its artillery battalion and II. Battalion/10. Rifle Brigade in fighting around Bihac in February and March 1945. The 11. Croatian Infantry Division was brought up to

strength to about 6,000 men by early May and assigned to the newly formed 5. *Ustaše* Corps.

6 Nigel Thomas, Krunoslav Mikulan, and Darko Pavlovic, *Axis Forces in Yugoslavia 1941-45.* London: Osprey Military Series, an imprint of Reed Consumer Books, 1995, p. 15.

7 Ibid.

8 Ekkehard Völkl, *Sauberungs in Europa: Die Abrechnung mit Faschismus und Kollaboration nach dem Zweiten Weltkrieg.* München: Deutscher Taschenbuch Verlag, 1991, p. 372.

9 Alex Buchner, 'Das kroatische Heer', in *Landser-Grossband.* Pabel Verlag GmbH: Rastatt, December 1982, p. 69.

10 Boro Mitrovski, Tomo Ristovski and Glišić Venceslav, *Bulgarska vojska u Jugoslavii 1941-1945.* Ljubljana: Medunarodna politika, 1971, p. 49.

11 Adolf von Ernsthausen, *Der Wölfe der Lika. Mit Legionaeren, Ustashi, Domobranen und Tschetniks gegen Titos Partisanen. Erlebnisse in Kroatien 1944.* Neckargemünd: Kurt Vowinckel Verlag, 1959, pp. 204–07, and 221.

12 Ivo Omrcanin, *Military History of Croatia.* New York: Dorrance Publishing, 1984, p. 157.

13 Josip Hecimovic, *In Tito's Death Marches. Testimony on the Massacres of the Croatian War Prisoners and Civilians after World War II.* United American Croats Central Committee. Chicago: Croatian Franciscan Press, 1961, p. 24.

14 Ibid., p. 24.

15 Ibid., p. 29.

16 Völkl, op. cit., p. 367.

17 Hecimovic, op. cit., pp. 30–1.

18 Hans Werner Neulen, *An deutscher Seite: Internationale Freiwillige von Wehrmacht und Waffen-SS.* München: Universitas Verlag, 1985, p. 219. Neulen quotes figures for deaths at Maribor, Kocevje, and St, Vid. Of those killed near Maribor, about 10,000 were found in an abandoned anti-tank ditch. This group included not only Croatian but German troops as well.

19 Hecimovic, op. cit., p. 16.

20 Neulen, op. cit., p. 219. Neulen also mentions the size of the civilian refugees who followed the Croatian Army into Austria at around 200,000 or roughly 10 per cent of the population. This may be a bit high, but certainly at least 100,000 civilians fled the communist advance.

21 Buchner, op. cit., p. 69.

22 Vladimir Zerjavic, 'Demografija o Bleiburgo', in *Bleiburg. Otvoreni dossier.* Uredio Marko Grcic, Zagreb: Stvarnost, 1990, (second printing), pp. 227–32.

23 Gerald Reitlinger, *The Final Solution: The Attempt to Exterminate the Jews of Europe 1939-1945.* New York: Thomas Yoseloff, second revised & augmented edition, 1968, p. 385. The first edition was published in 1953.

24 Edmond Paris, *Genocide in Satellite Croatia, 1941-1945.* Chicago: The American Institute for Balkan Affairs, 1961, p. 129.

25 Hans Safrian, *Die Eichmann Männer.* Zürich: Europa Verlag, 1993, p. 200.

26 Philip J. Cohen, *Serbia's Secret War. Propaganda and the Deceit of History.* College Station: Texas A&M University, 1996, pp. 1–10.

27 Paris, op. cit., p. 189.

28 Lothar Rendulic, *Gekampft, Gesiegt, Geschlagen.* Heidelberg: Verlag Welsermuhl, 1952, p. 161; and the Jasenovac Concentration Camp Memorial Site, as well as the United States Holocaust Memorial Museum..

29 Völkl, op. cit., p. 361.

30 Omrcanin, op. cit., p. 135.

31 Jozo Tomasevich, *The Chetniks: War and Revolution in Yugoslavia, 1941-1945.* Stanford: Stanford University Press, 1975, p. 258.

32 In September 1942, this officer's primary role was security and policing of prisoner of war and labour camps. The prisoner and labour camps were initially under the command of Eugen Dido Kvaternik, with Vjekoslav Maks Luburic taking command in the autumn of 1942. Prior to this, Luburic had been the commanding officer of the Croatian Home Guard 9th Infantry Regiment.

Appendix I: The Croatian Air Force, 1941–1945

1 At the time, the squadron was led by Lieutenant Djuro Svarc.

Index of Formations

1 Jozo Tomasevich. *War and Revolution in Yugoslavia, 1941–1945: The Chetniks.* Stanford: Stanford University Press, 1975, p. 350. In April 1944, Serbian Chetnik leader, Pavle Đurišić, established a pro-Axis collaborationist force in Montenegro with military assistance from the Serbian puppet government of Milan Nedic and the German Army. This collaboration with Axis forces was done to counter the growing communist partisan threat in the region, and represented in a way, the increasing desperation of the royalist Serbian Chetnik forces, as they saw the Tito communists eventually coming out on top and ruling Yugoslavia after the war. This ran counter to the Serbian Chetnik goal of placing the Serbian king back on the Yugoslav throne. At its height, this corps contained no more than 8,000 fighters, so it was the equivalent of about a division in strength.

BIBLIOGRAPHY

Primary Source Material

NARA

T-78, Roll 410

T-311, Roll 196, 285, 286, 447

T-314, roll 661

T-501, Roll No. 249, 256, 266

RG 226 and RG-331

Schramm, Ernst Percy, *Kriegstagebuch Des Oberkommandos Der Wehrmacht.* Munich: Bernard & Gräfe Verlag, 1982, 8 vols.

SS-Personnel Hauptamt, *Dienstalterliste der Schutzstaffel der NSDAP. SS Oberstgruppenführer bis SS Standartenführer, Stand von 9. November 1944.* Gedruckt in der Reichsdruckerei: Berlin, 1944.

Transcript of a speech given by Abraham Lincoln at the Illinois Republican State Convention, Springfield, Illinois 16 June 1858, Washington D.C.: Library of Congress.

Secondary Sources

Buchner, Alex, 'Das kroatische Heer', in *Landser-Grossband.* Pabel Verlag GmbH: Rastatt. December 1982.

Cohen, Philip J., *Serbia's Secret War. Propaganda and the Deceit of History.* College Station: Texas A&M University, 1996.

Colić, Mladenko, *Pregled operacija na Jugoslavenskumratistu 1941-1945.* Belgrade: Vojnoistorijski institut, 1988.

Dedijer, Vladimir, *Genocid nad Muslimanima, 1941-1945.* Sarajevo: Svjetlost, 1990.

Ernsthausen, Adolf von, *Der Wölfe der Lika. Mit Legionaeren, Ustashi, Domobranen und Tschetniks gegen Titos Partisanen. Erlebnisse in Kroatien 1944.* Neckargemünd: Kurt Vowinckel Verlag, 1959.

Gibson, Hugh and Sumner Welles (eds), *Ciano Diaries 1939-1943, Complete, Unabridged Diaries of Count Galeazzo. Italian Minister for Foreign Affairs 1936-1943.* New York: Doubleday & Co., 1946.

Hecimovic, Josip, *In Tito's Death Marches. Testimony on the Massacres of the Croatian War Prisoners and Civilians after World War II*. United American Croats Central Committee. Chicago: Croatian Franciscan Press, 1961.

Hnilicka, Karl, *Das Ende auf dem Balkan 1944/45*. Zürich: Musterschmidt-Göttingen Verlag, 1970.

Horstenau, Edmund Glaise von, *Ein General im Zweilicht: Die Erinnerungen Edmund Glaises von Horstenau (Veröffentlichungen der Kommission für Neuere Geschichte Österreichs)*. Wien: Böhlau Verlag, 1980, 3 vols.

Irvine, Jill A., *The Croat Question: Partisan Politics in the Formation of the Yugoslav Socialist State*. Boulder: Westview Press. 1993.

Jareb, Jere, *Pola stoljeća hrvatske politike 1895-1945*. 1960; reprint Zagreb: Institut za suvremenu povijest, 1995.

Jelić-Butić, Fikreta, *Ustaše i NDH*. Zagreb: Liber Zagreb-Skolska Knjga, 1978.

Klausch, Hans Peter, *Die 999er. Von der Brigade 'Z' zur Afrika-Division 999: Die Bewärungsbataillone und ihr Anteil am antifaschistischen Widerstand*. Frankfurt am Main: Roederberg Verlag, 1986.

Kumm, Otto, *7.SS-Gebirgs-Division ‚Prinz Eugen' im Bild*. Munin Verlag: Osnabrück, 1983.

Kumm, Otto, *Vorwarts, Prinz Eugen: Geschichte der 7. SS Freiwilligen Gebirgs Division 'Prinz Eugen'*. Osnabrück: Munin Verlag, 1984.

Likso, Tihomir and Danko Čanak, *Hrvatsko ratno zrakoplovstvo u drugom svjetskom ratu*. Self-published: Nova Gradiška, 1998.

Mazower, Mark, *Hitler's Empire. How the Nazis Ruled Europe*. Penguin Books: New York, 2008.

Meyer, Brün. *Dienstalterliste der Waffen SS. SS Obergruppenführer bis SS Hauptsturmführer. Stand vom 1. Juli 1944*. Biblio Verlag: Osnabrück, 1987.

Mitrovski, Boro, Tomo Ristovski, and Glišić Venceslav, *Bulgarska vojska u Jugoslavii 1941-1945*. Ljubljana: Medunarodna politika, 1971.

Neufeldt, Hans-Joachim, Jürgen Huck and Georg Tessin, *Zur Geschichte der Ordnungspolizei 1936-1945*. Boppard am Rhein: Schriften des Bundesarchiv, 1957.

Neulen, Hans Werner, *An deutscher Seite: Internationale Freiwillige von Wehrmacht und Waffen SS*. München: Universitas Verlag, 1985.

Newland, Samuel J., *Cossacks in the German Army, 1941-1945*. London: Frank Cass, 1991.

Omrcanin, Ivo, *Military History of Croatia*. New York: Dorrance Publishing, 1984.

Paris, Edmond, *Genocide in Satellite Croatia, 1941-1945*. Chicago: The American Institute for Balkan Affairs, 1961.

Ready, J. Lee, *The Forgotten Axis. Germany's Partners and Foreign Volunteers in World War II*. McFarland & Company: Jefferson, 1987.

Reitlinger, Gerald, *The Final Solution: The Attempt to Exterminate the Jews of Europe 1939-1945*. New York: Thomas Yoseloff, second revised & augmented edition, 1968.

Rendulic, Lothar, *Gekampft, Gesiegt, Geschlagen.* Heidelberg: Verlag Welsermuhl, 1952.

Safrian, Hans, *Die Eichmann Männer.* Zürich: Europa Verlag, 1993.

Schraml, Franz, *Kriegsschauplatz Kroatien: Die deutsch-kroatischen Legions-Divisionen 369., 373., 392. Inf.-Div (kroat.).* Neckargemünd: Kurt Vowinckel Verlag, 1962.

Strugar, Vlado, *Jugoslavija 1941-1945.* Belgrade: Vojnoizdavački zavod, 1969.

Thomas, Nigel, Krunoslav Mikulan, and Darko Pavlovic, *Axis Forces in Yugoslavia 1941-45.* London: Osprey Military Series, an imprint of Reed Consumer Books, 1995.

Tomasevich, Jozo, *The Chetniks: War and Revolution in Yugoslavia, 1941-1945.* Stanford: Stanford University Press, 1975.

Tomasevic, Jozo, *War and Revolution in Yugoslavia, 1941-1945: Occupation and Collaboration.* Stanford: Stanford University Press, 2002.

Trifkovic, Gaj, *Sea of Blood: A Military History of the Partisan Movement in Yugoslavia 1941-45.* Amherst: Helion and Company, 2002.

Various authors, *Oslobodilacki rat naroda Jugoslavije 1941-1945.* Belgrade: Vojnoistorijski intitut, two volumes, 1963.

Völkl, Ekkehard, *Sauberungs in Europa: Die Abrechnung mit Faschismus und Kollaboration nach dem Zweiten Weltkrieg.* München: Deutscher Taschenbuch Verlag, 1991.

Williamson, David G., *The Age of the Dictators.* New York: Routledge Publishing, 2007.

Zerjavic, Vladimir, 'Demografija o Bleiburgo', in *Bleiburg. Otvoreni dossier.* Uredio Marko Grcic, Zagreb: Stvarnost, 1990

INDEX OF FORMATIONS

Croatian Army Forces

Engineers

Labour/Construction Regiments

Mountain Infantry Formations

Mobile Formations

Artillery Formations

Garrison Brigades

Air Force Units

German Formations

Miscellaneous

Divisions

Brigades/Regiments/Battalions

German Luftwaffe Forces

Italian Army Units

Bulgarian Forces

Chetnik Formations

Tito's Partisan Army

Montenegrin Forces[1]

INDEX OF NAMES